Metaphysical
Baroque & Précieux
Poetry

Metaphysical Baroque & Précieux Poetry

BY

ODETTE DE MOURGUES

FELLOW OF GIRTON COLLEGE, CAMBRIDGE

OXFORD

AT THE CLARENDON PRESS

1953

Oxford University Press, Amen House, London E.C.4

GLASGOW NEW YORK TORONTO MELBOURNE WELLINGTON
BOMBAY CALCUTTA MADRAS KARACHI CAPE TOWN IBADAN

Geoffrey Cumberlege, Publisher to the University

PRINTED IN GREAT BRITAIN
AT THE UNIVERSITY PRESS, OXFORD
BY CHARLES BATEY, PRINTER TO THE UNIVERSITY

PREFACE

THIS work is a contribution both to the history of French poetry between Scève and La Fontaine and to the study of European literature in the late Renaissance. It is a deliberately limited contribution bearing only on the non-dramatic poetry of two countries, France and England, and taking as its centre a problem of terminology. In spite of this limited scope, I am only too well aware of the pitfalls lying in my way. To write on the précieux and particularly on the baroque is to plunge into very rough waters; too many of my readers have perhaps already made up their minds about these terms, even if in a purely negative way. It is probably the curse of a certain French tradition which makes me attempt to compel these elusive, complex terms to come into the category of *idées claires et distinctes*.

My task has been made both easier and much more difficult by the number of books and articles constantly appearing on subjects which cross this study at various points. Although there has been nothing in recent criticism to make me modify my point of view on terminology, I regret that while revising this work for publication I cannot give more space to critical appreciation of the latest articles; the reader will find them mentioned whenever they are relevant, either in the text or in footnotes. Especially in the case of the baroque, I had to deal with an enormous mass of documentation, and to face the threat of encumbering my work with the refutation of too many previous theories. I have therefore endeavoured to restrict the place of this lengthy preliminary work and to keep a fair balance between information and criticism, selecting in my bibliography the works which have proved of primary importance to the questions under discussion.

Since this study bears on a rather large period, it has seemed preferable to base my analyses on what can be considered either the best or the most significant poems of a given poet. My first debt of gratitude is to all the scholars and anthologists who have provided me with the material for my critical analyses.

I have also a general acknowledgement to make to the methods and suggestions of twentieth-century English criticism, which have been of such help in the study of the poetry of my own country; and a more special acknowledgement to Dr. F. R. Leavis for very generous encouragement and advice particularly during the difficult first stages of my research. Readers acquainted with modern criticism will appreciate my debt to him.

This work was first undertaken as a doctoral thesis, and I have particular obligations to the British Council for enabling me to come to England as one of their Research Scholars, and to Girton College where my tenure of a Research Fellowship made it possible for me to work on a subject which had been in my mind for several years. I am most grateful to Miss M. G. Lloyd Thomas and Professor F. C. Green, who supervised the initial stages of my work. For helpful criticism of the manuscript and precious encouragement towards publication I am deeply indebted to Professor P. Mansell Jones, Professor L. C. Harmer, Dr. R. W. Ladborough, Mr. W. G. Moore, Mr. R. A. Sayce, and Miss M. C. Bradbrook.

I owe so much to discussion with colleagues and friends interested in the same subject that I cannot give adequate and exhaustive acknowledgement. But I should like to mention Professor L. W. Forster for his kindness in inviting me to take part in lively weekly discussions on the baroque, held by germanists in Selwyn College in 1949 and 1950. Both in the text of my work and in the footnotes I have made due acknowledgement to Professor A. M. Boase's books and articles, but I wish to express my thanks to him more clearly for personal encouragement and stimulating conversations, as well as for his published work. It has been extremely gratifying to find that his studies, although not concerned with the question of terminology, have come very near my own position, and I am glad to be able to recall here how much every student of the poetry of the late Renaissance owes to his pioneer work and to his discoveries.

As for my debt to the patient English friends and colleagues who have spared so much of their time in order to suggest corrections and improvements in expression, it is impossible to thank them enough for having kindly accepted such a weary task. Among them, I have a very special acknowledgement to make: constantly, during all the years I have devoted to this work, my friend and colleague Dr. Alison Fairlie has given me invaluable help in every difficulty I met with, and I cannot adequately express how much I am indebted to her both in the writing of this study and in the preparation of the book for publication.

Finally, I would thank the Clarendon Press for their consideration, skill, and speed in producing this book.

O. DE M.

July 1952

CONTENTS

I

THE WELTER OF TERMINOLOGY

ONE of the prominent features of contemporary literary taste in France is the reawakening of interest in Scève and in the hundred years or so of literature which preceded Classicism. Evidence of the importance now attached to the period can be found both in academic circles and among the general reading public, in recent works such as the scholarly *Histoire de la littérature française au XVIIᵉ siècle—L'Époque d'Henri IV et de Louis XIII*,[1] or the special number of the *Cahiers du Sud* entitled *Le Préclassicisme français*,[2] destined for the wider public.

This reorientation of criticism has borne, to a large extent, on poets whom previous textbooks of literature had very often ignored or dismissed hastily as minor writers. Some of them were slumbering in the dusty oblivion of provincial libraries; others, stigmatized by the vague label *attardés et égarés* attached to them by Lanson, were left aside as puzzling oddities. It is perhaps not unnecessary to recall the flourish of trumpets which marked their triumphal reawakening, under the double name of précieux and baroques.

In 1941 M. Thierry Maulnier published his anthology *Poètes précieux et baroques*,[3] with a substantial introduction. This introduction is a brilliant piece of writing, a sweeping revaluation of the poets from whom, with a sure taste, he quotes the best lines, commenting upon them with keen appreciation of their artistic value. Such a revaluation was necessary, and it was probably necessary also that it should be done in this impressive rhetorical form and with such irresistible enthusiasm. But the careful reader cannot help feeling not only slightly dazed by the accumulation of qualifications with which the *poètes baroques et précieux* are endowed, but exasperated by the heterogeneous quality of the grist coming to the omnivorous mill. For the first part of the essay the terms précieux and baroque appear interchangeable, but later there seems to be an ill-defined distinction between the two words.[4]

---

[1] By A. Adam, 1948.   [2] Published in 1952.
[3] A revised version of the Introduction was published as an essay under the title 'Les derniers Renaissants' (*Langages*, 1946).

[4] M. Thierry Maulnier himself confesses the vagueness of the definition he gives; cf. 'Les derniers Renaissants', p. 41.

However, we are told that these poets are both précieux and baroque, and that they are more than that:

> Les poètes du temps de Louis XIII sont des Précieux; ils ne sont pas seulement des Précieux; ils sont des Baroques; . . . ils ne sont pas seulement des Baroques . . . Ils sont des pré-classiques et Faguet les a appelés, non sans raison, les Romantiques de 1630 . . . .[1]

They are everything: 'les plus artificiels de nos poètes et les plus naturels'. They are like Shakespeare, like Donne or Cowley. They conjure up Villon, they herald Racine, Musset, Baudelaire, and the symbolists, Hugo, Péguy, Lamartine, Apollinaire. They are, in short, an epitome of French poetry.

Although M. Thierry Maulnier was not the first critic to stress the necessity for a different attitude towards the poets of the late Renaissance,[2] his essay shows how, from the start, the revaluation of the poets called baroque and précieux was to be inextricably bound up with a confused, if enthusiastic, juggling with verbal offerings to these poets. It may be unfair to reproach M. Thierry Maulnier for not having been concerned with a problem of terminology, but it is a fact that the studies on the poetry of the period have not yet satisfactorily extricated themselves from the confusion of terms.

Since M. Thierry Maulnier's Introduction, a great deal of work has been done. Other anthologies have been published, in which sixteenth- and seventeenth-century poetry holds the most important place. Critical editions of rediscovered poets have appeared or are in the making. Articles, special numbers in reviews, courses of lectures, have shown either an interest in specific poets of the period or a wish to elucidate these shifting notions of baroque and précieux. Still the confusion persists. Sometimes the meaning of the two terms is taken for granted, at other times the two terms are taken as synonymous, or again the critic states a difference between the two terms but does not support his statement by any elucidation.

The confusion is made even greater by the addition of other terms, as if in their dazzled admiration for the riches of Renaissance

---

[1] 'Les derniers Renaissants', p. 43.

[2] As early as 1930 Professor A. M. Boase published an article on Sponde and on other poets of the same period which may be considered as the starting-point of the new criticism on late Renaissance poetry (*The Criterion*, Jan. 1930: 'Then Malherbe came').

and late Renaissance poetry critics had feverishly ransacked the western European storehouse of literary terminology in search of the right explanatory or laudatory epithet. Although the words précieux and baroque, however vague their signification, seem to be the most fashionable labels, they quickly call up references to Petrarchism, Gongorism, Conceptivism, Secentismo, Marinism. Comparisons with poets of later ages provide the insatiable critic with Romanticism, Symbolism, Surrealism, and so forth. Thus Scève is praised as being petrarchan or précieux, a *poète hermétique* or a symbolist, or even *mallarméen*, Saint-Amant as baroque or précieux, or as a disciple of Marino. The same poem will be given as an example of several categories of poetry: for instance Malherbe's *Les Larmes de Saint Pierre* is classified as an example of religious Petrarchism by Vianey,[1] as précieux by M. Thierry Maulnier,[2] and as baroque by M. Lebègue.[3]

One of the reasons for the difficulty in the use of terminology met by the student of the late Renaissance in France is that the problem he has to face refuses to limit itself to a problem of French terminology. The revaluation of the period is an international phenomenon and started in some countries earlier than in France. It was inevitable that there should be irritatingly close connexions between terms of literary criticism used in the various countries, since these connexions are based on the solid fact that the Renaissance and the late Renaissance were European literary movements/ We are by now used to thinking of the late Renaissance as a time when something important happened to the mind of Europe, and therefore any student in the field becomes to some extent a *comparatiste*. We have by now woven such an intricate network of connexions and analogies that it seems next to impossible to disentangle one term, detach it from the chain of its synonyms and study it with its own self-sufficient meaning. The result is that European terminology is a battlefield. In France the baroque and the précieux do not yield much ground to each other. In England baroque and, recently, its offspring Mannerism have slipped in as a menace to the well-defined word metaphysical. The influence of German terminology, where the term baroque is respectably established and reigns supreme, partly because of the absence of the terms

---

[1] J. Vianey, *Le Pétrarquisme en France au XVIᵉ siècle*, 1909, p. 313.
[2] 'Les derniers Renaissants', p. 31.
[3] R. Lebègue, *La Poésie française de 1560 à 1630*, 1951, vol. ii, pp. 13–20.

précieux and metaphysical, has a strong effect on other countries. Discussions between specialists of the various literatures prove of very little help; they are usually vitiated from the start by the fact that it is never clear whether the term discussed is taken as a 'historical' term or as a term characterizing a certain type of poetry.

It is not absurd to think that the types of poetry written in western Europe in the late Renaissance could probably be reduced to three or four clearly distinct categories, but it seems over-optimistic to hope for a standard European terminology.[1] Who would decide to what extent metaphysical poetry and Gongorism apply to the same type of poetry, and state that baroque and Marinism are synonymous? Would German terminology reduce the connotation of its term baroque, so as to leave room for other terms? Could French terminology adopt the term metaphysical, as we know of no French word that would enable us to dispense with it? Only a *comparatiste* of genius could consider the problem as a whole and suggest a complete and satisfactory solution.

Meanwhile we go on using these spurious counters. In spite of our good faith, they hamper research, or, what is worse, they offer a constant temptation to cheat. With the prestige of fashionable labels, they flow too glibly from the pen. Journalistic literature palms them off too easily on the general public. Our own students use them at random and are not alone to blame.

We may, however, attempt a partial solution, in the hope that it will be valid within certain limitations, and that it will help towards a more general revaluation of terminology. The present study is based on certain observations springing from an examination of the present state of French terminology.

Firstly, it seems that one of the reasons which explain why in France the struggle between the baroque and the précieux has come to a kind of dead end is that the two terms have not really been analysed in connexion with each other. The definition of baroque given by M. Lebègue includes as characteristics elements which M. Bray considers essential to his definition of the précieux —and vice versa. There seems to be almost a courteous gentleman's agreement between the two specialists based on the golden

---

[1] See *Dictionary of World Literature*, edited by J. T. Shipley, 1945. The definitions of baroque, Marinism, Gongorism, Secentismo, Préciosité, &c., are strangely similar, and to an incomplete definition is added: 'See *Préciosité*', 'See *Marinism*', 'See *Baroque*', so that the inquirer soon runs in a vicious circle.

rule: 'Let not thy left hand know what thy right hand doeth.' The danger of studying only one term lies in the irresistible temptation to gather around it all possible characteristics. Therefore I shall be concerned with the two terms, which I should like to see distinct from each other as well as clear in themselves.

The second danger to avoid lies, I think, in the question of inter-influences in western European literature. I shall allude to such influences in many places, taking into account the most reputable works of criticism written on the subject. Obviously it is extremely useful to know the sources of a poem, or whether a particular poetic theme was treated by a previous poet or not. But it is, per-haps, necessary to remark how many times the knowledge of the source of a poem has distorted the critical approach to it. There is not only the fact that its true original value runs the risk of being overlooked when the poem is considered primarily as the imitation of another piece of poetry, but there is also a particular danger in the field of terminology: one is too easily led to call a poem, say, petrarchan because it takes as its subject a theme to be found in an Italian poet of the fifteenth century; one may take too much for granted and so miss more important characteristics which would call for a different label. Accordingly I intend to attempt a classi-fication of French poems based not on sources and influences but on an analytical study of their individual characteristics.

At this point we may recall that, among the confusion of ill-defined terms, there is one term, at least, which has already been defined according to such a method of analytical study: the term metaphysical. It is the most solid strand in the skein of tangled terminology—and might well prove to be the thread of Ariadne. This third remark takes us back to comparative literature and to the possibility I mentioned before of classifying Renaissance and late Renaissance poetry under a limited number of headings. I think that the three terms, metaphysical, baroque, and précieux, would allow us to classify those French poets from Scève to La Fontaine who have up to now not found their proper place in the outline of French poetry. I think also that these three types of poetry, which are to be found in English literature as well as in French, might be found in other literatures besides.

Terminology is arbitrary, and the only basis on which terms of literary criticism can be accepted is their practical value as tools. In the present state of terminology, the terms baroque and précieux are bad tools. They stand for a vague and complicated accretion of ideas and theories, for an aggregate of emotional attitudes towards poets who attract us. We cannot adopt these indiscriminate labels in a history of French poetry; we cannot use such crude and blunted instruments to investigate the complex pattern of a very rich and confused period. I run the risk therefore of appearing harshly arbitrary to some of my readers, because I consciously react against the temptation of bringing every attractive connotation into my study of these fashionable terms. I think the risk is worth running.

It must be very clear from the beginning that this work is only an attempt to define as clearly as possible three different types of poetry. Because the task of defining will come foremost, I shall not be able to devote much time to justifiable likes or dislikes. The three categories: metaphysical, baroque, précieux, are not studied in an ascending or a descending order of merit; the order has been chosen for reasons of convenience and chronology. I do not intend to praise one kind of poetry at the expense of the others. As will appear from the following chapters, each type of poetry appeals to different tastes in the reader. Obviously within each category the artistic value of an individual poem still remains to be judged; the term baroque, for example, once it has been satisfactorily defined, will still cover good, bad, and indifferent baroque poets. Obviously, too, each reader may have good reasons for preferring one of these kinds of poetry to the others. But if I have not tried to compete with the prizegiving spirit which permeates so many studies on these very interesting poets, I hope the reader will agree with me that an attempt at clarification of terms and dispassionate analysis may help to stress the poetic achievements of one of the great periods of literature.

II

AN EARLY METAPHYSICAL POET—
MAURICE SCÈVE

I

THERE are two good reasons for beginning with the term metaphysical. One is the chronological sequence of the poets I
intend to study. The other derives from the preceding chapter. Of the three terms which are the object of this study, the term
metaphysical can boast of a well-defined and secure position in the
field of European terminology, supported by half a century of
analytical criticism in this country. Whatever the divergences of
critics, positive results have been obtained by now on which we
may rely for a definition.

The metaphysical poets—Donne, Herbert, Marvell, to mention
the most important—are characterized by

the more intellectual, less verbal, character of their wit compared with
the conceits of the Elizabethans; the finer psychology of which their
conceits are often the expression; their learned imagery; the argumentative, subtle evolution of their lyrics; above all the peculiar blend of
passion and thought, feeling and ratiocination which is their greatest
achievement; ... their desire to approximate poetic to direct, unconventional, colloquial speech.[1]

The 'peculiar blend of passion and thought' mentioned in this
well-known quotation has been analysed by many eminent critics
and we may safely consider it as one of the essential features of
metaphysical poetry. It is not an indifferent blend, but a perfect
poise between the play of intellect and the depth of emotion. This
poise has been given different wording by different critics, but
whether we adopt T. S. Eliot's definition of 'a tough reasonableness under the slight lyric grace' or that of other critics, we shall
always find that in metaphysical poetry passion is curbed by judgement, and judgement is illuminated by passion.

Such a balance implies on the part of the poet a successful
attempt at working out a complex experience into a coherent
pattern. The nature of the experience which will become ground

[1] H. J. C. Grierson, Introduction to *Metaphysical Lyrics and Poems of the
Seventeenth Century*, 1921.

for metaphysical poetry cannot be defined in terms of subject-matter or even of specific moods. But the experience expressed in the poem as well as the pattern chosen to express it may be characterized to a certain extent by the relation they bear to metaphysics. The epithet 'metaphysical', first used by Dryden[1] and by Johnson,[2] may well be misleading, for none of the metaphysical poets was a philosophical poet, like Dante, Milton, or Lucretius. But if on the one hand we do not find them expounding a philosophical system, on the other hand they were certainly concerned with ontological problems. We are familiar with such problems; we know that they come from an inherent and irreducible contradiction in the nature of things. But as a rule we do not connect them with experiences such as love or grief, and we do not choose to express them through the metaphor of a bed, or a pair of compasses or the colour green. Metaphysical poets did.

Mr. J. C. Smith[3] has shown how poetry handling ontological problems will possess the note of tension and strain which Professor Grierson finds in the metaphysical poets and calls 'the strain of passionate paradoxical reasoning'.

'Problems of this kind are not infinite in number and variety', says Mr. Smith. They are variations on the essential problem of the many and the one; they are the problems of time, space, and eternity. The problem of the unity and dualism of the spirit and the flesh, one of Donne's favourite themes, is a good example: the identity of lovers as lovers, their diversity as human beings.

In poets writing with such an overwhelming concern for argumentation on essences, differences, and causes, imagery will necessarily be used as a dialectical instrument. It will be functional, not merely decorative.[4] An image will be used in order to embody a particular metaphysical problem, and thus the 'metaphysical

---

[1] '[Donne] affects the metaphysics, not only in his satires but in his amorous verses, where Nature only should reign; and perplexes the mind of the fair sex with nice speculations of philosophy. . . .' 'A Discourse concerning the Original and Progress of Satire', *Essays of John Dryden*, ed. W. P. Ker, 1900, vol. ii, p. 19.

[2] Johnson's well-known attack on the metaphysical poets in his 'Life of Cowley'. See *Lives of the English Poets*, ed. G. Birkbeck Hill, 1905, vol. i.

[3] J. C. Smith, 'On Metaphysical Poetry', *Scrutiny*, Dec. 1933.

[4] See in Miss Rosemond Tuve's important work: *Elizabethan and Metaphysical Imagery*, 1947, the influence of Ramist logic on metaphysical imagery and the analysis of the functional value of such imagery. The characteristics of these images are 'aptness, subtlety, accuracy of aim, disregard of the superficially pleasing, logical power, ingenious or startlingly precise relationships or parallels, a certain "obscurity" due to logical complexity' (p. 353).

conceit' will offer the same 'puzzling' quality which characterizes metaphysics.

The elements of the conceit must be such that they can enter into a solid union and at the same time maintain their warring identity.[1]

Considered in this light the term metaphysical becomes a general term, since this kind of poetry is bound up with universal problems of mankind and may therefore be found in any country and at any time. And, in fact, French literature may offer us an example of a metaphysical conceit as good as those given by Mr. Smith to illustrate his demonstration: Pascal's *roseau pensant*. Pascal is certainly concerned with a metaphysical contradiction in man; he chooses to express it by the puzzling union of a reed (belonging to the vegetable kingdom) and of thought (belonging to the realm of the spirit). The two words clash, as clash in man the two aspects of his nature—his frailty and his strength; but the forced union of the words does not disintegrate, once the pleasurable shock of surprise has vanished. We go on accepting it as representing a reality of which Pascal is profoundly convinced: the double nature of man.

This metaphysical quality in the so-called metaphysical conceit being clear, it is easy to see that it accounts for the intellectual element in metaphysical poetry, its analytical tendency, its difficult subtlety, its use of scholastic modes of reasoning, and its learned imagery.

There is another characteristic of metaphysical poetry to be found especially in Donne. It is the way in which the poetic medium (rhythm more than anything else) is based on living speech. Famous quotations from Donne such as

For Godsake, hold your tongue, and let me love[2]

[1] Mr. Smith takes the most famous metaphysical conceits in Marvell and Donne, explaining how each can be reduced to a metaphysical problem:
'Annihilating all that's made
To a *green Thought* in a green Shade'   (thought and extension)
Marvell, *The Garden* (*Metaphysical Lyrics and Poems of the Seventeenth Century*, ed. Grierson, p. 210).
'This bed thy center is, *these walls, thy spheare*'   (man and universe)
Donne, *The Sunne Rising* (*The Poems of John Donne*, ed. Grierson, 1929, p. 11).
'. . . her pure, and eloquent blood
Spoke in her cheekes, and so distinctly wrought,
That one might almost say, her body thought.'   (body and mind)
Donne, *The Second Anniversarie* (ibid., p. 234).
[2] Donne, ibid., p. 14.

or

> I wonder by my troth, what thou, and I
> Did, till we lov'd? . . .[1]

illustrate this 'colloquial' element as opposed to the musical element of Spenserian poetry.[2]

That a similar sort of poetry might exist in France in the sixteenth and seventeenth centuries has in general[3] been either overlooked or openly denied:

We shall look in vain in France for any parallel to the movement which sprang up meanwhile. For 'Metaphysical' poetry owes its character to the peculiar genius of one man, John Donne.[4]

My theory is that there exists in French poetry, not a metaphysical school, but a metaphysical 'line' beginning as early as 1544 with Scève's *Délie*, dodging the Pléiade, running in an underground way through scientific poetry, coming to the surface again at the end of the sixteenth century and giving its last scattered manifestations in some minor poets of the mid-seventeenth century.

2

From his own age onwards, Scève has perplexed and disheartened many readers by the difficulty of his poetry.

Ceux-cy au commencement firent profession de plus contenter leurs esprits, que l'opinion du commun peuple. Le premier qui franchit le pas fut Maurice Scève Lionnois, le quel ores qu'en sa jeunesse eust suivy la piste des autres, si est-ce qu'en arrivant sur l'aage, il voulut prendre un autre train. Se mettant en butte, à l'imitation des Italiens, une Maistresse qu'il célébra sous le nom de Délie . . . *avecques un sens si ténébreux et obscur, que le lisant, je disois estre très content de ne l'entendre, puisqu'il ne vouloit estre entendu . . . et toutesfois la vérité est qu'il affecta une obscurité sans raison.* Qui est cause que son livre mourut avec luy, au moins ne vois-je point que depuis il ait couru par nos mains.[5]

In some ways the present-day student is better able to understand

[1] Donne, ed. Grierson, p. 7.

[2] '. . . Donne uses in complete dissociation from music a stanza-form that proclaims the union of music and poetry. The dissociation is positive; utterance, movement and intonation are those of the talking voice' (F. R. Leavis, 'The Line of Wit', *Revaluations*, 1936, p. 11).

[3] Except for the important article by Professor Boase mentioned above. See p. 2, n. 2.   [4] J. Stewart, *Poetry in France and England*, 1931, p. 57.

[5] 'De la grande Flotte de poètes que produisit le règne du Roy Henri deuxième', Pasquier, *Recherches de la France.* Quoted by R. J. Clements, *Critical Theory and Practice of the Pléiade*, 1942, p. 113.

him than his contemporaries were. The competent studies of the sources by Eugène Parturier who produced the first critical edition of *Délie* in 1916 explain the conceits borrowed from the symbolism of minor Petrarchists. Bertrand Guégan's introduction to his edition of the *Œuvres poétiques de Maurice Scève* in 1927 gives more exact biographical data than had previously been available. A great deal, too, has been done towards the rehabilitation of Scève.[1] The efforts of his admirers have naturally been centred on the obscurity of his verse. The fact that interpretations have turned in such varying directions—towards symbolism, magic, mysticism, or transcendentalism—seems to indicate that Scève's obscurity is complex, and that each of his critics has endeavoured to meet the complexity with a single interpretation. In one of the following chapters I shall come back to the different kinds of obscurity or difficulty in poetry, not as a side-issue, but as part of the problem of terminology. We need only note here that Scève is obscure for very varying reasons: there are the grammatical difficulties (the syntactic ambiguities for instance); there are the semantic difficulties (one does not always know the real meaning and import of a given word); there is his learned imagery which is not entirely explained by the symbolism of the petrarchists (valuable clues will probably be discovered in the domains of alchemy and emblematic literature). Another difficulty lies in the philosophical theories (pseudo-platonic for the most part) permeating his poetry. But even without these difficulties Scève would remain a difficult poet, because the extreme concentration of thought, the subtle relations between the abstract and the concrete, and the argumentative quality in his verse, require an intellectual effort of logic and imagination on the part of the reader. Such difficulty is not deliberate or arbitrary. It is inherent in a form of poetry which does not rely on musical effects, decorative patterns, plain statements, or rhythmical repetitions to convey an emotional experience; a form of poetry which, having complex problems to translate into poetic language, can express that complexity only by means of a somewhat elaborate synthesis, thus demanding that the reader should grasp the intellectual content behind the emotion if he is to be moved by it at all. To this extent,

---

[1] Until these last years, the most interesting commentary on the evolution of criticism on Scève was to be found in Valéry Larbaud's 'Notes sur Maurice Scève' (*Ce vice impuni, la lecture, Domaine Français*, 1941). Now the standard work on Scève is M. V.-L. Saulnier's thesis: *Maurice Scève*, 1948.

metaphysical poetry is difficult; and if Scève's poetry is, in some respects, metaphysical, this will account for at least one layer of obscurity.

3

If the line of metaphysical poetry begins in France with Scève's *Délie* (1544), this means that it begins earlier than in England, where we have to look as late as Sidney to find a poet who, it is sometimes suggested, might stand as a forerunner of the metaphysical poets. As Scève and Sidney have written poems which in many ways resemble each other, comparisons between Scève's *Délie* and Sidney's *Astrophel and Stella* as possible metaphysical poetry may well seem a suitable starting-point.

Both works are sequences of love-poems having common Italian models. Sidney's hundred sonnets and Scève's four hundred *dizains* are both loosely linked together by a love-story which consists of the courtship of two lovers; the ultimate failure of this courtship in Sidney's case, its success in the case of Scève. A few sonnets or *dizains* have an anecdotal interest, as they relate certain precise incidents in the everyday relationship between the lover and the lady, for instance a tournament at the English court or a fishing-party on the Rhône. But as a rule the themes are the conventional ones of their Italian models: petrarchan (hyperbolical praise of the lady's beauty, virtue, and wisdom; respectful adoration by the lover; expression of his sufferings—pangs of desire and of jealousy, separation, alternation of hope and despair) or anacreontic (brief incidents relating to Cupid, Venus, or Diana). This is not, of course, an exhaustive list of the themes treated. In the same way, the short remark about the love-story—the plot linking the sonnets or the *dizains*—leaves aside the question of the biographical element in the poems. But our immediate interest is not the themes but the treatment, and more particularly two important features of the two poets' technique: their choice and use of conceits, and the intellectual element in the construction of each sonnet or *dizain*.

To mention conceits may suggest once again the question of Italian influence, since we know of the Italian origin of the conceit. We know also of the endless ratiocination and love-casuistry in petrarchan poetry. The problem of influences, however, is not our immediate concern. We may admit that both Sidney and

Scève wrote poetry with borrowed materials and according to a certain book of literary recipes, borrowed too: the whole question of what they did with their borrowings remains a problem on its own, and it is this problem that will here be discussed.[1]

Sidney's poetry has often been praised as being 'packed with thought',[2] a compliment which implies either that Sidney was concerned with very important problems or that he applied a great deal of creative intelligence to the service of his courtship of Stella. It has been said that 'passionate thinking is always apt to become metaphysical',[3] and it is thus worth trying to decide whether the intellectual element in Sidney's sonnets does in fact have this result.

Outward signs of this intellectual element appear undoubtedly in the structure of each sonnet; all possess strong articulations such as the conjunctions 'but', 'for', 'so that', 'thus', and so on; unmistakable signs of an attempt to prove something. Many of the sonnets are constructed like a demonstration, even like a theorem, and one might reduce them to the categories of formal logic. There would be the reasoning by analogy,[4] the reasoning by elimination,[5] or the deduction from the general to the particular.[6] The

---

[1] Certain relevant aspects of Petrarchism will, however, be discussed in Chapter VIII.

[2] 'The poetry of Sir Philip Sidney is packed with thought of this deep interrogative-speculative type' (Introduction to Grosart's edition of the *Complete Poems of Sir Philip Sidney*, 1877).

[3] H. J. C. Grierson, Introduction to *Metaphysical Lyrics and Poems of the Seventeenth Century*.

[4] Sonnet XLIX (Sidney, *Complete Poems*, vol. i, p. 68):

> I on my horse, and Loue on me, doth trie
> ·Our horsemanships, while by strange works I proue
> A horsman to my horse, a horse to Loue. . . .

The whole sonnet demonstrates the analogy with horsemanship.

[5] Sonnet LXXV, in praise of Edward IV:

> *Not for* his faire outside, nor well-lined braine, . . .
> *Nor* that he could . . .
> *Nor* that he made . . .
> *Nor* this, nor that . . .
> But only for this worthy knight durst proue
> To lose his crowne, rather than faile his loue.

[6] Sonnet LXXVIII states the general characteristics of the monster Jealousie: 'other's harme', 'Beautie's plague', 'Vertue's scourge', 'succour of lies', and by logical steps brings the conclusion which is a particular feature of jealousy:

> Who, since he hath, by Nature's speciall grace,
> So piercing pawes as spoyle when they embrace;
> So nimble feet as stirre still, though on thornes; . . .
> *Is it not* euill that such a diuell wants hornes?

syllogistic form is also used as a means of demonstration, as in Sonnet XXV: (A) Plato said that if we saw Virtue she would raise Love in us, but man cannot behold the skies in which Virtue dwells; (B) Virtue has chosen to take Stella's shape; (C) therefore since I saw Stella 'I do burne in loue'.

This is obviously the conventional love-casuistry of the Petrarchists. Can we expect more from Sidney's logic? Even when we turn to apparently elaborate reasoning that might lead to a fine apprehension of some subtle problem, we are disappointed. We may take for example Sonnet V:

I   *It is most true* that eyes are form'd to serue
      The inward light, and that the heauenly part
      Ought to be King, from whose rules who do swerue,
      Rebels to nature, striue for their owne smart.

II   *It is most true*, what we call Cupid's dart
      An image is, which for ourselues we carue,
      And, fooles, adore in temple of our hart
      Till that good god make church and churchmen starue.

III   *True*, that true beautie vertue is indeed
      Whereof this beautie can be but a shade,
      Which elements with mortall mixture breed.

IV   *True*, that on earth we are but pilgrims made,
      And should in soule vp to our country moue:
      True, and *yet true*—that I must Stella loue.

We have here four propositions and a conclusion. The fourth is merely a repetition of the first (the heavenly part ought to be King). As it is, the sonnet is a false syllogism, the conclusion standing in contradiction to the premisses. The reasoning runs as follows: the heavenly part ought to be King (that is, we must serve Virtue); earthly beauty is just an image; it is the image of true beauty which makes one with virtue; and then the conclusion: 'True, and yet true that I must Stella love'. We should expect the conclusion to be: I must love Stella because she is not earthly beauty but true beauty. But there is no such proposition in the sonnet and the conclusion means: in spite of all these arguments and in spite of Stella's being only earthly beauty, I cannot help loving her. This is perhaps coherent enough and done with some nimbleness of mind (except for the weak repetition of the fourth proposition). But one may question the seriousness of the argument: a comparison between this sonnet in which Stella is not true beauty but earthly beauty and Sonnet XXV (summed up on the previous page) shows clearly how the platonic doctrine is used both ways, as a handy device, and this illustrates the rather unconvincing character of Sidney's reasoning.

This display of logic does not appear a very successful attempt to grasp real problems and to solve them by a strong movement of the intelligence. The more we study the argumentative strain in Sidney the more we become convinced that it is a mechanical trick of style, destined to lead up to an extremely weak conclusion: the inevitable petrarchan *pointe finale*.[1]

For eminent critics and particularly for M. C.-M. Garnier[2] the only way of being fair to Sidney's 'passionate thinking' is to consider the last sonnets of *Astrophel and Stella*, which offer not only the most sincere intensity of passion but also deep insight into the problems of love. It is precisely these sonnets, the themes of which are night, absence and presence, that I propose to compare with some of Scève's *dizains* written on the same themes.

Here is Sidney on absence:

Sonnet LX

When my good angell guides me to the place
Where all my good I doe in Stella see,
That heau'n of ioyes throwes onely downe on me
Thundring disdaines and lightnings of disgrace;
But when the ruggedst step of Fortune's race
Makes me fall from her sight, then sweetly she,
With words wherein the Muses' treasures be,
Shewes loue and pitie to my absent case.
Now I, wit-beaten long by hardest fate,
So dull am, that I cannot looke into
The ground of this fierce loue and lovely hate;
Then, some good body, tell me how I do,
Whose presence absence, absence presence is;
Blest in my curse, and cursèd in my blisse.

This sonnet is based on an antithesis; presence in absence, absence in presence: just one antithesis (the antitheses fierce love—lovely hate, bliss—curse, are only illustrative of the basic

[1] Moreover, the note of a mere intellectual game is very plain in several sonnets, for instance in the 'grammatical' sonnet on Stella's having said 'No, no', which ends with 'two negatives affirm' (Sonnet XLIII; *Complete Poems*, vol. i, p. 84).

[2] C.-M. Garnier, Introduction to his edition of Sidney's *Astrophel and Stella*, 1939.

antithesis). We might be tempted to think that Sidney is dealing here with one of the *essential* metaphysical problems of love: the union of the lovers when they are separated or the impossibility when in each other's presence of realizing perfect unity. But this is not the case. The problem here is not that of absence and presence, but rests only on the *accidental* fact that Stella feels better disposed towards Astrophel when he is absent, so that the antithesis is not the expression of metaphysical difficulties implied by love;[1] the sonnet only expresses two particular moods of Stella's and the lover's reaction to them.

Here is Scève on the same theme:

Dizain CXLIV

En toy je vis, ou que tu sois absente:
En moy je meurs, ou que soye present.
Tant loing sois tu, tousjours tu es presente:
Pour pres que soye, encores suis je absent.
  Et si nature oultragée se sent
De me veoir vivre en toy trop plus, qu'en moy:
Le hault povoir, qui ouvrant sans esmoy,
Infuse l'ame en ce mien corps passible,
La prevoyant sans son essence en soy,
En toy l'estend, comme en son plus possible.

This *dizain*, which may seem distressingly abstract, is not given as a sample of Scève's best poetry, but only to show the seriousness with which he approaches the problem of absence.

The first four lines are statements, made in an antithetical form, of the irreconcilable results of love: the two lovers are always present to each other in spite of absence (ll. 1 and 3), but in this constant union the lover loses his own individuality and yet retains it (ll. 2 and 4)—the problem of the one and the many, as Mr. J. C. Smith would say.

The solution given in the second part of the poem is borrowed from platonic doctrine: by the will of some supreme power, the essence of the lover's soul can only develop fully in the other lover's self.

Leaving aside the platonic solution, it is clear that whereas Sidney's concern is with the accidental, Scève's is with the essential.

---

[1] It is undoubtedly the expression of *psychological* difficulties. The word *accidental* must not be misunderstood. The contradiction between the two attitudes of Stella may be of a general psychological interest, but, as regards metaphysics, it does not spring from the essential nature of love.

Let us now take two other poems, in which absence is illustrated by the image of darkness.

Sonnet LXXXIX

Now that of absence the most irksom night
With darkest shade doth ouercome my day;
Since Stella's eyes, wont to giue me my day,
Leauing my hemisphere, leaue me in night;
Each day seemes long, and longs for long-staid night;
The night, as tedious, wooes th' approach of day:
Tired with the dusty toiles of busie day,
Languisht with horrors of the silent night;
Suffering the euils both of day and night,
While no night is more darke then is my day,
Nor no day hath less quiet then my night:
With such bad-mixture of my night and day,
That liuing thus in blackest Winter night,
I feele the flames of hottest Sommer day.

Once given as a premiss that the absence of Stella turns day to night, the whole poem is nothing but a play on the two words 'day' and 'night' in order to have them come at the end of every line, with the feeble addition of winter and summer in the last two lines. It is a thoroughly static poem in which the original metaphor—absence equals darkness—is not developed, and it cannot even avoid flat repetition (ll. 2 and 10).

Here is Scève:

Dizain CXXIX

Le jour passé de ta doulce presence
Fust un serain[1] en hyver tenebreux,
Qui fait prouver la nuict de ton absence
A l'œil de l'ame estre un temps plus umbreux,
Que n'est au Corps ce mien vivre encombreux,
Qui maintenant me fait de soy refus.
    Car dès le poinct, que partie tu fus,
Comme le Lievre accropy en son giste,
Je tendz l'oreille, oyant un bruyt confus,
Tout esperdu aux tenebres d'Egypte.

The starting-point is the same as Sidney's: absence is night, and darkness, and winter too; the memory of the day (*jour* in the first line, taken at once in the metaphorical and the real sense, has

---

[1] *Serain*, used as a substantive.

C

the three meanings: a certain day, my state or position, the day-light given by the presence of Délie, meanings which in Sidney are taken one after the other) in the presence of Délie is like an isolated moment of luminous peace in the darkness of winter and proves that compared to it absence is as dark as night.

Then the poet goes further into his analysis: the darkness in his soul during Délie's absence is much worse than the physical weariness of going on living when she is gone, when the body separated from the soul by absence is a living corpse. And the experience of darkness in the soul and physical helplessness is stressed by the final metaphor: we have a rather strange shift from the image of bodily anxiety and immobility given by the frightened hare crouching in its hole, to the anxiety of the soul lost (*éperdu*) in the ominous gloom of a far-off land of exile (the word *Egypte* bringing with it, quite unexpectedly, biblical and geographical associations). The surprising enlargement of the metaphor is worked out perfectly satisfactorily through *oyant un bruit confus*, which applies at the same time to the hare frightened by any noise, to the lover's body to which auditive perceptions become meaning-less, and to the soul to which absence brings confusion and chaos. To sum up: Scève has condensed into three lines everything Sid-ney puts in a whole sonnet, and treats in the rest of the *dizain*, in a far from conventional form, two fundamental aspects of absence: the split between the body and the soul and the frightful feeling of strangeness and chaos in the lover's universe during absence.

One may notice, by the way, that whereas Sidney usually begins a sonnet with a metaphor (and some of them make a good start, such as the abrupt: 'I on my horse and love on me' already quoted) and spends the rest of the sonnet pulling the conceit to pieces until nothing is left of its original strength (the sonnet 'I on my horse' is a typical example), Scève, as a rule, keeps his startling conceit to the end of the *dizain* so that it works like a spring, as if his highly-strained dialectic became so tense that it needed a jump into another field of expression.[1] His imagery is far from being

---

[1] It would be a study in itself to note all the startling final conceits in Scève. Yet it is worth mentioning *Dizain CXLIII* ending with the surprising

> En mon penser soubdain il te regarde,
> Comme au désert son Serpent eslevé.

and *Dizain CLXVI*:

> Et le flagrant de sa suave alaine
> Apovriroyt l'odorante Sabée.

mere decoration and is an imperious necessity of thought which cannot express itself otherwise.

Sidney and Scève have both chosen the end of the night as the subject of a poem. Here is Sidney's sonnet:

Sonnet XCIX

When far-spent Night perswades each mortall eye,
To whome nor Art nor Nature graunteth light,
To lay his then marke-wanting shafts of sight,
Clos'd with their quiuers, in Sleep's armory;
With windowes ope, then most my mind doth lie,
Viewing the shape of darknesse, and delight
Takes in that sad hue, which, with th' inward night
Of his mazde powers, keepes perfet harmony:
But when birds charme, and that sweete aire which is
Morne's messenger, with rose-enameld skies
Cals each wight to salute the floure of blisse;
In tombe of lids then buried are mine eyes,
Forst by their lord, who is asham'd to find
Such light in sense, with such a darkned mind.

This is the decorative pageant of 'Sleep's armory'. The decorative element is the most striking feature of the sonnet ('rose-enameld skies', 'floure of blisse', &c.). The theme, very thin, is the harmony between 'the shape of darknesse' and the inward confusion of his mind. It ends on the antithesis between the darkness of his thoughts and the external light of the day.

Scève treats a similar experience: the moment when the lover passes from the dark confusion of night to rosy morning. But against the loveliness of daybreak he sets much more than a vague 'darkned mind':

Dizain CCCLXXVIII

La blanche Aurore a peine finyssoit
D'orner son chef d'or luisant, et de roses,
Quand mon Esprit, qui du tout perissoit
Au fons confus de tant diverses choses,
Revint a moy soubz les Custodes closes
Pour plus me rendre envers Mort invincible.
  Mais toy, qui as (toy seule) le possible
De donner heur a ma fatalité,
Tu me seras la Myrrhe incorruptible
Contre les vers de ma mortalité.

Scève begins with a picture of dawn which is as mythological and conventional as Sidney's 'rose-enameld skies'; this consciously literary beginning is, of course, destined to form a contrast to the gruesome realism of the last line.

In Scève, too, night was in harmony with the 'inward night of his mazde powers' (l. 4: 'Au fond confus de tant diverses choses'). But in the *dizain*, the shock provoked by the sudden passage from nocturnal numbness and dreamy uneasiness to a state of lucid consciousness brings to the lover's mind the problem of how to transcend death. Awakening thus takes the form of a metaphysical crisis which results in a sort of morning prayer: the proud assurance that love transcends man's mortality.

And if we compare the light airiness, the graceful, almost casual movement of the first two lines with the slow ponderous rhythm of the last four, we not only feel the strength of the antithesis *incorruptible—vers*, but we realize also what solid assurance is contained in the precious substance of the myrrh, while the golden haloes and roses of actual dawn recede into a dreamlike universe.[1]

It is no doubt time to stop crushing Sidney with such comparisons and to carry on the demonstration with Scève alone. Sidney had probably in him the makings of a metaphysical poet (his intellectual nimbleness is significant), but he was a court poet and was not sufficiently great to break with the conventions which were the literary fashion of the courtly friends for whom he wrote. He gives the impression of an immature poet who has not yet taken full advantage of the possibilities offered by the alertness of his mind. Moreover he is more inclined to courtly wooing than to writing poetry, more satisfied with the prettiness of expression (whether it be ornamental imagery or subtlety of reasoning) than interested in the importance of the content of the poem. Yet one should not be unjust towards him, and the fact that his attempts to be a metaphysical poet (however unconscious they may seem) come short of Scève's achievements should not lead us to a condemnation of the kind of poetry he wrote.[2]

[1] The *dizain* evidently hinges on the seventh line:
Mais toy, qui as (toy seule) le possible,
which gives the full dramatic value to man's appeal to love for immortality.

[2] A metaphysical poet can also be a poor poet, though metaphysical, and a poet can be a great poet, though not a metaphysical poet in the sense defined above. The fact is that Scève is a greater poet than Sidney, but it is scarcely fair to Sidney to judge him solely in connexion with metaphysical poetry. In my

Although the *dizains* quoted up to now are sufficient proof that qualities are to be found in Scève that are akin to those of the metaphysical poets—investigation of experience, compressed passionate reasoning, functional rather than merely decorative conceits, special awareness of the metaphysical problems underlying the problems of his love—a further analysis, this time of one of his greatest poems, may not be altogether superfluous:

Dizain CCCLXVII

Asses plus long, qu'un Siecle Platonique
Me fut le moys, que sans toy suis esté:
Mais quand ton front je revy pacifique,
Sejour treshault de toute honnesteté,
Ou l'empire est du conseil arresté
Mes songes lors je creus estre devins.
   Car en mon corps: mon Ame, tu revins,
Sentant ses mains, mains celestement blanches,
Avec leurs bras mortellement divins
L'un coronner mon col, l'aultre mes hanches.

(It may be noted in passing that Scève's *dizains* possess, as well as Sidney's sonnets, a robust external structure. This particular *dizain* is strongly articulated on the two conjunctions *mais* and *car*.)

The subject-matter is the meeting of the two lovers after a month's separation. The first two lines express the torturing power of time which expands from the actual lapse of a month to the longest possible lapse of time imagined by the scientists of the age (and there is also the ambivalence of the word *platonique*).

The following lines characterize the presence of Délie which represents the presence of her moral qualities: serenity, virtue, supreme wisdom. But the presence of these becomes a reality only with the actual proof of physical presence: Délie's arms and hands.

This *dizain* might seem to be nothing more than a variation on the theme absence–presence, but even a first reading, if careful, shows clearly that Scève is giving expression to a very particular experience which I will call ecstasy. This will help to point out more effectively the metaphysical quality of the *dizain*, as the word ecstasy, which refers to similar experiences of unusual happiness and peace, is usually, in non-metaphysical poetry, characterized by the overwhelming intensity of the emotion, the almost

opinion, his poetry belongs to the category of précieux poetry, and within this category, as I shall hope to show later, Sidney is a good poet.

total escape from reality and the wild impulse to lose oneself in the unknown.[1]

Here the lover's ecstasy offers the opposite characteristics; it is made of a clear awareness of the ever-existing problems threatening love: the divorce between the body and the soul during absence, the opposition between the physical perishable nature of man and the divinity of his soul, between the desire of the flesh and the purity of platonic love. The ecstasy is not in the denial of such conflicting pairs, but in a perfect poise between them and inside each of them, a balance that reunites the body and the mind ('Car en mon corps, mon Ame, tu revins'), reconciles the dream of absence to the reality of presence ('Mes songes lors je creus estre devins') and annihilates the conflict between lust of the flesh and honesty of the soul by giving to the flesh the immortal quality of the soul (*bras divins, mains celestes*) and to the soul a physical power of touch (*mon Ame . . . sentant ses mains*[2]). This poise is a very delicate one. We are made aware of the momentary and precarious perfection: for while the lover reconciles the bodily quality of Délie's arms with the divine element, he does not forget their inevitable fragility (*bras mortellement divins*), and we may even suspect that the celestial quality of her hands is due to their earthly whiteness.

So consummate is the balance and so intense the tension that the bold concrete picture of the two lovers' embrace which ends the *dizain* does not in the least point the way to further embraces, nor does it hang on to the poem like an additional grace. It possesses a marble-like quality, as if time had stopped and perfection were achieved in this self-sufficient and fully significant gesture.

4

If the demonstration attempted above proves sufficiently that Scève's poetry has a metaphysical quality, on the other hand his *dizains* do not offer the 'colloquial' element which is the second characteristic of English metaphysical poetry. Although his verse never aims at musical effects or at loveliness for loveliness' sake, its roughness, abruptness at times, is not that of the spoken language. It possesses almost 'unfrench' characteristics which make

---

[1] The Shelleyan ecstasy would afford a fair example.

[2] This is a metaphysical conceit similar to Donne's 'her body thought'. Cf. Ch. II, p. 9, footnote.

it quite removed from the natural, spontaneous utterance of ordinary speech.[1]

Fulke Greville is the only English poet who could be compared with Scève. Even more than in Scève's, we find in his poetry a modification of the normal syntax, a natural liking for knotty expressions; and if Scève may seem, at times, rigid in his stiffness, Fulke Greville is as a rule slow, archaic, stiff and stately to a greater degree.

Fulke Greville, like Scève, is a difficult poet. He may have had personal reasons for being deliberately obscure. But we are struck, when reading his poems and tragedies, by a sort of natural passion for making the most of his intellectual powers and exacting the same effort from the reader, while Ronsard, Spenser, Sidney, and also, in another direction, the Emblem Books and the purely baroque poets, were endeavouring to catch the reader's ear or to attract his eyes.

Contrary to the opinion expressed by Mr. J. M. Purcell in his article 'Sidney's "Astrophel and Stella" and Greville's "Caelica"',[2] I think that the second half of *Caelica* would be enough to convince anybody that Greville was not writing a rather poor imitation of his friend's *Astrophel and Stella* and that if one of them is to be considered as a forerunner of the metaphysical poets, it is Greville and not Sidney.

It seems that Greville does not work at ease among the conventional themes, that the conventional mood breaks vigorously into irony, protest, and increased claims upon the working of the lucid intellect; that his imagery discards Italianate prettiness and fanciful decoration, to borrow, as the metaphysical poets were to do (and as Scève does for that matter), from science, geography, astronomy, and everyday life.

Relatively varied as the themes of his poems and of his dramatic productions are,[3] the poet's mind seems to be haunted by one metaphysical problem, the problem of knowledge. Whether he is

---

[1] To a lesser degree, however, than Milton and Góngora are removed from ordinary English or Spanish, by their latinisms.

[2] *Publications of the Modern Languages Association of America*, vol. 1, 1935.

[3] Fulke Greville's tragedies lie outside the scope of this work, yet would corroborate the remarks made in this section about his poems. See F. L. Lucas, *Seneca and Elizabethan Tragedy*, 1922, and U. M. Ellis-Fermor, *The Jacobean Drama: an Interpretation*, 1936. The poems were written roughly between 1580 and 1610.

concerned with death or love, religion or politics, he gives vent to feelings of passionate uncertainty as to the condition of humanity or of bitter mistrust of man's reason:

> Now in this *twilight* of Deliberation,
> Where Man is darke, because he will not see:
> Must he not trust to his selfe-constellation?
> Or else grow confident, he cannot be?
> Assuming this, hee makes himselfe his end,
> And what he understands, that takes to friend.
>
> *(Fame and Honor)*[1]

There is not space enough to dwell on the different aspects the same problem takes in Greville's poetry, but the following sonnet will illustrate the metaphysical quality this poetry can at times possess.

Sonnet LXXXVII

> When as Mans life, the light of humane lust,
> In socket of his earthly lanthorne burnes,
> That all this glory unto ashes must,
> And generation to corruption turnes;
>   Then fond desires that onely feare their end,
>   Doe vainely wish for life, but to amend.
>
> But when this life is from the body fled,
> To see it selfe in the *eternal Glasse*,
> *Where time doth end and thoughts accuse the dead,*
> *Where all to come, is one with all that was;*
>   Then living men aske how he left his breath,
>   That while he lived never thought of death.
>
> *(Caelica)*[2]

As in Scève's *dizains*, the thought here is concentrated to the extent of distorting slightly the normal syntax of the language, and the complete meaning of the poem is difficult to grasp at a first reading. The first stanza expresses the panic which seizes man when, on the point of dying, he wishes for the first time to atone for an ill-spent life, but in vain. The conventional comparison with the candle is worked out in a very powerful way through the alliance of concrete terms and abstract qualities: 'the *light* of humane *lust*', 'this *glory* unto *ashes*', with an effect of sober dramatic irony in the

[1] *Poems and Dramas of Fulke Greville First Lord Brooke*, ed. G. Bullough, 1938, vol. i, p. 194.   [2] *Ibid.*, vol. i, p. 136.

connexion between *lust* and this *glory*. This *glory* appears even more futile in the next line, 'And generation to corruption turnes', which has the ponderous finality of a knell.

More impressive still is the second stanza which translates the idea of the soul's confrontation with itself after death. Here also Greville's achievement lies in the blend of the concrete and the abstract. The particular horror he wants to impart is impossible to express in terms of earthly experiences, for it is a kind of 'metaphysical' horror: the unexperienced feeling of finding oneself in a world where time does not exist and where thoughts, assuming a life of their own, turn against man. Yet the image of the Glass enables the poet to suggest this horror: the Glass is like a wall shutting out the possibility of any future and checking what was the supple line of development in life with the barrier of a flat opaque surface. The Glass is also the mirror in which the dead man sees not what he used to see of himself, but his own thoughts changed into as many enemies. And while, in a terrible loneliness, man is thus confronted with the Glass, living men wonder only what his last moments were like. The whole metaphysical content is intensified by the poignant irony of the contrast between the timeless state into which he is hurled and their preoccupation exclusively with the temporal consideration of a virtuous deathbed.

The sonnet shows how, for Fulke Greville, the death of the unregenerate man, which is in itself a moral theme, is inseparable from metaphysical problems: so that he conceives the punishment in terms of mental torture, as the agonizing state of the mind suddenly shifted from the notion of human time to that of the absence of time.

In his poetry the metaphysical strain is already, as it will be in Donne, the reflection of the philosophical pessimism of the late Renaissance, centred in this particular case on the problem of knowledge.

III

THE INTERLUDE OF SCIENTIFIC POETRY

SCÈVE failed to create a tradition. Critics have tried to trace his influence, at least on the poets of his own city, on Pontus de Tyard or Louise Labé, or on later poets, very minor ones such as Philibert Bunyon, Guillaume de la Taissonnière, and Claude de Taillemont.[1] Actually the resemblances between the poetry of these poets and Scève's are merely external (Platonism and Petrarchism). It would be idle to speculate on what chances there would have been of a Scèvian line of poetry had the Pléiade not interfered. On the one hand, Scève's contemporaries failed to understand his conception of poetry, seem to have considered that he wrote only for himself rather than to impart anything to the reader, and attacked his obscurity mainly on the ground of incoherence of ideas. On the other hand, the Pléiade poets brought forth a new kind of poetry, the aesthetics of which were incompatible with the tenets of Scèvian 'metaphysical' poetry, and they were so successful that Scève's would-be disciple Pontus de Tyard was won over to the new school of poetry at a very early stage.[2]

Although the poetry of Ronsard and Du Bellay lies outside the scope of the present study, it is necessary here to examine briefly how the new school was running counter to any possible form of metaphysical poetry, and more especially to consider that criterion of beauty which was the basis of their poetical endeavours.

The beauty of poetry had been revealed to them by their classical studies. To create, in their own language, a literature as perfectly beautiful as those of Greece and Rome became the be-all and end-all of their efforts. To put it more bluntly, they did not write poetry because poetry appeared to them the satisfactory medium through which they could express particular problems or their particular vision of the universe, but because poetry would bring a new dignity and grandeur to their native tongue, would produce

---

[1] M. Raymond, *Influence de Ronsard sur la poésie française*, 1927, vol. i, pp. 72–95.

[2] Not only does his second book of the *Erreurs amoureuses*, published 1550, include praise of Du Bellay and Ronsard, but the influence of the Ronsardian odes is easily perceptible (Pontus de Tyard, *Œuvres poétiques*, ed. Marty-Laveaux, 1875).

something beautiful, and would eventually bring them fame. The nobleness of their motives is not to be questioned; but it is obvious that such a starting-point was bound to shift the stress from the intellectual content of a poem to its form, from the intrinsic value of the experience it expressed to its delightfulness.

To begin with, the poetry of the Pléiade presents itself as an experiment in language and imagery, along the lines set out clearly by Du Bellay in his *Deffence et Illustration*:

> ... qu'il n'y ait vers, ou n'aparoisse quelque vestige de rare et antique érudition. . . . Sur toutes choses, prens garde que ce genre de poeme soit eloigné du vulgaire, enrichy et illustré de motz propres et epithetes non oysifz, orné de graves sentences, et varié de toutes manieres de couleurs et ornementz poetiques . . . .[1]

We have seen that Scève uses imagery very sparingly, uses it in fact when it is the only possible way to convey his thought. With the Pléiade imagery tends to become decorative instead of functional, and also to be more lavishly used because it is a means of enriching, illustrating, and adorning. It is, in fact, the extraordinary profusion and variety of images which constitute the undeniable interest of Ronsard's and Du Bellay's first poems. Let us take, for instance, Sonnet LXXXIII from Du Bellay's *Olive*:

> Deja la nuit en son parc amassoit
> Un blanc troupeau d'etoiles vagabondes,
> Et, pour entrer aux cavernes profondes
> Fuyant le jour, ses noirs chevaulx chassoit;
>
> Deja le ciel aux Indes rougissoit,
> Et l'Aulbe encor' de ses tresses tant blondes
> Faisant gresler mile perlettes rondes,
> De ses thesors les prez enrichissoit:
>
> Quand d'occident, comme une etoile vive,
> Je vy sortir dessus ta verde rive,
> O fleuve mien! une Nymphe en rient.
>
> Alors voyant cette nouvelle Aurore,
> Le jour honteux d'un double teint colore
> Et l'Angevin et l'Indique orient.[2]

---

[1] J. du Bellay, *La Deffence et Illustration de la Langue francoyse*, ed. H. Chamard, 1948, pp. 113–14.

[2] Du Bellay, *Œuvres poétiques*, ed. H. Chamard, 1908, vol. i, p. 97 (I have adopted the variant 'blanc' for 'grand' in line 2).

The imagery is effective not because it helps us more adequately to grasp the subject-matter (which is no more than a praise of his lady's beauty worked out through a conventional petrarchan fiction), but because it sets the imagination wandering along many different paths which are not closely connected with the subject. It is the more effective and the more pleasurable as, in this particular sonnet, metaphors are mixed according to a rather complicated pattern, interacting on one another: the *white* flock of the stars is set in contrast with the *black* horses of the night, but these *black* horses are themselves antithetical to daylight (*fuyant le jour*). The *etoiles vagabondes* (in itself a pleasantly unexpected adjective, as we think of the stars as dutifully bound to follow their courses) are connected with *night*, whereas the *etoile vive* (*vive* suggesting both the general quality of living being and liveliness) appears at *daybreak*, and asserts its personality by rising in the west, contrary to all astronomical laws. We pass with incredible quickness from the sheep-fold of the stars to the caverns of Night, from the idea of sheep to the vision of horses, from the personification of the sky to that of dawn, and from the star to the nymph.

The complexity may even be greater when the interplay of metaphors is still further reinforced by the possibility of several associations attached to an image. Thus, in the last lines of another sonnet of Du Bellay's *Olive* (a sonnet in which absence is compared to a storm, the poet to a bark, and his lady's eyes to the stars),

> Lors tout soudain je voy' le ciel changer,
> Et sortir hors de leurs nubileux voyles
> Ces feux jumeaux, mes fatales etoiles,[1]

feux means at the same time the brightness of the eyes and the beacon; *feux jumeaux*, the two eyes and the constellation of the *Gémeaux*; and the expression *fatales etoiles* is antithetic to *feux jumeaux* if one takes the trouble to remember that the welfare of navigators was precisely the charge of the *Gémeaux* (Castor and Pollux).

Similar examples could be chosen from Ronsard's sonnets to Cassandre. In his sonnets, as in Du Bellay's, the learned complexity does not arise, as it does in metaphysical poetry, from the complexity of a problem dealt with by the poet. It shows, as we have seen, that the subtle art of the 'quintessence' (so it was called

---

[1] Sonnet XI, *Œuvres poétiques*, vol. i, p. 36.

then), which Scève had applied to the poetic expression of difficult problems, was being applied to imagery itself, thus giving
that rich and lovely world of Du Bellay's *Olive* and of Ronsard's
Premier Livre des Amours, in which mythological associations,
notations of colours and sounds, strong feeling for nature, and
intellectual subtlety blend in a sometimes startlingly condensed
form.[1]

But most of the time the prevalent concern for enrichment and
illustration was destroying any attempt at condensation, by over-
burdening the poem with images. Thus a disciple of Ronsard,
Etienne Forcadel, who had written first the following lines about
a fisherman who is on the point of yielding to the charms of the
mermaids:

> . . . esmeu de grand désir
> De voir de près qui cause tel plaisir,
> Trois fois sa nef abandonner voulut . . .

modified them by intercalating between the second and third lines:

> Et cuidant voir Venus, celeste fille,
> Née en la mer, et la ronde coquille
> De blanche nacre avec ses goderons
> Qui lui servit de barque et d'avirons,
> Trois fois . . . .[2]

Ronsard disapproved of such padding and repented the pedantry
of his earliest odes, but poetry had nevertheless lost the quality of
concentration it had in Scève. It was to lose its characteristic of
complexity also. Ronsard used classical allusions more and more
discreetly, rejected the mixed metaphors, and came to prefer the
more logical and more lengthy development of the simile. At the

---

[1] These manifestations of the enthusiastic and youthful seething of the
imagination at the outset of the Pléiade's poetic career show what possibilities
the two poets had before them. It may be deplored, in the case of Du Bellay,
that when, later on, he chose to write of actual experiences, the vein of his
wonderful imagination was almost exhausted. As for Ronsard's first poems, it is
interesting to note here what a critic who was one of his contemporaries wrote
about them: 'Il est bien vrai qu'au jugement de Pasquier, dans la Cassandre de
Ronsard il se trouve cent sonnets qui prennent leur vol jusques au Ciel et qui
passent de bien loin tous ceux qu'il composa depuis pour Hélène et Marie; sur
ce que Ronsard en ses premières amours voulut contenter son esprit, et que dans
les secondes et les troisièmes il n'écrivit seulement que pour faire plaisir aux
Seigneurs et Dames de la Cour' (*L'Art poétique du Sr. Colletet*, 1658: 'Traité
du Sonnet', pp. 34–35).
[2] Quoted by Raymond, *L'Influence de Ronsard*, vol. i, p. 53.

same time, with the same general principles behind his metrical reforms as behind the experimentation in imagery, Ronsard had swept away the intricacies of metre, insisted on the test of the ear, and, with a rare sensitiveness to verbal music, produced most successful examples of imitative harmony. This marked concern for the musical arrangement of sounds and rhythms was part of the more general idea that poetry must be, in the first place, delightful; and the concept of *sweetness* (expressed by the recurrent motifs of the bee, of honey, of the swan, of the rose, which are key-images in Ronsard) was equally applied to thought, themes, imagery, sounds, and cadences.[1]

This criterion of delightfulness naturally ran parallel to the criterion of aptness. Indeed, it was part of the delightfulness of an image or of a musical pattern that it should be in perfect harmony with the thought expressed.

These exigencies were bound to limit the poet's choice of subjects, not to those which were vitally important in his own experience or in the experience of his age, but to those which lent themselves to classical allusions and references to delightful things (the perfect blend of nature and learning)—that is, to a certain number of commonplaces. Thus the transitory quality of youth would conjure up the image of the rose and the rose would be perfectly satisfactory, because of its sensuous concreteness as a delightful thing, because of its sensual suggestion as an erotic symbol, because it is the rose of Horace and Catullus, and because it is also the rose of the Vendômois and the Ile-de-France. There are no better examples of what Ronsard could achieve in this way than the famous 'Sonnet à Hélène' or the sonnet to Marie 'Comme on voit sur la branche au mois de mai la rose'.

At the same time, Ronsard was making it almost impossible for French poetry ever to have that colloquial element, which, as we have seen, is one of the characteristics of metaphysical poetry; the exclusion of this colloquial element was implicit in his reform— the opposite of that later effected by Wordsworth—the creation of poetic diction. 'Le style prosaïque est ennemi capital de l'éloquence poétique.'[2] He thus opened the door to the grand style of the

[1] See in Clements's *Critical Theory and Practice of the Pléiade*, an excellent study of the concept of sweetness, pp. 123–86.

[2] Although 'éloquence' here is used by Ronsard with its old meaning of effective verbal expression, it reminds us of a certain high-flown fluency typical of some aspects of Ronsard's poetry, and there is little doubt that the Pindaric

seventeenth and eighteenth centuries, though the classicists of the seventeenth century, in their unfairness to Ronsard, did not realize how much they owed him in that respect.

Such were the main trends of the new school that proved fatal to a possible Scèvian line of poetry. In 1560 there was a sudden drop in the production of French poetry; but ten years had been enough to change the whole direction of the evolution of poetry, and the after-effects of the Ronsardian doctrine were in fact much more lasting and important than may appear from the study of Ronsard's immediate successors.

2

That the poetry of Du Bellay and Ronsard reflected the golden days of the Renaissance is evident enough: the quest for beauty, the belief in immortal fame, the enthusiasm of creative imagination, the intoxication of learning all point to the self-assurance of the new-born Renaissance man firmly planted as the centre of the universe, proud of his newly acquired knowledge, his mind freed from the obsession of death, his body restored to pagan nobleness. But very soon the men of the Renaissance were to find themselves in the midst of such conflicting forces that the enthusiasm would flag and self-assurance disappear. As such conflicts reacting upon sensibility have been the cause ascribed to metaphysical poetry, it is worth examining how, the first wave of well-being once past, French poetry reacted to the first difficulties.

It reacted very early and inside the Pléiade itself—with a concern for metaphysics and a need for some intellectual grasp of the situation. The efforts to reconcile the pagan and the Christian worlds, the new learning and the old philosophy, produced what is usually called the scientific poetry of the sixteenth century. Thanks to the exhaustive study of M. A.-M. Schmidt,[1] that scientific poetry has been brought to our knowledge with excellent analyses of poems and indications of sources. I now propose to examine this poetry in search of possible metaphysical elements.

The first stage of this scientific poetry is, characteristically enough, to attempt an ambitious compendium of all that Renaissance man

'divine fury' which appealed so much to the Pléiade was directly antagonistic to metaphysical poetry (cf. Ronsard's *Ode à Michel de l'Hospital* and *Ode à la Reine*).

[1] A.-M. Schmidt, *La Poésie scientifique en France au seizième siècle*, Paris, 1938.

knew about philosophy and science, in order to build up a coherent vision of his universe. Peletier's *L'Amour des Amours* (1555),
Ronsard's *Hymnes* (1555–6), and Scève's *Microcosme* (1562) are
three Towers of Babel raised as high as the stars by the pride
of the Renaissance; they were to share the fate of that Tower. But
they show how, at that stage, man had the illusion of planning the
world in perfect harmony round himself. With an ardent desire for
order, they collected all the materials available, philosophy, theology, physics, astronomy, mathematics, arts . . . and, piling them up,
endeavoured to explain away all the metaphysical contradictions
and to rejoice in the harmony of the whole.

Peletier's synthesis is based on neo-platonic philosophy and on
astronomy: Love guides him not to the world of Ideas but to the
kingdom of Numbers and Stars; his lady, the celestial Urania,
communes with him through the music of the spheres,[1] and teaches
him the harmony of the cosmos through the praises of the elements
and meteors.[2] Ronsard's universe is organized by his demonology.[3]
The phenomena of the universe, set to work by the *daimons*, are
ruled by the stars which act as the agents of Fate, helped by Nature,
and Power keeps the balance of cosmic forces: these gods being
only the personifications of a supreme invisible god: Eternity. But
Ronsard being a true humanist centres his universe on man who
must, with the help of the ministering *daimons*, fulfil his ethical
object and achieve his true vocation of Master. The *daimons* will
give him science and poetry; all knowledge, from pharmacology to

[1] Here is a sample of Urania's astral song:

> Elle chante des Feux Mondains
> Les mouvements et les pratiques
> Et mêmement des Erratiques
> Les cours paresseux et soudains;
> Elle chante du Sinifère
> Les domiciles apparents
> Qui cernent, ordonnés par rangs,
> En écharpe toute la sphère.

(Quoted by Schmidt, p. 33.)

[2] Here are some lines in praise of Air:

> Air qui est meilleur ou pire,
> Clair, obscur, libre ou enclos,
> Que l'âme aspire et respire
> Par longs ou fréquents sanglots (pp. 36–37).

(I have modernized the spelling in these two quotations which were otherwise
particularly difficult to follow.)

[3] On Ronsard's demonology, apart from Schmidt, see H. Busson, 'Sur la philosophie de Ronsard' (*Revue des cours et conférences*, 1929–30).

astrology, will enforce his power over the world. Scève's synthesis is also based on a humanist attitude, the microcosmic philosophy,[1] which implies that God has placed Adam in the centre of the world; by not making him wholly terrestrial or celestial, mortal or immortal, he has allowed Adam to choose the sphere of his existence; Adam makes his own decisions by means of the free will God has given him; not only does man contain the whole universe because he can contemplate it, not only can he progress in the hierarchy of species, but Scève endows him with a certain purpose and power of organizing the world, and Scève's universe is a progressive one, constantly improved by man's workmanship through science and art, man being God's delegate.[2]

This rough outline was necessary to show in what sense we must take the term scientific poetry. Certainly these poets were interested in what we call scientific facts, that is mechanico-materialistic explanations of the phenomena of the physical world; but at the same time they could only be satisfied by linking these mechanical explanations to a comprehensive metaphysical system.

There is undoubtedly in this poetry a prevalent concern for metaphysics and a great intellectual effort to express in verse the quintessence of the threefold platonic, rhetorical, and humanist tradition. But nothing in these poems would suggest metaphysical poetry as we have defined it. They do not aim at pointing to metaphysical contradictions inside a definite experience; metaphysics comes into them as a postulate, as a system taken for granted. Where metaphysical poetry is dialectical, scientific poetry is dogmatic; metaphysical poetry is subjective and based on psychology, scientific poetry is objective and based on knowledge of the external world, and if 'thought' is present in it, 'passion' seems lacking. Moreover, the use of imagery is in itself sufficient to prove our point. No metaphysical conceit can be found among the metaphors. A study of the image-technique in Ronsard's *Hymnes* or Scève's *Microcosme* reveals a kind of straightforwardness very remote from the sophistication of metaphysical 'wit'. In fact the stylistic instru-

---

[1] The notion of the little world (*microcosmos*) goes back to the Middle Ages, but received its full philosophical meaning in the works of Pico della Mirandola, more particularly in his *Oratio de hominis dignitate* (1486).

[2] The key-lines in Scève's *Microcosme* are the following:
  Ne vois-tu, ô Adam, que ton Dieu se dispose
  A travailler en toy, comme en soy il repose?
                              (*Microcosme, Œuvres poétiques*, p. 206.)

ments these poets handle are mostly either similes or personifications (of the elements: Water, Earth, &c., or of abstractions: Eternity, Time, &c.).

Here is a passage from Ronsard's *Hymne des Astres*, in which
the Stars and the Hours are personified and are at the same time
compared to a flock and its shepherds:

> Quand le Soleil hurtoit des Indes les barrieres
> Sortant de l'Ocean, les Heures ses portieres
> Couroient un peu devant son lumineux flambeau
> R'amasser par le Ciel des Astres le troupeau,
> Qui demenoit la danse, et le contoient par nombre,
> Ainsi que les pasteurs, qui, le matin, souz l'ombre
> D'un chesne, vont contant leurs brebis et leurs bœufz,
> Ains que les mener paistre aux rivages herbeux.[1]

It seems that the relation borne by learning to imagery is exactly
the opposite in the cases of metaphysical poetry and of scientific
poetry. On the one hand metaphysical poetry uses learned imagery
in order to illuminate human experience: for instance Donne's
well-known choice of a compass to illustrate the experience that
two lovers are one. Scientific poetry, on the other hand, will take
images from human relationships to illustrate learning: for instance, the difficult lines of Scève in which he seeks to describe an
astronomic phenomenon (the alterations of the sun when in the
neighbourhood of Mars) and uses the image of anger reddening
a human face:

> Et l'autre ardemment sec pour à guerre s'armer
> Rougement enflammé en sa colere amer
> Rend son prochain chaud, sec, et sur le teint estrange.[2]

It is not part of our study to pass judgement on the artistic value
of Ronsard's, Scève's, and Peletier's scientific poetry; but there
seems little doubt that (if we except some of Ronsard's *Hymnes*

---

[1] Ronsard, *Œuvres complètes*, ed. P. Laumonier, 1935, vol. viii, p. 151; and
also in later scientific poets, this simile of Baïf on the Milky Way:
> Comme en la grande mer une suyte chenüe
> D'ecume blanchissant longue se continüe
> Derrière un galiot qui souflé d'un bon vent
> Depart les flots ronflans et s'en vole au Levant:
> Ce long chemin aussi de sa lumiere blanche
> En deux egales parts tout ce grand monde tranche.
Quoted by Schmidt, p. 175.)

[2] *Microcosme, Œuvres poétiques*, p. 257.

and a few lines of Scève's *Microcosme* and of Peletier) its main interest does not lie in the aesthetic pleasure it can offer, although it undoubtedly furnishes precious documents on the spirit of the age, and thus on the evolution of the poetry which expresses the age.

These versified encyclopaedias of human knowledge have been compared above to the Tower of Babel; but, as we consider them, beneath the magnificent arrogance of these monuments of self-reliance seems to lurk an unmistakable sense of failure.

Scève's *Microcosme*, in spite of the apparent optimism of its humanistic vision, leaves the impression of a sort of heaviness, as though the author of *Délie* had lost faith in his own genius, had accepted the lack of understanding of his contemporaries, and was, with a sort of detachment, cutting himself off from them by an increased use of neologisms and abstruse vocabulary, plodding his way, in proud loneliness, towards his own ideal of perfection, out of reach not only of the average man of his age but of later critics.

Peletier was driven, through his passion for the sciences, to a self-imposed mutilation of his poetic talent, and, as an ultimate result of his feverish researches, to an almost complete metaphysical scepticism. His tremendous effort toward generalization and harmonious synthesis led him to the humble and disillusioned confession:

> La Vérité n'est point, sinon de quelque fait.[1]

More impressive still is the attitude of Ronsard, as in his case the sense of failure, lending an accent of pathos to certain lines of the *Hymnes*, prevents them from being cold objective poetry. As a consequence of his pantheistic synthesis, astral fatalism darkens the last part of his life; the acknowledgement of the inexorable limitations of man's intelligence and power assumes a more bitter form than in Peletier:

> Nostre mere Nature entre les Dieux et nous
> Que fist Deucalion du get de ses caillous,
> Mist la Lune au milieu qui nous sert de barriere,
> Afin que des mortels l'imbecille lumiere
> S'exerce à voir la terre, et d'art audacieux
> N'assemble plus les monts pour espier les Cieux.[2]

Ronsard's theories about the *daimons* assume lurid aspects. He

[1] Quoted by Schmidt, p. 67.
[2] From *Discours à Monsieur de Cheverny* (1584), quoted by Schmidt, p. 101.

can no longer fight them, sword in hand.[1] He becomes superstitious almost to the point of mania, mortally afraid of bad omens. Hence the tone of pathetic nervousness which pervades his poem on the cat.[2] Helpless before his horoscope (he is under the sign of Saturn) he depicts himself as

Farouche, soupçonneux, triste et mélancolique
(*Elégie à Jacques Grévin*)

and loses that *joie de vivre* which was one of the main features of the Pléiade's poetry:

Ah, et en lieu de vivre entre les Dieux,
Je deviens homme à moy-même odieux.
(*Elégie à Belot*)

It seems rather significant that the poet who had been the embodiment of Renaissance self-assurance and boundless ambition should in the end be driven to despair and brought down to the level of the lower occultism.

The further developments of scientific poetry are none the less significant as regards the evolution of French poetry. There was reason to expect that once the enthusiasm and passion for a unified universe which were the framework of Peletier's, Scève's, and Ronsard's poems had collapsed, later poets would be left to work on fragments. And, in fact, the second phase of scientific poetry bears the unmistakable signs of specialization.

Baïf is interested in atmospheric phenomena (*Le Premier des Meteores*, 1567); Belleau's poems are a textbook of lapidary science (*Les Nouveaux Eschanges des Pierres Precieuses*, 1576); La Boderie deals with psychology (*L'Encyclie*, 1571). It was a natural develop-

---

[1] In his poem *Les Daimons* (1555), Ronsard tells how once, at midnight, he met a ghostly hunt and, although desperately afraid, drew his sword and scattered the spectres (*Œuvres poétiques*, ed. Laumonier, 1935, vol. viii, pp. 134–5).

[2]   Mais par-sus tous l'animal domestique
Du triste Chat a l'esprit prophetique,
.   .   .   .   .   .
Homme ne vit qui tant haïsse au monde
Les chats que moy d'une haine profonde;
Je hay leurs yeux, leur front et leur regard,
Et les voyant je m'enfuy d'autre part,
Tremblant de nerfs, de veines et de membre',
Et jamais chat n'entre dedans ma chambre,
Abhorrant ceux qui ne sçauroient durer
Sans voir un chat aupres eux demeurer . . .

(*Le Chat*, à Remy Belleau, 1573, *Œuvres complètes*, ed. P. Blanchemain, 1857, vol. vi, p. 70.)

ment that certain characteristics of scientific poetry already found in Scève and Peletier should get the upper hand and that it should become merely didactic and descriptive. It is not proposed to discuss here whether science is a proper subject-matter for poetry,[1] but in the case of these poets, the 'remotest discoveries of the Chemist,[2] the Botanist, or Mineralogist' (to use Wordsworth's expression) taken as 'objects of the Poet's art', did not seem to open up any new poetic field, were without any contact with human joys or sufferings, and could very well have been stated in prose, poetry coming in only as a technical difficulty to be overcome. This particular distortion of poetic creation, which delights in the *difficulté vaincue*, that is, in choosing subjects which, by their nature, do not lend themselves to poetry, not only accounts for a very important feature of sixteenth-century scientific poetry,[3] but heralds later eighteenth-century[4] and even nineteenth-century[5] poetry.

Among the fragments left over from the great encyclopaedic poems, there was also the germ of a certain kind of descriptive poetry which was to be characteristic of early seventeenth-century

---

[1] 'The remotest discoveries of the Chemist, the Botanist, or Mineralogist, will be as proper objects of the Poet's art as any upon which it can be employed, if the time should ever come when these things shall be familiar to us, and the relations under which they are contemplated by the followers of these respective sciences shall be manifestly and palpably material to us as enjoying and suffering beings' (Wordsworth, Preface to *Lyrical Ballads*).

[2] In their case we should perhaps say the Alchemist.

[3] Scève, for instance, must have taken an almost perverse pleasure in dealing in verse with the problem of adjacent angles.

> . . . La perpendiculaire
> Joignnant la base au bout se parfait angulaire
> S'aguisant droite, ou non, en maints angles pointus
> Par contingence plaine, et plus, ou moins obtus.
> (*Microcosme, Œuvres poétiques*, p. 243.)

[4] The following titles speak for themselves: *Ode sur les causes physiques des tremblements de terre*, by Lebrun; *Epître à Monsieur Laurent à l'occasion d'un bras artificiel qu'il a fait pour un soldat invalide*, by Delille; *L'Utilité des découvertes faites dans les sciences et dans les arts sous le règne de Louis XV*, by Lemierre. And one thinks, of course, of such gigantic productions as Roucher's *Les Mois*, Saint-Lambert's *Les Saisons*, and Delille's *Les Trois Règnes*, so aptly summed up by Sainte-Beuve: 'Il fabriqua en quelque sorte les jouets d'une époque encyclopédique, et, par lui, Lavoisier, Montgolfier, Buffon, Daubenton, Lalande, Dolomieu, que sais-je? eux et leurs sciences furent modelés en figurines de cire et mis pour les salons en airs de serinette . . . le dernier triomphe et comme le bouquet du genre est aussi la dernière grande production de Delille, *Les Trois Règnes*, qu'on peut définir la mise en vers de toutes choses, animaux, végétaux, minéraux, physique, chimie, etc. . . .' See L. Bertrand, *La Fin du Classicisme*.

[5] Cf. C. A. Fusil, *La Poésie scientifique de 1750 à nos jours*, 1918.

poets (and, in its final stage of sophistication, would lead to La Fontaine's *petits tableaux champêtres*): a small picture of a limited landscape, the ingenuity and pleasantness of the description making up for the diminutive quality of the object. Thus the following lines of Baïf:

> Voy l'écarboucle fine et regarde l'eau claire
> Que l'on distile afin que de nuit elle eclaire:
> Voy le bois vermoulu, les mailles des poissons,
> Un petit ver qui luit bloti sous les buissons . . .[1]

already suggest the sort of landscape-painting Théophile and Saint-Amant will indulge in: pastoral poems, in which nature is depicted with all the diminutive detail of a Chinese garden, and which represent, as we shall see, one of the multiple aspects of baroque poetry.

We can also expect, from the fall of the Tower of Babel, that is, from the bursting of that cosmic unity so dear to Ronsard or Peletier, a kind of poetry which will reveal a chaotic state of the cosmos; we shall find this too as one of the main features of baroque poetry. Cosmic poetry did not die with scientific poetry. Fragments of the cosmos, magnified by anxiety and made more terrifying by their isolation, suns, stars, inter-planetary spaces, will haunt later poets, and provide them with a rich store of poetic themes and images. It is the natural fate of fallen monuments to be looted. A huge number of broken pieces was lying within reach; they had lost their objective value, but could become serviceable material for late Renaissance imagery.

But before crumbling away, scientific poetry had other possibilities to offer to poets, and none was overlooked. When the pagan universe of Renaissance man had receded into the background and, for historical reasons, religious problems came to be among the main preoccupations of writers, some poets found in scientific poetry a ready-made weapon for apologetics. It gave them the opportunity for praising the beneficent harmony of God's creation, and for building up a Christian cosmology on a firm and reassuring basis of learned scientific dissertations. Of that third and last stage of scientific poetry (roughly from 1578 to 1610), the most important work is Du Bartas's well-known *La Semaine ou la Création du Monde* (1578). This bulky compendium, which relates and ampli-

---

[1] *Premier des Meteores*, quoted by Schmidt, p. 173.

fies the creation of the world and the first stages of its existence, by its optimism and the lofty picturesqueness of its descriptions gave renewed strength to scientific poetry, while at the same time burdening it with the fatal shackles of heavy moralizing and bombastic rhetoric.

Du Bartas was a disciple of Ronsard. He carried out the Pléiade's theories of 'illustrating' and 'adorning' to the extent of creating a poetic diction which can be at times abominable fustian. Although he has been partly rehabilitated recently,[1] even his best lines reveal in what direction the stylistic decadence of the Pléiade's followers was operating. If we compare in Du Bartas's *Hymne du Ciel* (in the *Seconde Journée*), a passage rightly praised for its powerful grandeur:

> O beau rond cinq fois double, ennemy du sejour,
> Vie de l'univers, sacré père du jour,
> Sacré père de l'an, de toy-mesme modelle,
> Qui ne changes de place, et toutesfois ton aile
> Sur nous vole si tost que nostre entendement
> Seul peut, comme tien fils, suivre ton mouvement;
> Infiniment fini, franc de mort, d'accroissance,
> De discord, de langueur, aime-son, aime-danse,
> Tousjours semblable à toy, tout à toy, tout en toy,
> Cler, transparent, leger, du bas monde la loy,
> Qui borne, non borné, d'un grand tour toute chose . . .[2]

with Ronsard's *Hymne du Ciel*:

> O Ciel net, pur, et beau, haute maison de Dieu,
> Qui prestes en ton sein à toutes choses lieu,
> Et qui roules si tost ta grand'Boule esbranlée
> Sur deux essieux fichez, que la vitesse aislée
> Des Aigles, ny des ventz par l'air, ne sçauroient pas
> En volant egaller le moindre de tes pas.
> Seulement le penser de l'humaine sagesse
> Comme venant de toy, egalle ta vitesse . . .[3]

what is worth looking into is precisely how Du Bartas 'improves' on Ronsard. We find in Du Bartas a strong tendency to repetitions, either on the side of redundancy ('*sacré père* du jour, *sacré père* de

---

[1] *Du Bartas, Poète chrétien*, présenté et édité par Michel Braspart, 1947 (Introduction: 'Du Bartas et la condition du poète chrétien').
[2] *The Works of Guillaume de Salluste Sieur du Bartas*, ed. U. T. Holmes, J. C. Lyons, R. W. Linker, 1938, vol. ii, p. 259.
[3] *Œuvres complètes*, ed. Laumonier, 1935, vol. viii, pp. 141–2.

l'an'), or mechanical verbal witticisms ('*infiniment fini*, qui *borne non borné*'); then an instance (very mild here) of his taste for newly coined compound adjectives (*aime-son, aime-danse*); and a rather heavy scientific image in the first line ('O beau rond cinq fois double'). Ronsard relieves the abstractness of his praise by a few concrete images (*maison, grand'Boule, essieux, aigles, pas*), whereas there is in Du Bartas's lines a dull uniformity which does not even succeed in creating a harmonious whole. The quality of harmony, of wholeness, is fatally endangered by a broken rhythm: from the line 'Infiniment fini . . .' onwards, the reader's mind, constantly stopped by recurrent commas, and, moreover, hampered by the repetitions already mentioned, is left without any valuable thread to follow or key-word to pause on; hence an unpleasant effect of disconnected enumeration or juxtaposition (although, to be fair, there are connexions in that juxtaposition: for instance, *aime-son* refers back to *discord, aime-danse* to *langueur*). Ronsard on the contrary remains a perfect master of caesura and sound, and makes a rhythmical success of the two lines (so different in the use of pauses):

> O Ciel net, pur, et beau, haute maison de Dieu
> Seulement le penser de l'humaine sagesse.

This passage of Du Bartas is a fair example, as he is at his best in these lofty incantations. Another example will show the ultimate result of that stylistic decadence, the germs of which were already perceptible in the lines quoted above:

> Mais tairay-je l'eymant, dont l'âme morte-vive
> De raison ma raison par ses merveilles prive?
> L'honneur magnesien, la pierre qui s'armant,
> D'un attrait sans attrait, d'un mousse acrochement,
> D'aveugles hameçons, de crochets insensibles,
> De cordeaux incognus, et de mains invisibles,
> L'esloigné fer attire . . . .[1]

These lines do not require any comment.

I do not propose to study here Du Bartas's imitators in France (such as Du Monin or Du Chesne), or in England.[2] But there is still an important remark to be made on this scientifico-religious

---

[1] *Works*, ed. Holmes, vol. ii, pp. 296–7.
[2] The clearest account of Du Bartas's influence is to be found in A. H. Upham, *The French Influence in English Literature*, 1908.

poetry. Just as renewed religious activity was characterizing the last stage of scientific poetry, with very poor artistic results, thus putting a heavy seal upon the decline of the Pléiade, the same religious spirit was gaining ground over the whole field of poetry; and by turning really creative poets to religious thoughts, was destined to produce, in the following fifty years, some of the masterpieces of metaphysical and baroque poetry.

As far as French 'metaphysical poetry' is concerned, the case has still to be examined. For the moment it may suffice to mention that in England, among the spiritual or divine poems for which this religious activity is responsible, we find a recognized metaphysical work in Donne's *Holy Sonnets*.

3

There remains a last question concerning sixteenth-century scientific poetry which, although it has a rather subsidiary importance in the study of scientific poetry as a whole, brings out a problem closely connected with this present work; the question of hermetic poetry.

It requires some effort on our part to connect the term 'scientific poetry' with those various forms of occultism which our modern scientific mind dismisses as mere superstitions. We have already seen the part played by demonology in Ronsard's poetry. We know also that, in spite of the immense sum of enlightened learning collected by the sixteenth century, in the later part of that century, and in the early years of the seventeenth, witch-burnings reached their maximum and magical practices (crystal-gazing, 'sympathized dials', and so on) were perfectly seriously discussed; and as poets were attracted by conjectural sciences such as astrology, they were also attracted by alchemy. Hermetic poetry is basically connected with hermetic philosophy[1] and with writings inspired by neo-platonic philosophy, Philonic Judaism, and Cabbalistic theosophy, dealing with the creation of the world, the fall of man, and the regeneration of the soul (subjects which could not fail to interest a scientific poet of the sixteenth century). It is also, in a derived and slightly wider sense, related to the occult sciences and in particular to alchemy. Accordingly, a scientific poet could find in the hermetic tradition

[1] From Hermes Trismegistus (the thrice great Hermes), an honorific designation of the Egyptian Hermes, the god of Wisdom. See Nicolas Lengley-Dufresnay, *L'Histoire de la philosophie hermétique*, Paris, 1742.

both a metaphysical explanation of the world and a treasury of complex and coloured allegories and symbols. For instance, the colours black, white, red, which characterize the three stages of the philosophers' stone—putrefaction, ablution, rubification—symbolize the alternating of death and resurrection, and may also include sexual symbolism.

This literature of alchemy in the sixteenth century needs the erudition of a specialist if it is to be fully appreciated.[1] One may simply refer to Nuysement's poem, *Les Visions hermétiques* (as late as 1610), as a characteristic work of this kind, and in two lines from another poem of Nuysement,

> Je parle aux entendus, esloignez-vous prophanes,
> Car mon âme s'esleve aux plus secrets arcanes,

we have his own expression of the attitude of intentional obscurity.

As the term 'hermetic' is often loosely applied to any kind of difficult poetry, and the criterion of difficulty or obscurity is often used as a means of distinguishing one kind of poetry from another, it is perhaps not unnecessary, in a study which deals mainly with terminology, to make some very simple remarks on the different categories of obscurity which may be found in poetry.[2]

One can first dismiss the kind of obscurity which comes from defects or shortcomings in bad poets: unintentional and unconscious obscurity due to improper use of vocabulary, poorly ordered combination of words, or illogical development. The attempted classification will deal only with *conscious* obscurity (conscious, not necessarily *intentional*).

(*a*) The first kind of difficulty in poetry has already been described, that of metaphysical poetry. The poet, having complex problems to translate into verse and aiming at concentration, will necessarily evolve elaborate poetry and in his verse mixed imagery, excessive brevity, ambiguities may appear to be obscure to some readers. But the degree of obscurity of such poems depends only on the degree of intelligence or attention of the reader.

---

[1] There does not exist, to my knowledge, any general study on the relationships between alchemy and imagery in sixteenth-century poetry. It would throw an interesting light on some rather obscure symbolism (in Scève, for instance). For the study of the three alchemist-poets of the late sixteenth century, see Schmidt, op. cit.

[2] These remarks will have to be extremely simplified ones, the matter of obscurity in literature, as discussed by theorists from the remotest antiquity to modern times, providing an enormous bulk of critical literature in itself.

(*b*) The second kind is the case in which poems require, if they are to be understood, a certain amount of knowledge of the materials handled. As a matter of fact all poetry draws upon a store of knowledge, but the difficulty begins when the poet exacts from his reader a degree of culture above that of the average man. In that respect Ronsard's poetry is obscure, because of his mythological allusions, to a reader who does not possess a classical background; but Ronsard wrote for the cultured man of the Renaissance and his exigencies are reasonable. T. S. Eliot's poems are obscure for a similar reason: they suppose in the reader a good classical training, a knowledge of English literature and of Western religious traditions. This second category of obscurity is also a fair one. As in the first case, the difficulty is part of the rich complexity of the texture of the poem.

(*c*) Very different is the category of 'obscurity for obscurity's sake'. It goes back to a very ancient literary tradition (the Orphic) and rests on the two ideas that (*a*) the poet addresses himself only to the initiated, (*b*) only difficulty is beautiful.

The poet may require his reader's initiation into occult sciences; and this is hermetic poetry proper, that of Nuysement and that of Gérard de Nerval in *Les Chimères*.[1] Or it may be initiation into any kind of particular science. Thus La Ceppède's poems, which will be discussed in the next chapter, make considerable use of symbolism drawn from the Catholic liturgy. In the same way emblematic literature is partly hermetic whenever the emblem results from an arbitrary relation between the image and its significance.[2]

In the same category we may also place poems which may be obscure because the imagery and even the language are peculiar to a certain set of people; because the initiated readers—that is the members of a restricted set—have in common not only a certain vocabulary, but specific interests involving allusions which the general public can only fail to understand. This will be studied

[1] See Georges Le Breton, 'La Clé des Chimères: l'Alchimie', *Fontaine*, 1945. But Nerval's case is more complex; his poems are destined to be enjoyed in different ways according to the reader: the innocent reader will read them as pleasant poetical divagations (and Nerval was very careful not to give the key to his obscurity); the reader who knows the secret will, with the use of Pernety's *Dictionnaire mytho-hermétique*, appreciate the extremely rigorous art with which Nerval uses alchemy as convenient imagery.

[2] It is to be regretted that we do not possess a proper study of sixteenth- and seventeenth-century emblematic literature in France comparable to Miss R. M. Freeman's *English Emblem Books*, 1948.

later as a characteristic of précieux poetry. It implies both initiation and the pleasure of *la difficulté vaincue*.[1]

The stress put on this second characteristic of deliberate obscurity—the conviction that only difficulty is beautiful—assumed in the Middle Ages the aspect of a cunning pastime. Everybody knows of the acrostics, equivocations, anagrams, complex verse forms, all devices enthusiastically adopted by the *rhétoriqueurs*. In the sixteenth century the wilfully obscure poets did not look on obscure poetry as providing amusing brain-teasers, but with the loftier conviction that the poet was a man of mystery.[2] This mania for obscurity may explain how the difficulty of the English poet Chapman is different from the difficulty of metaphysical poetry. There is in Chapman the theory that poetry must be to some extent 'dark' in order that it may be understood only by the right people (initiation),[3] and also for the arbitrary pleasure of a subtlety that 'cloaks the truth' rather than advancing thought.[4]

As a result of such an attitude, the poet who aims at being obscure may use any sort of obscurity belonging to any of the categories which have been examined: in particular the subtlety and concentration of metaphysical poetry (category (*a*)) or the learned imagery and associations provided by high culture (category (*b*)). The difference between this poet and poets of the categories (*a*) and (*b*) is that the latter have to be obscure because of their purpose, whereas this poet has chosen obscurity as a purpose in itself. But the external resemblances of the devices sometimes make the distinction between these two sorts of obscurity

[1] See below, Ch. VII.

[2] According, of course, to the Pindaric tradition that the Bard must cloak the truth which, as an interpreter of divine wisdom, he communicates to men.

[3] Which we find also very clearly stated in Peletier's *Art poétique* (1555): 'L'intention du bon Poète n'est de non estre entendu, ny aussi de se baisser et accommoder à la vilté du vulgaire pour n'attendre autre jugement de ses œuvres que celuy qui naistrait d'une tant lourde cognoissance.' (Peletier, *Art poétique*, ed. J. Boulanger, 1930, p. 126.)

[4] See *Ovids Banquet of Sence*: Introductory Letter: 'The prophane multitude I hate, and onelie consecrate my *strange* Poems to these serching spirits, whom learning hath made noble, and nobilitie sacred; endevoring that materiall Oration, which you call *Schema*; varying in some *rare* fiction, from popular custome, even for the pure sakes of ornament and utilitie; . . . Obscuritie in affection of words, and indigested concets, is pedanticall and childish, but where *it shroudeth it selfe in the hart of his subject*, vtterd with fitness of figure, and expressive Epethets; with that darkness wil I labour to be shadowed; rich Minerals are digd out of the bowels of the earth, not found in the superficies and dust of it' (*The Poems of George Chapman*, edited by Phyllis Brooks Bartlett, 1941, p. 49).

(the conscious non-arbitrary one and the conscious arbitrary one) a delicate question. That is one of the reasons why the question of placing Chapman among the metaphysical poets has been such a controversial one. But the reading of his works after a study of French scientific poetry brings strange connexions. In him we find, reunited in one poet, the main tendencies we have seen separately in the French poets: the all-embracing didacticism of Renaissance Humanism, the prophetical and mystical fervour of the Christian, the learned imagery borrowed from Antiquity, and the esoteric strain tending towards hermetic poetry not only by an essentially difficult symbolism but also because a particularly knotted quality of the style makes the image so difficult to grasp that it distracts our attention from the main statement.

4

This chapter may seem to yield merely negative results as far as our quest for metaphysical poetry goes. Scientific poetry, while interrupting in many ways the natural evolution of the Pléiade poetry, failed on the other hand to link up with the metaphysical poetry of Scève. Yet the striking features of scientific poetry in the course of its development—its lack of homogeneity, its ambiguous and wavering literary tenets,[1] the fact that it raises such problems as the possibility of true scientific poetry (science as an object of poetry) or the relative value of obscurity in verse, that it offers many possible poetic themes and genres—show to what an extent it had enlarged the scope of poetry and the creative initiative of the poet. With its blundering endeavours it played the part of an energizing agent. The Pléiade poets, by the somewhat limited character of their ideals of form, beauty, and verisimilitude, were classicists, and time was not ripe for Classicism. If their doctrine had succeeded in retaining its sway over the late Renaissance, we should have had not the harmonious development of the Pléiade movement ripening into seventeenth-century Classicism, since harmony supposes the concord of literature with the problems of the age and the problems of the late Renaissance were of a particular kind, but a static and artificial condition of French poetry.[2]

[1] Which, if we except some clear professions of faith made by the hermetic poets, the scientific poets hesitated to formulate, holding a perfunctory belief in the Pléiade's literary doctrine.

[2] Such as was the case with eighteenth-century poetry.

But by breaking down the barriers which the Pléaide had built up round the garden of its poetry and thus transforming it into a sort of rather disorderly tilt-yard, scientific poetry had made it possible for any kind of poetry to exist, metaphysical poetry included.

IV

METAPHYSICAL POETRY

I

As has been noted in the preceding chapter, one of the most conspicuous trends in the literature of the end of the sixteenth century is the florescence of Christian poetry which attained, by the first decades of the seventeenth century, fabulous proportions. This religious poetry has been studied in various ways: as scientific poetry,[1] as the imitation of Italian Petrarchism,[2] as a manifestation of the great current of devout humanism;[3] its historical causes have been proved;[4] the many existing collections of verse (called *La Muse chrétienne, Le Parnasse séraphique, Œuvres chrétiennes, Sonnets spirituels*) are constantly being increased by the rescue from oblivion of works unearthed from remote provincial libraries by patient scholars, thanks to whose labours we now possess, in various anthologies, a choice of the best of these religious poems.[5] Even a superficial and incomplete survey of these Christian lyrical works reveals that they range not only from execrable to excellent poetry but from childish and touching praise of a popular saint to passionate reflection on difficult religious problems; that among the dominating tendencies of this vast literary movement the part played by imagination, feeling, or intelligence is extremely variable; and that, accordingly, to write a history of the religious poetry of this period would amount more or less to writing a history of the literary tendencies of the time. Yet a closer study of certain poems shows the existence in them of qualities not to be found in the non-religious poems of the same period: a keen awareness of insoluble problems lurking beneath accepted truths and a reflective interest in subtle argumentation on such problems.

[1] See the works mentioned in Ch. III.

[2] J. Vianey, *Le Pétrarchisme*, ch. iv.

[3] H. Bremond, *Histoire littéraire du sentiment religieux en France*, vol. i: *L'Humanisme dévot*, 1916.

[4] G. Dejob, *L'Influence du Concile de Trente sur la littérature et les beaux-arts*, 1884.

[5] H. de la Maynardière, *Poètes chrétiens du XVIème siècle*, textes choisis publiés avec notices, 1908; Dominique Aury, *Anthologie de la poésie religieuse française*, 1943; Thierry Maulnier, *Poésie du XVIIe siècle*, 1945.

These particular qualities can to a certain extent be traced back to the later scientific poetry. Le Fèvre de la Boderie wrote the following sonnet:

Aux Naturalistes et Mécréants

Comme le beau Soleil de surgeon pérennel
Dardant son rais subtil pénètre une verrière
Sans le verre casser, et sans que sa lumière
Il retranche d'avec son pur rayon isnel;

Ainsi nous envoya Dieu le Père éternel
Son Verbe et sa splendeur dedans la Vierge entière,
Sans fendre son cristal ni rompre sa barrière
Et sans se séparer du surgeon paternel.

Vous qui ne donnez foi à la sainte écriture,
Remarquez ce mystère au livre de Nature,
Ouvrez les yeux de l'Ame afin d'apercevoir

Le Soleil du Soleil qui dans les cœurs veut naître,
Et n'attribuez plus au serviteur qu'au maître:
Puissant doit être cil qui donne à tous pouvoir.[1]

It is a piece of argumentation for the benefit of atheists and materialists. The poet has chosen for his subject delicate points of Christian dogma: that God sent us His Son, who is Himself without ceasing to be One with God; that Mary conceived her divine Son without ceasing to be a Virgin.

The poet knows that such statements are mysteries, that is, part of the dogma which must be believed although they shock the reason; he knows that the new learning would oppose them by adducing the laws of nature; and it is through a learned image borrowed from the natural and recognized qualities of the sunlight that he means to prove that the mystery of the Incarnation is acceptable to reasonable minds. This is different from the usual apologetic religious poetry of the time. Here we have not the crude, straightforward praise of God's works, but a real intellectual effort to reconcile contradictory statements and a rather subtle use of an image which is not only scientific but decorative, and enables him also to round off his sonnet by a praise of God's majesty and by

[1] *Encyclie des secrets de l'éternité*, 1571; in D. Aury's *Anthologie de la poésie religieuse*, p. 56.

the final argument: what you accept of the sun, you must accept of
God who is the 'Soleil du Soleil'.

Alongside this intellectual aspect of poetry, there appears also
in some poets a tendency to express a passionate religious feeling
in a violent and somewhat rugged form:

> Souffle dans moi, Seigneur, souffle dedans mon âme
> Une part seulement de ta sainte grandeur;
> Engrave ton vouloir au rocher de mon cœur
> Pour assurer le feu qui mon esprit enflamme.
>
> Supporte, Seigneur Dieu, l'imparfait de ma flamme
> Qui défaut trop en moi: rends-toi le seul vainqueur,
> Et de ton grand pouvoir touche, époinçonne, entame
> Le feu, le cœur, l'esprit de moi, ton serviteur.
>
> Elève quelquefois mon âme dépêtrée
> Du tombeau de ce corps qui la tient enserrée;
> Fais, fais-la comparoir devant ta Majesté:
>
> Autrement je ne puis, ne voyant que par songe,
> D'avec la chose vraie éplucher le mensonge
> Qui se masque aisément du nom de Vérité.
>
> (GRÉVIN)[1]

These two examples are not given as samples of metaphysical
poetry, but as landmarks on the way to metaphysical poetry.[2] For
if a poet were to appear who, working on similar religious themes
(mysteries and personal religious experience), were to reunite the
craving for intellectual argumentation and the passionate feeling,
he might write a kind of poetry which would deserve the qualification of metaphysical. At the turn of the century two poets at least
went as far as they could towards what Professor Grierson calls
'the blend of passion and thought, feeling and ratiocination': La
Ceppède and Sponde.

2

La Ceppède (1550–1622) published three centuries of sonnets
on the Passion: *Théorèmes sur les sacrés mystères de notre rédemption*.[3] The title is unusual, somewhat startling, and even ambiguous,

[1] D. Aury, *Anthologie de la poésie religieuse*, p. 67.
[2] The Grévin sonnet, particularly towards the end, does, however, come very
close to metaphysical poetry.
[3] *Les Théorèmes de Messire Jean de la Cépède sur les sacrés mystères de notre*

but at the same time no title could better express what La Ceppède will endeavour to do in his poems. The word *théorème* bears its mathematical sense, that is, a proposition which is not self-evident (like the axiom) but is demonstrable by argument. But the word also retains its original meaning of a contemplative attitude towards a certain truth (as the Greek verb from which it comes means to contemplate, to consider), as opposed to a practical attitude. The word *mystère* means: (*a*) a religious truth known only from divine revelation, involving difficulties which human reason is incapable of solving, such as, for instance, the mystery of one God in three persons; (*b*) an incident in the lives of our Lord or the Saints regarded as an object of commemoration in the Christian Church and having a mystical significance; (*c*) the everyday meaning of the word, something baffling to our reason. All these different meanings of the words *théorèmes* and *mystères* apply to La Ceppède's poems. Some are argumentation, others purposeful contemplation. The spiritual activity of the poet takes as its object either a doctrine of faith puzzling to our reason, or an episode taken from the life of Christ (the Mount of Olives or the betrayal by St. Peter), or anything mysterious to be found in the Gospel story (for as he says, speaking of the story of the Passion: 'Tout est plein de mystère en cette tragédie').[1]

The poet's mind is thus intent on deciphering the secrets of the Old and New Testaments, and also on giving artistic shape to the contradictions enclosed in mysteries. But, while doing so, he is actuated not only by intellectual curiosity but also by passionate feelings, as the ultimate aim of the poet is not knowledge but love, and as the stake of this struggle between intelligence and mystery is the culmination in God of his own personal religious experience.

> Les marqués de ton coin n'eurent jadis à craindre;
> Je ne craindrai non plus, s'il te plaît de t'empreindre
> Par le burin d'amour sur le roc de mon cœur.[2]

La Ceppède's poems are not very easy to understand at a first reading. He may seem in a way hermetic, by his erudite symbolism and his biblical allusions. All the connexions he stresses between

---

rédemption, Toulouse, 1613. An edition of this work is being prepared at the moment. The best sonnets from the *Théorèmes* can be found in the various anthologies mentioned above and in Bremond (op. cit.).

[1] *Les Théorèmes*, I. ix, quoted by Bremond, vol. i, p. 349.

[2] *Les Théorèmes*, III. xxi, quoted by Bremond, vol. i, p. 357.

the Old and New Testaments demand from the reader a knowledge
of the Bible. For instance, lines such as:

> Le vieux pal, sur lequel jadis fut agencé
> En Eden le serpent aux mordus secourable,
> Elève ores celui qui piteux a pansé
> Du Vieux serpent d'Eden la morsure incurable ...
> Le pressoir de la vigne en Calvaire est dressé ...
> L'échèle israelite est posée en ce lieu,[1]

connect the serpent in Eden, Aaron's serpent in the desert, the
wine-press of the Old Testament prophets, and Jacob's ladder
with the Cross and Christ the True Vine.

His use of symbolism is also a source of difficulty, as he is never
satisfied with using symbols incidentally or accidentally with a
single meaning attached to each symbol; but in some poems the
symbol constitutes the basic principle of construction of the poem,
thus playing the part that the pulley and the church-floor play in
Herbert's famous poems. And also in the course of the poem the
poet makes every effort to include the greatest possible number of
significances attached to the symbol. In this way he writes a poem
which is entirely based on the number 3 (the Trinity, the three
theological virtues, the three times Christ went to see his friends
asleep in the garden of Gethsemane . . .).[2] Elsewhere his meditation on the white robe thrown by Herod's soldiers over Christ's
shoulders inspires him with a sonnet which Bremond calls a symphony in white, for white is also the colour of the Dove, and of the
Lamb, of the High Priest's and the Pope's garments, of innocence
and of victory:[3]

> Blanc est le vêtement du grand Père sans âge,
> Blancs sont les courtisans de sa blanche maison,

---

[1] *Les Théorèmes*, III. XXIII; Thierry Maulnier, *Poésie du XVIIᵉ siècle*, p. 39.

[2] This *ternaire* may be compared to Jodelle's *Sonnet à la Triple Hécate* in
which Ronsard's friend weaves a very elaborate pattern of triple adjectives and
images, on a ternary rhythm, to celebrate the three aspects of the Moon as
Hecate, Luna, and Diana. Jodelle's sonnet is certainly more skilful. But the
great difference is that Jodelle, a characteristic Pléiade poet, is merely interested
in the decorative value of mythological conventions, whereas La Ceppède's mood
is that of convinced admiration for divine logic.

[3] Bremond suggests, quite rightly, that this symphony in white is a transposi-
tion to a religious subject of a favourite theme of the Renaissance. It is quite
true that white as opposed to black was a usual symbol with Shakespeare, Sidney,
and other poets. The poem may therefore be considered as still enriched by
non-religious associations.

Blanc est de son ésprit l'étincelant pennage,
Blanche est de son Agneau la brillante Toison.
Blanc . . . .[1]

(Religious symbolism and Biblical allusions are still further complicated by the use of mythological names, such as *gouffres plutoniques* or *Averne* for Hell, references to the shears of Atropos or to Phoebe.)

This obscurity in La Ceppède does not spring from any desire to be hermetic; he took the trouble to write long commentaries on each poem. Far from trying to 'cloak the truth' from all but the initiated few, he was showing the way to a more satisfactory understanding of what in the Scripture may seem to human reason mysterious, illogical, disconnected, or gratuitous.

If we come back to the various meanings of the words *théorèmes* and *mystères*, and think of all the possibilities they offer to a poet for whom poetry is ultimately a prayer, we shall not be surprised to find that some of his sonnets are mere descriptions of episodes in the story of the Passion. In these we have not the application of intelligence, but the application of the senses to the contemplation of mysteries. The result is that many of his sonnets—in which he visualized the Passion, describing with vivid imagination the physical sufferings of Christ, or the Virgin's attitude when she stood at the foot of the Cross —bind him to a kind of pictorial and emotional religious poetry, working through the senses on sensibility, in the manner of Crashaw and Southwell. This aspect of his poetry may be left aside for the present, to be considered later in the chapter on baroque poetry. It is nevertheless worth indicating it here, if but to point out how comprehensive is his treatment of religious themes and how he enlists in his work at the same time his erudition, his sensuous imagination, his feelings, and his intelligence. And also one might be misled by the pictorial side of his poetry into overlooking his more intellectual attempts.

Here is a sonnet which is this time a symphony in red, but in which the symbolic colour does not lead to a simple enumeration of objects attached to the symbol (as in the white sonnet):

Aux Monarques vainqueurs la rouge cotte d'armes
Appartient justement. Ce Roi victorieux
Est justement vêtu par ces moqueurs gens d'armes
D'un manteau qui le marque et Prince et glorieux.

[1] *Les Théorèmes*, II. LIV; D. Aury, *Anthologie de la poésie religieuse*, p. 148.

O pourpre, emplis mon test de ton jus précieux
Et lui fais distiller mille pourprines larmes,
A tant que méditant ton sens mystérieux,
Du sang trait de mes yeux j'ensanglante ces carmes.

Ta sanglante couleur figure nos péchés
Au dos de cet Agneau par le Père attachés:
Et ce Christ l'endossant se charge de nos crimes.

O Christ, ô saint Agneau, daigne-toi de cacher
Tous mes rouges péchés, brindelles des abîmes
Dans les sanglants replis du manteau de ta chair.[1]

From the crimson cloak derisively thrown over Christ's shoulders by the soldiers, the poet draws a certain number of conceits all connected with the colour red: royal purple, scarlet sin, and the carmine Passion of Christ. The last three lines are destined to express, through an extremely concise fusion of the three reds, the mystery of the Redemption: the red of our sin (a symbolic red) will disappear in the red of Christ's blood (an actual red), those red sins which would without the Redemption be so many firebrands in Hell (and a fourth kind of red, that of fire, is added to translate the idea of damnation). The final image implies a contradiction which is the essence of the mystery of the Redemption, that Christ should both be white as the spotless Lamb and red with His blood and our sins, contradictions which the words *manteau de ta chair* express in a startling but perfectly satisfactory way, the more effective as, while *manteau* stands at the same time for the idea that underneath it the Lamb is as white as ever, for the red cloak flung over Him by the soldiers, and for the royal purple of Him who triumphed over Hell, the *chair* stands out, at the end of the line, with its one meaning of poor human flesh. It seems, from this analysis, that we find in the last line of the sonnet an unmistakable quality of surprise, tension, and unity, which is not very different from the quality which makes Donne's *her pure, and eloquent blood /Spoke in her cheeks*, a recognized metaphysical conceit.[2]

[1] *Les Théorèmes*, II. LXIII; ibid., p. 149.
[2] John Davies of Hereford attempted a similar treatment of the colour red. But although his lines display subtlety and fine quaintness, he does not achieve the powerful concentration of La Ceppède:

> And deeply die each object of my Sense,
> In tincture of the Sonnes all saving Blood:
> By which Aspect my Mindes reminiscence
> May ruminate the vertue of that good

Another sonnet reveals a similar attempt to bring together elements belonging to very different orders of things, and that in order to express the puzzling quality of religious mysteries:

> Cette rouge sueur goutte à goutte roulante
> Du corps de cet Athlète en ce rude combat,
> Peut être comparée à cette eau douce et lente
> Qui la sainte montagne en silence rebat.
>
> L'aveugle né, qui mit tous les siens en débat
> Pour ses yeux, fut lavé de cette eau doux-coulante,
> Et dans le chaud lavoir de cette onde sanglante
> Toute l'aveugle race en liberté s'ébat.
>
> Et l'un et l'autre bain ont redonné la vue.
> Siloé du pouvoir dont le Christ l'a pourvue;
> Et celui-ci de sang de son propre pouvoir.
>
> Aussi ce rare sang est la substance même
> De son cœur, qui, pour faire à nuit ce cher lavoir
> Fond comme cire au feu de son amour extrême.[1]

Here the blood of Christ is compared to the miraculous water of Siloam and cures the blind race of men as Siloam cured the man who had been born blind. The line 'Et celui-ci de sang de son propre pouvoir'[2] brings the words *sang* and *pouvoir* into specially close contact, to the extent that even the suggestion of 'blood of

> That is our *Summum bonum* and the rate
> Of Sinne, Gods wrath, and just, though heavy, hate.
> O holy God! then looke, O looke on me
> Through the through-wounded Sides of thy deere Sonne;
> O let my Scarlet Sinnes, pure purple be
> In his deere Blood, my Sinnes Purgation:
> For ev'n as through redde Glasse, Things red do seeme,
> So, through that Blood, my workes thou good wilt deeme!
> (*The Holy Roode*, 1609.)

John Davies of Hereford, *The Complete Works*, ed. A. B. Grosart, 1878, vol. i, pp. 28–29. (We shall see later that Christ's wounds and blood are a popular theme in the late Renaissance—as a matter of fact a baroque theme—but what interests us here is that the theme is treated by La Ceppède in a metaphysical way and by John Davies of Hereford with a great deal of intellectual subtlety.)

[1] *Les Théorèmes*, I. xxxix; D. Aury, *Anthologie de la poésie religieuse*, pp. 146–7.

[2] I interpret its possibly ambiguous construction as follows:
'Both these baths have restored sight;
[the bath of] Siloam through the power with which Christ endowed it;
[the bath of] blood by its own power.'

his own power' (which would be a typical metaphysical conceit) seems to creep into the meaning of the line, if not grammatically, at least in keeping with some inner logic of the miracle which re-unites the abstract quality of power to the physical fact of a bath of blood. The ultimate effect of the line is, in its bold condensation, remarkably vigorous and of the same kind as that produced by a metaphysical conceit.

Here we must refer to the definition of the metaphysical conceit given in Chapter II: 'the elements of the conceit must be such that they can enter into a solid union, and at the same time main-tain their warring identity. . . . Metaphysical problems rise out of pairs of opposites that behave almost exactly as do the elements of a metaphysical conceit'.[1]

La Ceppède is not concerned with metaphysical problems proper, but with problems offering singular resemblances to metaphysi-cal ones: the mysteries of religion. The problem of identity, for instance, may be evoked by the mystery of one God and three persons. The contradiction, in mysteries as in metaphysics, springs from essence, and is not accidental. La Ceppède's conceit of the 'manteau de ta chair' and bold syntax of 'de sang de son propre pouvoir' seem to deserve the qualification of metaphysical. There is no difference in nature between the '*rouges* péchés dans les *san-glants* replis du manteau de ta chair' and Marvell's '*green* thought in a *green* shade'.

The difference between La Ceppède's poetry and the English poetry generally accepted as metaphysical is that in the case of the latter the problems spring from a reality which is in the very nature of things and which nobody can possibly deny, whereas in the case of La Ceppède the reality from which the problems origi-nate is grounded on faith; but, for the believer, the doctrine of faith is reality.

Another resemblance between La Ceppède and metaphysical poets like Donne is that he repudiates the Pléiade's poetic diction, and that for him language is above all an instrument of expression rather than a source of delight. Even colloquial or low words are used if found necessary:

Couvrant de vos parfums mon vieux *pus* qu'il déteste (I. LXXXV);

. . . *hé!* dites-le Seigneur,
C'est afin d'accomplir mainte vieille écriture (I. LXXVII)

[1] J. C. Smith, 'On Metaphysical Poetry', *Scrutiny*, Dec. 1933.

> Et vous, Jean, qu'il aimait plus singulièrement,
> Lâchez-vous ce bon maitre à ces cruels gendarmes? (I. LXXX)

It is the tone, vocabulary, and rhythm of spoken French.[1] He does not hesitate to use puns:

> Arbre trois fois heureux, qui vois pendre à tes branches
> La rançon de ce Tout, tu *balances* ce corps
> Qui nos péchés *balance*.[2]

Moreover (as already suggested), he indulges in certain syntactical audacities destined to make the expression impressive; such as the opening of his poem *Vexilla Regis*:

> Les Cornettes du Roi volent par la campagne
> La Croix mystérieuse *éclate un nouveau jour*.[3]

or:

> Mais toujours, mais toujours, vos ennemis divers
> *M'empoignant au linceul* m'ont la force ravie.[4]

Professor Boase remarks on La Ceppède's boldness of syntax in his article on Sponde,[5] and Sponde is in fact the other poet of the same period in whom we can find something very near to metaphysical poetry.

3

Sponde (1557–95) is a late-sixteenth-century poet whom we know today thanks to the discovery made by Professor Boase, who is also the first critic to consider Sponde as a metaphysical poet.[6] His love-poems are not strikingly metaphysical. Except for certain

---

[1] Bremond sees in La Ceppède's use of the colloquial a Provençal characteristic: 'C'est un lettré, fervent admirateur des modèles classiques, diligent, raffiné même; néanmoins il reste peuple. On sait que la langue provençale reflète à merveille cette heureuse combinaison: nulle préciosité ne lui coûte, et d'un autre côté, rien n'est trop libre pour elle' (op. cit., p. 347).

[2] *Vexilla Regis*; Thierry Maulnier, *Poésie du XVIIe siècle*, p. 48.

[3] Quoted by Professor Boase in 'Jean de Sponde, un poète inconnu', *Mesures*, no. 4, 15 Oct. 1939.

[4] *Les Théorèmes*, I. LXXXVIII; D. Aury, *Anthologie de la poésie religieuse*, p. 145.   [5] See n. 3, above.

[6] 'Then Malherbe came', *Criterion*, 10, 1930–1; 'Jean de Sponde, un poète inconnu', *Mesures*, 15 Oct. 1939. Sponde's poems are to be found in various anthologies. See also *L'Œuvre poétique de Jean de Sponde*, ed. M. Arland, 1945. Professor Boase has since published a study of Sponde's life and works (François Ruchon et A. Boase, *La Vie et l'œuvre de Jean de Sponde*, 1949) and a critical edition of Sponde (*Sponde, Poésies*, 1949).

lines of his *Stances*[1] they seem to be good examples of Petrarchism at its best; but here and there a tense line such as

> Je suis cet Acteon de ces chiens deschiré![2]

is perhaps superior to Du Bellay's and Ronsard's efforts during their first stage of condensed and striking imagery.

His religious poems broke away from any literary convention. They would all deserve to be commented upon. But a few examples will sufficiently show why Sponde has been called by Professor Boase 'un Donne manqué'.

He is not interested, as La Ceppède was, in the mysteries of theology. His one theme is Death and rests on the conflict between the Christian acceptance of death and the natural human reaction to it. Let us examine a sonnet which is one of his masterpieces:

> Mais si faut-il mourir! et la vie orgueilleuse,
> Qui brave de la mort, sentira ses fureurs;
> Les Soleils haleront ces journalieres fleurs,
> Et le temps crevera ceste ampoule venteuse.
>
> Ce beau flambeau qui lance une flamme fumeuse,
> Sur le verd de la cire esteindra ses ardeurs;
> L'huile de ce Tableau ternira ses couleurs,
> Et ses flots se rompront à la rive escumeuse.
>
> J'ay veu ces clairs esclairs passer devant mes yeux,
> Et le tonnerre encor qui gronde dans les Cieux,
> Ou d'une et d'autre part esclatera l'orage,
>
> J'ay veu fondre la neige et ses torrents tarir,
> Ces lyons rugissans, je les ay veus sans rage.
> Vivez, hommes, vivez, mais si faut-il mourir.[3]

The theme of this sonnet is a very simple one: the transitory quality of life and the unescapable triumph of death. What is less simple is the way in which the theme is sharply forced upon our consciousness. The basic process is, naturally enough, as stated in the first two lines, to contrast the pride and boastfulness of life with the fury of death. On the whole Sponde makes use of the very conventional metaphors which have always served to express life, death, and the passing of time: the flower, the torch, the

---

[1] 'Et les champs repoussaient un doux printemps de fleurs' (noted by Professor Boase).   [2] *Poésies*, ed. Boase, p. 177.   [3] Ibid., p. 234.

picture, the waves. But the use he makes of these metaphors is all his own.

The effect of a line such as 'Les Soleils haleront ces journalieres fleurs' does not depend on any of these words taken in particular but on the connexion between them: the quality of *journalieres* ascribed to flowers reducing their beauty to insignificance as *journalieres* stands out in devastating opposition to *Soleils* (the plural suggesting, rather than the repetition of the rising of the sun and its daily value, a time measured in astronomical figures), while much of the effect also depends on the concrete and precise value of the verb *haleront* connected with flowers.

For one of the most powerful devices used in this poem is to produce an effect of dramatic irony by connecting the conventional symbol with some concrete fact, thus destroying its romantic glamour:

> Ce *beau flambeau* qui lance une *flamme fumeuse*
> Sur *le verd de la cire* esteindra ses *ardeurs*.

So too the rapid and unexpected succession from *fleurs* to *ampoule venteuse*. The dramatic effect is still further enhanced by the brutality of the verbs chosen: *crevera, lance, se rompront, eclatera*, and the irony reinforced by using these verbs in the active form; it is the torch which puts itself out, the picture which tarnishes itself, and life destroys itself, so to speak, from within.

The abruptness of the whole poem is to be found also in the absence of transition between one image and the next, or in breaks like the last line of the poem; it translates a particular urgency, and death must be felt as a devastating force, which bursts, distorts, and breaks. We must be made to feel the pressure of impending catastrophe and the futility of what stand as proud symbols of human life. It is evident that we are very far from the Pléiade's treatment of the theme of death, from Ronsard's sonnet 'Comme on voit sur la branche . . .' in which the slow movement and melody, the use of delightful imagery, and the tendency to a gently elegiac note produce an effect distinctly opposite to that of Sponde's sonnet. There is no irony in Ronsard's sonnet: the value of the rose as a thing of beauty for ever will not be impaired by its frailty or by the death of a hundred Maries. In Sponde the irony is both serious and destructive, and flowers when he uses them belong rather to the category of 'lilies that fester'.

Another sonnet will show even more clearly to what extent
Sponde breaks away from the Ronsardian tradition:

> Et quel bien de la Mort? où la vermine ronge
> Tous ces nerfs, tous ces os; où l'Ame se depart
> De ceste orde charongne, et se tient à l'escart,
> Et laisse un souvenir de nous comme d'un songe?
>
> Ce corps, qui dans la vie en ses grandeurs se plonge,
> Si soudain dans la mort estouffera sa part,
> Et sera ce beau Nom qui tant par tout s'espard,
> Borné de vanité, couronné de mensonge.
>
> A quoy ceste Ame, helas! et ce corps desunis?
> Du commerce du monde hors du monde bannis?
> A quoy ces nœuds si beaux que le Trespas deslie?
>
> Pour vivre au Ciel il faut mourir plustost icy:
> Ce n'en est pas pourtant le sentier racourcy,
> Mais quoy? nous n'avons plus ny d'Henoc, ny d'Elie.[1]

The general movement of this sonnet, with its brusque elliptical
questions, is that of impatient colloquial speech and recalls Donne's
similar movement: 'I wonder by my troth . . .'. The ironical and
dramatic treatment of death is worked out through the same
devices as in the preceding sonnet: the contrast between noble
poetic symbols (*les grandeurs, ces nœuds si beaux* . . .) and words
which are either familiar (*le sentier racourcy*) or brutally concrete
(*la vermine ronge, orde charongne*).

What strikes me particularly in this sonnet is that Sponde not
only breaks away from Ronsard but goes back in some respects to
a fifteenth-century tradition in poetry. He not only uses, to describe
the physical facts of death, exactly the gruesome words Villon and
fifteenth-century poets used (*orde charongne, vermine*), but his
particular blend of familiar tone, colloquialism, dramatic irony,
and sometimes fantastic imagination is precisely what constitutes
Villon's technique.

In the line: 'A quoy ceste Ame, *helas!* et ce corps desunis?' the
helas! breaking through the sentence annihilates the value of the
soul deprived of its body in the same simple and overwhelming way
as Villon's *Helas!* in

> Le roi de Chypres de renom,
> Helas!

[1] *Poésies,* ed. Boase, p. 243.

consigns royal splendour, a thousand battles and palaces to the nothingness of oblivion.

When Villon, having described the horrible and painful act of dying, wished that there should be a *sentier racourcy* (as Sponde puts it)—at least for the *tendre corps feminin*—the movement of his imagination is parallel to that of Sponde:

> Te faudra-t-il ces maux attendre?
> *Ouy, ou tout vif aller es cieux.*

> Ce n'en est pas pourtant le sentier racourcy,
> Mais quoy? *nous n'avons plus ny d'Henoc, ny d'Elie.*

It would be preposterous to carry the comparison between the two poets any farther. These remarks were meant to suggest that French poetry, from time to time, offers that particular blend of familiar tone, colloquial turn of the sentence, and dramatic irony to be found in both Villon and Sponde[1] and that direct and homely speech and abrupt vehemence are not necessarily incompatible with the essence of French poetry.[2]

However, if Sponde's divorce from the Ronsardian tradition is relatively easy to prove, it is a much more delicate question to decide whether or not the problems which form the subject of his poetry are metaphysical ones. The one theme of Sponde's religious poetry is death; death is not in itself a metaphysical problem: it is a fact. Disgust with life because it is doomed to destruction, or fear of death because of the revolt of our senses confronted with decaying bodies, is not metaphysical. Metaphysics comes into the theme in so far as death is connected with such problems as the relationships between the body and the soul or the contradictions of the two concepts of time and eternity. In part, Sponde's treatment of the theme of death gives no more than the conventional commentaries on the *Memento, homo*, which were the leit-motifs of fifteenth-century poetry: Remember you must die: remember that all your earthly possessions, so dearly bought, treasures, honours, will be of no avail to you; remember that your body will be a prey to worms; that life is like a dream, a shadow, and the world has no more reality than the wind. But what distinguishes Sponde from his predecessors is that the impulse does not entirely

[1] As more sophisticated representatives of such a vein in French poetry we have, later, Laforgue and Apollinaire.

[2] This question will be discussed more thoroughly at the end of this work.

spring from the ordinary automatic reactions concerning death (horror of physical death and bitter awareness of the illusory character of earthly riches) or from a didactic intention. For not only does he report common experiences concerning death but they arouse speculation in his mind, and speculative thought on death is bound to hit on metaphysical problems. One of the problems he dwells upon most passionately is that, although we usually consider life and death as mutually exclusive, experience shows that death exists within life; moreover, philosophy and religion assert that death is another life. This contradictory interplay of life and death is expressed in his first sonnet in an extremely strong and concentrated way:

> Mortels, qui des mortels avez pris vostre vie,
> Vie qui meurt encor dans le tombeau du Corps,
> Vous qui r'amoncelez vos tresors, des tresors
> De ceux dont par la mort la vie fust ravie.[1]

That such lines imply neo-platonic philosophy (the body as a prison, a tomb) is irrelevant to their value as a passionate attempt to think out a contradiction. The tension of the first two lines, due to the sharpness with which not only the elements inside a line are opposed but also the second line collides with the first, is of the kind we find in metaphysical poetry.

If Sponde is considered as a metaphysical poet, his limitations are impossible to overlook and they account for the name of 'Donne manqué' given to him by Professor Boase. The range of inner experiences expressed in his poetry is a narrow one; he is but occasionally aware of metaphysical problems lurking behind the theme he develops; his lines do not always deserve to be qualified as 'packed with thought'; his weakness is on the intellectual side. Although one of his best claims to a resemblance to Donne lies in his power of finding a rhythm that will express the passionate fullness of his mind, it sometimes happens that a felicitous rhythm takes hold of a whole sonnet, thus sacrificing sense and emotion to the perfection of a rhythmical pattern:

> Tout s'enfle contre moy, tout m'assaut, tout me tente,
> Et le Monde, et la Chair, et l'Ange revolté,
> Dont l'onde, dont l'effort, dont le charme inventé,
> Et m'abisme, Seigneur, et m'esbranle, et m'enchante.

[1] *Poésies*, ed. Boase, p. 233.

Quelle nef, quel appuy, quelle oreille dormante,
Sans peril, sans tomber, et sans estre enchanté,
Me donras tu? Ton Temple où vit ta Sainteté,
Ton invincible main, et ta voix si constante?

Et quoy? mon Dieu, je sens combattre maintesfois
Encor avec ton Temple, et ta main, et ta voix,
Cest Ange revolté, ceste Chair, et ce Monde.

Mais ton Temple pourtant, ta main, ta voix sera
La nef, l'appuy, l'oreille, où ce charme perdra,
Où mourra cest effort, où se perdra ceste onde.[1]

This is the perfect ternary poem: the powerful assaulting waves of temptation, whose restless ebb and flow are expressed most strikingly in the first stanza by means of imagery (*s'enfle, onde*) and ternary rhythm, progressively vanquished, abate at the end of the sonnet still following the same pattern. It is a superbly constructed poem, but one may, without unfairness, wonder whether the movement of the verse, the constant working out of the ternary pattern do not attract our attention (and perhaps that of the poet) in themselves rather than as a medium of a compulsive force in the experience expressed, thus destroying the feeling of great immediacy we may experience when reading the first two lines of the poem.

But within these limitations, if he is compared with many other French religious poets, there is in Sponde intense personal experience which, if it may lapse somewhat in the enthralling rhythm of his own invention, never allows itself to borrow spurious dignity from the thud of conventional rhythm or to be cheated by sentimental, ready-made phrases as an equivalent for feelings. He may lack variety in the field of his experiences and depth in the grasping of essential problems; his dramatic, ironical, tormented, unconventional treatment of problems concerning death, of the struggles between the spirit and the flesh within him,[2] is enough to give him a place among those of the French who have come very near the English metaphysical poets.

---

[1] *Poésies*, ed. Boase, p. 244.
[2] See his *Stances de la Mort*, ibid., pp. 228–32, which we have no space to examine here.

4

In both Sponde and La Ceppède we have noted the tendency to a broken, abrupt rhythm. It is equally to be found in the sonnet by Grévin quoted at the beginning of the chapter.[1] It is an interesting feature of the post-Ronsardian and pre-classical poetry that a great number of religious poets rejected the melodious and ample rhythm of Ronsard, and experimented along their own lines, almost in opposition to it.

Some of them stiffened the rhythm into the rigid and robust homophony of litanies. For instance Du Perron's *Cantique de la Vierge*:

> C'est celle dont la foi dure éternellement,
> C'est celle dont la foi n'eut jamais de pareille,
> C'est celle dont la foi pour notre sauvement
> Crut à la voix de l'Ange et conçut par l'oreille . . .[2]

or Bertaut's

> Soit à jamais sa gloire en notre âme adorée,
> Soit à jamais son nom par nos chants célébré:
> Soit l'honneur de son los d'éternelle durée;[3]

and even La Ceppède does not hesitate to make use of this sort of rhetoric:

> L'amour l'a de l'Olympe ici bas fait descendre:
> L'amour l'a fait de l'homme endosser le péché:
> L'amour lui a déjà tout son sang fait épandre:
> L'amour . . . .[4]

Others, like Sponde, Grévin, and La Ceppède (in other sonnets), wishing to express not the serene and solemn mood of ritualistic prayer but the tormented, restless passion of the soul struggling towards God, dislocated the rhythmical outline of the verse, mainly by the device of an enumeration and juxtaposition of verbs and nouns separated by commas:

> Et de ton grand pouvoir touche, époinçonne, entame
> Le feu, le cœur, l'esprit de moi, ton serviteur.[5]

[1] See above, p. 49.
[2] *Cantique de la Vierge*; *Œuvres*, 1622. In D. Aury, *Anthologie de la poésie religieuse*, p. 115.
[3] *Paraphrase du Psaume CXLVIII* (*Recueil des œuvres poétiques*, 1605), ibid., p. 143.
[4] *Les Théorèmes*, III. xx; Thierry Maulnier, *Poésie du XVIIᵉ siècle*, p. 38.
[5] Grévin, quoted above, p. 49.

Conjunctions and prepositions, those words usually weakly
stressed, having disappeared, the lines give an effect of what is
sometimes called in English prosody sprung rhythm—which
means, as far as French poets are concerned, that although the line
remains in keeping with French scansion (the number of syllables
has not changed) it seems at the same time to include more words
and to run at a quicker tempo, and both results translate admirably
feelings such as urgency, violence, and pressure from within.

Here we need but a few examples to illustrate the resemblance
to Donne's technique:

> Or sus donc serrez fort, liez fort, ô canaille, . . .
> Combattez, abattez, celui-ci qui bataille
> Pour abattre, abattu, vos antiques haineux.[1]

> Ceste Terre, et ce Feu, ce Ciel qui ceint le Monde,
> Enfle, abisme, retient, brusle, esteint tes desirs.[2]

> That I may rise, and stand, o'erthrow mee, and bend
> Your force, to breake, blowe, burn, and make me new.[3]

5

We cannot speak of La Ceppède or Sponde as forming a school
of poetry. This chapter aims at nothing more than showing how
religious poetry, at the end of the sixteenth century, was, in certain
poems of certain poets, metaphysical. Strangely enough, no such
metaphysical aspect is to be found in the love-poetry of the same
period. Religious poetry, after Malherbe, was to lose its intellectual
subtlety, its homely speech, and sophisticated use of imagery. As
a matter of fact the last metaphysical accents in religious poetry
are still to be found in Malherbe himself (but, of course, in an
early poem, more or less contemporary with those of Sponde and
La Ceppède):

> Beaux pas de ces beaux pieds, que les astres cognoissent,
> Comme ores à mes yeux vos marques apparoissent!
> Telle autresfois de vous la merveille me prit,
> Quand desjà demy-clos sous la vague profonde,
> Vous ayant appelez, vous affermites l'onde,
> Et m'asseurant les pieds m'estonnastes l'esprit.[4]

[1] *Les Théorèmes*, I. xci; Thierry Maulnier, *Poésie du XVII⁰ siècle*, p. 32.
[2] Sponde, *Stances de la Mort*; *Poésies*, ed. Boase, p. 232.
[3] Donne, *Holy Sonnets*, xiv; *Poems*, ed. Grierson, p. 299.
[4] *Les Larmes de Sainct-Pierre* (1587), text of 1607; *Les Poésies de M. de Malherbe*, ed. J. Lavaud, 1936, vol. i, p. 20.

The purpose of these lines is to make the reader share St. Peter's admiration for Christ's feet, not so much because of their sensuous beauty as because of their miraculous quality. The whole effectiveness depends on having the reader's attention focused on the miracle and at the same time making him accept that feet could, so to speak, be personified. Such personifications are extremely common in a certain kind of baroque poetry and are apt to degenerate into bad taste if not absurdity.[1] But here personification is made quite satisfactory by the clever use of ambiguities, which never allow the reader's mind to dwell too heavily on the concrete picture of the feet. The word *pied* (concrete) is so closely associated with the word *pas* (more abstract and vaguer)—'Beaux *pas* de ces beaux *pieds*'—that it is difficult to decide which will be the subject of the ensuing action. Grammatically these lines are extremely ambiguous. In 'telle autresfois de *vous* la merveille me prit', *vous* stands logically for *pas*, but might as well be the *pieds* or *vos marques*. (In line 4 *demy-clos* ought to refer to *vous*, the subject of the main verb, that is Christ's feet, but makes sense only if it refers to St. Peter who was on the point of sinking when Christ rescued him.) The fact that this *vous* is vague enough makes it acceptable that it should have *affermi l'onde*, supported the feet of St. Peter, thus striking him with astonishment. Apart from such grammatical ambiguities, ambiguities in meaning are to be found as well: the word *marques* suggests both footprints and marks, and the word *merveille* may mean the wonderful quality of Christ's feet or St. Peter's amazement. Nobody would assert that in itself the use of ambiguities is the sign of great or even of very intellectual poetry (it may indicate that the poet has not been able to master matters that were conflicting or alternating in his mind), but in the present case the working out of alternative meanings in some words and the grammatical looseness of the sentence appear as a very effective device in the treatment of a difficult subject. The difficulty lies not so much in the awkward concreteness of the feet as in the fact of the miracle. The miracle is here the basis for a kind of metaphysical poetry (in the same way as in La Ceppède it was the mystery which constituted the basis). In point of fact it is the whole miraculous person of Christ who is implied by that synecdoche, Christ as both Man and God, walking on earth (an actual fact), walking in interplanetary space (a figurative way of asserting His heavenly power),

[1] See Ch. VI, § 1.

walking on the waters (the actual miracle related in the Bible); the ultimate result of these puzzling qualities being concentrated in the last line of the stanza, with the clash of physical security and extreme mental disturbance.

But this is not, in the period covered by the present study, the last example of a kind of poetry which deserves, in some respects, to be called metaphysical. Later on, in the first half of the seventeenth century, poems can be found that show in a very different way the characteristically metaphysical 'reconciliation of opposites', this time in non-religious poetry. For chronology's sake and also because the particular value of this later 'metaphysical' poetry needs the whole background of late Renaissance poetry in order to be appreciated, it is advisable now to turn to what might come under one of the favourite labels applied to late Renaissance literature: the baroque.

V

THE QUESTION OF THE TERM BAROQUE

I

THE term baroque has been mentioned in Chapter I as one of those elusive words which contribute to the chaotic state of terminology concerning the poets of the late Renaissance. Either the meaning of the word is taken for granted and the term applied, without any preliminary explanations, to various kinds of poetry; or theories about the baroque are formulated, none of which succeeds in providing us with a safe criterion for the term. A whole book could be written simply by collecting the different uses of the word baroque in literary criticism and indicating the weak points of the theories about this term. The scope of this study precludes an exhaustive examination of what might be called the negative side of the question.[1] Nevertheless, the main difficulties must be stated as clearly as possible.

To begin with, there is controversy about the origin of the word.[2] The etymology which is generally admitted is that it comes from a Portuguese word *barroco*, which in the technical vocabulary of the jeweller means a pearl of irregular shape, not perfectly round, and it has retained this technical meaning in French and in English also. It has also been suggested that the word might come from the mnemonic name of a syllogistic figure in scholastic logic (*baroco*) meaning a special kind of tortuous argument. Both etymologies would impart the same idea of irregularity, distortion, and

[1] To the best of my knowledge the most complete survey and summary of international theories on the baroque is to be found in a Portuguese work by Afrânio Coutinho: *Aspectos da Literatura Barroca*, 1950.

[2] The word baroque is found for the first time in French in 1531. See A. Dauzat, *Dictionnaire étymologique*, 1949, and also O. Bloch and W. von Wartburg, *Dictionnaire étymologique de la langue française*, 1950: 'Baroque, 1531, en parlant de la perle baroque (ou irrégulière). Emprunté du portugais *barroco*, nom masculin de même sens, d'origine inconnue, auquel correspond l'espagnol *barrueco*, de même sens. Le lieu d'origine de *baroque* est démontré par la présence, dans un des premiers textes, d'*ajorffe*, autre sorte de perle, portugais et espagnol *aljofar*. Quant au sens figuré qui n'apparaît qu'à la fin du XVIIe s. (Saint-Simon), les textes ne permettent pas actuellement de reconnaître s'il s'est développé spontanément ou s'il est postérieur à son application au style architectural de Borromini, XVIIe (sens qui a été emprunté de l'italien *barocco*, qui vient aussi du portugais).'

lack of proportion. Moreover, there are the ordinary associations of the word as part of everyday French vocabulary (meaning queer, quaint, crazy) which obviously come into play if it is used without definition.

The main trouble with the term is that it first belonged to the field of art criticism, where it was harmless enough for a time, being applied in a derogatory way by classicist critics of the eighteenth century to denounce the non-classical taste in which the preceding period had indulged. But at the beginning of the present century the baroque style was analysed in an objective and masterly way by the art-historian Wölfflin.[1] Wölfflin's criteria for the baroque are based on a symmetrical opposition between Renaissance and baroque art. For instance, Renaissance art is 'linear', 'closed', 'flat', 'clear', whereas baroque art is 'painterly', 'open', 'deep', 'blurred'. The transfer of Wölfflin's categories to literature immediately became an irresistible temptation to literary critics. Mr. R. Wellek in an article on 'The Concept of Baroque in Literary Scholarship'[2] has analysed the dangers of such parallelism between the different arts. When we consider not only the examples given by Mr. Wellek but even more recent attempts, we can see that the results obtained by this transfer of Wölfflin's categories are unsatisfactory, even in the most interesting and very subtle article by M. Marcel Raymond, 'Propositions sur le Baroque et la Littérature française'.[3] It seems first that some of Wölfflin's categories cannot be transposed to literature, or would become completely distorted or ambiguous if this were attempted (such are, for instance, the concepts of 'flatness' or 'depth'); secondly, that if we apply those which prove more tractable, they seem to help us merely to arrange works in two categories which correspond roughly to Classicism and Romanticism, with the opposition between the static linear classical poem and the dynamic restless poetry of the romantics. It is significant that M. Raymond, who is yet one of the best scholars on the period, should in 1949 come back in a way to the theories of Eugenio d'Ors (he even mentions him), who wrote in the thirties and proposed a concept of the baroque as an historical constant alternating with the classical.[4]

[1] H. Wölfflin, *Kunstgeschichtliche Grundbegriffe*, 1915, translated into English as *Principles of Art History*, 1932.

[2] In the *Journal of Aesthetics and Art Criticism*, vol. v, p. 2 (1946).

[3] In the *Revue des sciences humaines*, July–Dec. 1949.

[4] E. d'Ors, *Du baroque*, Version française de Mme A. Rouardt-Valéry, 1935.

Yet when we think of Eugenio d'Ors we are taken back to the beginning of the baroque controversy, as his book is, for the greater part, an account of the famous 'Querelle de Pontigny', which occurred when a group of eminent professors and art critics, Dutch, French, German, and Spanish, met in order to form a general criterion for the baroque and failed after the most amusing incidents.[1]

There is also a new danger lurking in the field of art criticism for those who try to pursue the parallelism between art and literature in the late Renaissance. Professor Pevsner, in his lectures in Cambridge and in articles, has shown in a most convincing way how a style different from the baroque, namely Mannerism, separates the Renaissance from the baroque. The term Mannerism has almost immediately been adopted by literary criticism.[2]

It seems impossible to rely on art criticism to find a safe criterion for the baroque in literature. It seems also very difficult, at the present stage, to look for help and more clarity in the terminology of German, Spanish, and Italian literatures. The use of the term baroque in the terminology of German literature, in particular, appears to be of no value for the present study, as it covers all the poetry of the seventeenth century and acquires a wider connotation in a field of literary criticism in which the words metaphysical and précieux do not exist.[3]

It may be wondered why the word baroque should not be used in the terminology of French and English literature, as it is in German, to designate simply an historical period, which would correspond roughly to the late Renaissance. In fact there has always been a strong tendency to use the term with this historical connotation. But there is such a marked hesitation in recent criticism between the baroque as an era and the baroque as a type of

[1] The Querelle de Pontigny has become the prototype and caricature of a baroque conference, and a warning too. It is probably because of that warning that the Deuxième Congrès des Études Françaises, held in Paris in September 1950, in order to discuss the term baroque, assumed a sober tone, a certain self-consciousness, and a complete absence of the picturesque. Perhaps also because of certain memories of Pontigny, there was only one art critic present.

[2] See M. M. Mahood, *Poetry and Humanism*, 1950.

[3] This particular point (the dismissal, painful as it may be, of all that the specialists on German literature have concluded about the baroque) has been very clearly stated in a study on the baroque, 'Baroque Literature in England', by Mr. Marco Mincoff, which I have been privileged to read in manuscript. My own experience of discussions with specialists on German literature, stimulating as they were, has convinced me that we cannot apply their criteria outside the field of German literature.

literature that we cannot possibly consider that there is a clear acceptance of the baroque as a synonym for the late Renaissance, outside Germany.[1] It is only too clear that if the baroque is an aggregate of the manifestations of the late Renaissance spirit, we must look for a general criterion which would cover all the manifestations of the period, including literature, philosophy, music, and the sciences. The quest for this general criterion was responsible for the failure of the Pontigny conference; it inevitably leads to those parallels between literature and the other arts which have proved so unsatisfactory. Modern criticism, on the one hand, longs for some unified interpretation of the late Renaissance characteristics which would establish the term baroque on a solid historical basis;[2] but, on the other hand, so much attention has been devoted to the baroque as a specific type of literature that it is very difficult to deny the fact that by now the word has its place in the aesthetic categories of literary terminology.

Even if we limit ourselves to the literatures of France and England, it is not easy to find an acceptable criterion for the use of the term baroque. The criterion of the Counter-Reformation has to be discarded; for if baroque were Counter-Reformation only, a baroque poet would necessarily be a Catholic; but of the three English poets usually considered baroque—Southwell, Giles Fletcher, and Crashaw—Fletcher was a Protestant and not particularly High Church, and Crashaw wrote a great deal of his poetry before he was converted to Roman Catholicism. On the French side, d'Aubigné was a Protestant, and Sponde (if we include him in the baroque) a converted Protestant.

One cannot even say that baroque poetry must be religious, since what is considered as one of the first examples of baroque poetry in France, d'Aubigné's *Printemps*, is a sequence of love-poems; and the poets Théophile and Saint-Amant, considered also as baroque, were suspected of being free-thinkers.

One may face the problem in another way and try to find the criterion of baroque literature, and especially baroque poetry, from within, that is, in a certain number of themes or stylistic

[1] And even among the specialists on the German baroque, some confess, with some uneasiness, that inside the period labelled baroque there are literary manifestations which express a kind of baroque within the baroque.

[2] This wish, voiced so many times, has been expressed recently by Mr. Wolfgang Stechow in an article on 'Definitions of the Baroque in the Visual Arts' (*Journal of Aesthetics and Art Criticism*, vol. v, p. 2).

characteristics. This is the line taken by some critics: Mr. Wellek in America, M. Lebègue in France, and a small number of English critics. The themes which are considered baroque are more or less the features held to be characteristic of the late Renaissance: death, violence and passion, feeling of insecurity, effort at reconciling the macrocosmos and the microcosmos, contradiction and tension. As far as the style is concerned, the stress is put on the use of the conceit, the far-fetched metaphor, the hyperbole, and other ornaments.

It is certainly impossible to disprove the contention that the baroque has something to do with such themes, or that baroque poetry uses conceits. My objection to such a description of the baroque is that it does not make the term baroque sufficiently clear and distinct from other terms. The very obvious proof is that it has led in English criticism to the confusion between baroque and metaphysical. Miss Kathleen Raine in 'John Donne and the Baroque Doubt'[1] is an example of the tendency to ascribe a recognized metaphysical poet's characteristics to the baroque. Mr. T. S. Eliot in 'A Note on Richard Crashaw'[2] calls this poet both metaphysical and baroque, implying, it seems, that baroque is the European term and metaphysical the English one. Mr. Mincoff does not hesitate to state: 'The most obvious characteristic of the baroque lyric both in Italy and Germany is the metaphysical conceit that we find in England in the poetry of Donne and his followers.' For Mr. Mincoff the metaphysical style is only one of the streams of baroque culture.[3]

In France the most noticeable event has been the controversy between M. Lebègue and M. André Chastel,[4] as a result of which M. Lebègue has been led to the following conclusions. He defines the baroque as: (a) 'l'abondance luxuriante et désordonnée'; (b) 'die

---

[1] *Horizon*, 1943. [2] In *For Lancelot Andrewes*, 1928.

[3] Miss Mahood's recent book has something of the same confusion between baroque and metaphysical; see particularly in the chapter 'Donne, the Baroque Preacher', pp. 145–6.

[4] R. Lebègue, 'Le Théâtre baroque en France', *Bibliothèque d'humanisme et renaissance*, 1942; A. Chastel, 'Sur le baroque français', 1944; R. Lebègue, *La poésie française de 1560 à 1630*, 1951. See also P. Kohler, 'Le Classicisme français et le problème du baroque', *Lettres de France — Périodes et Problèmes*, 1943. There is also a most interesting contribution to the problem of the baroque in M. G. de Reynold's *Le XVIIᵉ Siècle*, 1944. I shall state later the extent to which M. de Reynold's views on the baroque are of particular interest to me (see below, p. 75).

Lebensfülle', or, more exactly, the hyperbolical representation of intense feelings; (c) the straining after the surprising, the subtle, the new, and after an original way of expressing a commonplace thought. Such a definition worked out by an eminent specialist on the poetry of the period and proposed with a great deal of caution is extremely valuable, but not altogether satisfactory. Some of the characteristics which M. Lebègue claims to be those of baroque poetry—such as an ornate style and a hyperbolical representation of feeling, the straining after the surprising, the new—are precisely the characteristics which M. Bray considers as the very essence of the précieux.[1]

Within the last year or two the term baroque has become one of the most widely discussed in literary studies, but there seems to have been little development towards a more precise definition of the word. A special number of the *Revue des sciences humaines*[2] was devoted to the baroque, and during the Deuxième Congrès des Études Françaises[3] the baroque was one of the main subjects for discussion. It appears from the articles contained in the *Revue des sciences humaines*, as well as from the papers read at the conference, that the specialists of the baroque are maintaining the positions they had previously assumed.

After such fruitless researches concerning the exact place of the term baroque in the two terminologies (the French and the English) where it seems constantly to be confused with either the précieux or the metaphysical, one would be tempted to agree with Mr. J. Mark that in literary criticism the word baroque means nothing.[4]

In spite of these discouraging remarks, an attempt can perhaps be made to propose a criterion which tries both to take into account the results obtained by the specialists of the baroque question and to differentiate between the baroque, the metaphysical, and the précieux.

[1] M. Bray's theories on the précieux will be discussed in Chapter VII.

[2] July–Dec. 1949. See particularly '*Les Larmes de Saint Pierre*, poème baroque', by M. Lebègue; M. Raymond's article 'Propositions sur le baroque et la littérature française', already mentioned; and Professor Boase's article 'Poètes anglais et français de l'époque baroque' (I would very readily agree with a great number of his remarks, although they are not immediately relevant to the problem of terminology studied here).

[3] This conference has already been mentioned. See the account written by M. Lebègue in *Revue d'histoire littéraire de la France*, Oct.–Dec. 1950.

[4] J. Mark, 'The Uses of the Term Baroque', *Modern Language Review* vol. xxiii, 1938.

2

To begin with, I think that part of the confusion is due to a careless use of stylistic devices as a means of providing a criterion for the baroque. Many critics base their distinctions on the presence or the predominance of figures of speech such as the conceit or the hyperbole, instead of studying the nature and the function of a given figure of speech in a given poem. I shall come back to this point, which I consider particularly important, when studying the rhetoric of précieux poetry. But even at this stage this remark may show how easily one can be led to confuse a metaphysical conceit and a non-metaphysical conceit, and to overlook the fact that the use of the hyperbole is very different in a metaphysical poet like Marvell from what it is in a 'salon' poet like Voiture.

There is another reason which might explain why there has been a growing refusal to distinguish clearly between the baroque and the metaphysical. More and more we think of the poets whom we call metaphysical, or baroque, or both, mostly in connexion with the problems of their age. Therefore we want to see in all of them, whether baroque or metaphysical, the poetic expression of the spirit of the age. We are tempted to unify their reactions to these problems into one typical attitude and to gather their stylistic characteristics into one sheaf of similar poetic devices. To a certain extent this is a reasonable view, and, if one were content to accept baroque as a vague synonym for late Renaissance, one might leave the question there. But this can hardly satisfy those for whom a term is only clear when it is also, in the Cartesian meaning of the word, distinct.

It is, I think, possible to distinguish between different attitudes and responses to the same problems in the late Renaissance. As is well known, this was a time of great confusion, of spiritual crises, of religious wars, and of bitter disillusionment after the exhilaration of the Renaissance.[1] With the conflict between Humanism and Religion, and, inside Religion, between Reformation and Counter-Reformation, the poets had to deal with the impossible tripartism: Platonism, Natural Sciences, Religion; and out of this conflict of elements there emerged, inevitably, a sort of poetry reflecting the efforts of the poet's intelligence, stimulated by the hardships of the age, to grasp the eternal problems of man's destiny, that is

[1] See above, Ch. III.

the metaphysical ones. These conflicts provided then the most favourable climate for metaphysical poetry. We have seen that metaphysical poetry was characterized by its intellectual emphasis, that 'the distinctive note of metaphysical poetry is a distinctive blend of passionate feeling and paradoxical ratiocination', and that the metaphysical conceit has in the same way been defined as a sort of balance between conflicting elements. Such perfect poise constitutes the achievement of a Donne, a Herbert, a Marvell. But it is a very delicate poise, and it is perfectly understandable that the balance might be destroyed and that sensibility and imagination might have a firmer hold upon the poet than an intellectual desire for the reconciliation of opposing forces.

I should like to limit the meaning of the term baroque and to apply it only to the poetry in which, although the problems of the age are reflected, the perfect poise between intelligence and sensibility is either destroyed or not achieved or not attempted, with the result that the poet has a distorted vision of life, distorted through imagination and sensibility, without any apparent care for proportions or balance. Two comments should perhaps be made: first, that a 'distorted' vision may, of course, carry its own poetic value and, secondly, that I take sensibility in the widest connotation of the word, including the senses as well as the emotions.

This definition puts baroque poetry into an aesthetic category different from that of metaphysical poetry. In metaphysical poetry we judge a poem by the art with which the poet achieves the reconciliation of clashing opposites. In baroque poetry we should judge a poem by the art with which the poet expresses the experiences of a sensibility determined to go, unchecked, to the bitter end of its reactions to the problems of the age.

The baroque poet thus depends on his power to carry his reader into his own world which is often a sort of surreality, and to light up for him those strange vistas which such baroque sensibility can open up both in the concrete world of nature and in the recesses of man's consciousness. Accordingly the stylistic devices used by the baroque poet will work mostly on the imagination and the emotions of the reader, and as powerfully as possible. Hence, perhaps, that impression of violence, restlessness, or vehemence which is often linked with the term baroque.

This definition does not go against M. Lebègue's statement that the baroque aims at calling forth astonishment: unchecked sensibility will naturally indulge in its distorted vision and enjoy making it as uncouth or appalling as possible. Nor does it reject altogether the characteristics of 'subjectivism and introspection' which Mr. Mincoff considers as primarily important; although it will make a clear distinction between the introspective attitude of the meta-physical poet who is trying to control his inner world and the introspective attitude of the baroque poet who gives himself up to his own visions.[1]

The notion of a certain distortion, of a lack of balance, is in keeping with the original meaning of the word baroque. It also takes into account the sharp contrasts, never reconciled, which we are going to find in baroque poetry.

The aspects of baroque poetry which I propose to analyse are the mystical, the morbid, the macabre, the cosmic, the apocalyptic, and the absurd. Yet, as will be seen, more important than these descriptive labels, or than the themes chosen by the poets I call baroque, is the way in which such visions are offered to us, each constituting a world in itself, with its own one-sided logic, and cut off from the control of reasonable intelligence.

[1] Although I find extremely valuable the chapters which M. de Reynold has devoted to the baroque in his book *Le XVIIe Siècle*, particularly the pages on the contrasts in the baroque (pp. 133 and 138), I cannot agree with him that will-power is an essential characteristic of the baroque (p. 134), since it is precisely in the fact that they do not bring their sensibility under the control of will-power that there lies for me the essential characteristic of the baroque poets. The clear-sightedness and will-power of Corneille's heroes are, for me, very far indeed from the baroque spirit. If there are some aspects of baroque sensibility in Corneille, I would see them in the theme of illusion and reality which can be found in his comedies. But it seems to me that his haughty *culte du moi* is, on the contrary, a typical seventeenth-century attempt to check baroque sensibility.

VI

SOME ASPECTS OF BAROQUE POETRY

I

The Mystical

THE first distorted vision of life to be met with in baroque poetry is the best known. It is the aspect of the baroque which, in painting and architecture, identifies itself with the Catholic Counter-Reformation, with the Emblem Books of the Jesuits, with Correggio, Bernini, and many others: angels among rosy clouds, the Infant Jesus, the Sacred Heart, the Holy Innocents, the crucified Saviour from whose wounds flow water and blood, the Pietà, the repentant Magdalene, the ecstatic Teresa, the mystics receiving the stigmata . . .[1] These religious themes, characteristic of Counter-Reformation baroque in the visual arts, are to be found also in the poetry of a certain number of English and French poets.

The theme of the Holy Innocents and of St. Peter's complaint inspired Southwell's *The Slaughter of the Innocents*, Malherbe's *Les Larmes de Saint Pierre*, and La Ceppède's *Sonnet XXX* (livre II). The crucifixion of Christ is depicted by Southwell, Fletcher, Crashaw, and La Ceppède. St. Mary Magdalene, a favourite saint of the time (a theme for painters like Rubens, Ribeira, and Van Dyke), weeping and meditating in the wilderness, became the subject of innumerable poems;[2] among them we have in England Crashaw's *The Weeper*, and on the French side poems straggling from the

---

[1] The most representative example of baroque sensibility in art is the famous St. Teresa by Bernini; and the best description of this is given by Mr. Austin Warren: 'In the most celebrated of her visions she saw a seraph holding in his hand a fire-tipped dart of gold which he thrust several times through the heart of the saint. . . . It is this celebrated "transverberation" which Bernini translated into flowing, undulating marble. The bare-footed saint, floating among the clouds, but with one foot swinging free from even this security, falls back in a swoon, her mouth agape, her eyes almost shut. The face is relaxed; but rapture speaks in the writhing swirl of her garments and the tumult of folds. To her left stands the winged seraph, bearing his golden wand and ready to inflict the sweet pain of love's wound' (A. Warren, *Richard Crashaw, A Study in Baroque Sensibility*, 1939, p. 140).

[2] See A. Warren, op. cit., pp. 134–6, and Bremond, 'Sur la littérature magdaléenne', op. cit., vol. i, pp. 383–5.

beginning of the century (Durant's *Magdaliade*, 1608) to the *Madeleine au Désert de la Sainte-Baume*, by le Père Pierre de Saint-Louis (1668).

It is, of course, generally agreed that the epithet baroque may be applied to the poetry which derives directly from the aesthetico-religious creed and culture of the Counter-Reformation, which takes as its subjects the physical sufferings of Christ and the raptures of saints, which is roughly characterized by sensuous decoration and symbolic metaphor, and of which the most representative poet is Richard Crashaw.

German exponents of *Geistsgeschichte* have pursued the ramifications of 'Barock' as Browne pursued the quincunx, with a heavier foot and with equally specious and elliptical logic, but for us the simplest definition is 'poetry like Crashaw's'.[1]

I do not propose here to dwell at length on Crashaw's verse, which has been thoroughly analysed and commented upon, more particularly by Mr. Austin Warren in *Richard Crashaw, a Study in Baroque Sensibility*. I am indebted to him for his excellent criticism of Crashaw's poetry, and the greater part of his conclusions do not invalidate my own theory of the baroque as a distortion of the universe through sensibility. All I intend to do in this section is to sum up the characteristics of such poets as Crashaw and show in what the distortion of their vision lies.

As a preliminary remark, it must be recalled that this baroque vein, in poetry as in art, sprang, after the Council of Trent, from a very natural desire on the Catholic side to emphasize the traditional Catholic use of the arts and also to stress almost systematically both what the Reformers had attacked in the Church of Rome (for instance, the use of painting and sculpture) and the practices and doctrines they had rejected. In this way the Catholics would stress the Sacrament of Penance by praising the repentant sinners, saved by their contrition, like Mary Magdalene or St. Peter. In a more general way, visual arts and poetry would make more obvious the fundamental difference between the Calvinistic belief that the senses are enemies of the spirit and not to be indulged in any way, and the Catholic affirmation that the senses are an integral part of man and can in their humble way contribute to God's glory. We can perceive in the position thus taken up by the Catholic poets a

---

[1] D. Bush, *English Literature in the Earlier Seventeenth Century*, 1945, p. 141.

possible element of distortion, since the control of reason has less power when it runs the constant risk of being overcome by party spirit.

But this narrow view does not enable us to understand fully the causes which account for this baroque poetry. The latter did not derive merely from party warfare and the desire to oppose the Reformers in all possible ways. There was the chaos of the late Renaissance universe, of which the conflict between Reformation and Counter-Reformation was the most spectacular but by no means the only aspect. Either mingling with that conflict or transcending it was the almost unattainable aim of reconciliation between the old Christian world and the new pagan one cherished by the Renaissance. Although it seems that the Catholics solved the problem by gratifying Renaissance appetites in integrating them into religious practice (thus producing the *humanisme dévot*),[1] the dangers of this integration were only too obvious.[2] On the other hand, the problem existed also for the Protestants (which explains why we find Protestant poets unexpectedly in the camp of the baroque). Hence that marked hesitation, in baroque religious poetry, between the material and the spiritual, between the unreal world and the real, which will be analysed later. Metaphysical poetry, dealing with the same problems, tried to reconcile contradictory worlds in the metaphysical conceit. Baroque poetry relied on unbridled fancy to bridge the gap between the pagan and the spiritual world, and it is the disorders of this imagination enlisted in the service of God which will account for the main features of baroque mystical poetry.

The first remarkable feature of this kind of poetry is its direct appeal to the senses—the sense of sight to begin with, and there the similarity borne by baroque poetry to the visual arts is good evidence of its pictorial characteristic. The reader is invited to concentrate upon some sensuous object described by the poet:

[1] See in Bremond this reconciliation of the pagan and Christian worlds in devout humanism, and the optimism of the latter: men are (according to le Père Alexis, quoted by Bremond, p. 359) '. . . aimés et prisés du ciel et de la terre, contents et heureux *au Paradis de tous les biens de cette vie, en attendant un autre encore meilleur*'.

[2] See later, p. 83, footnote, Bremond's conclusions on the dangerous use some philosophers and poets made of it: unwholesome mysticism, perverse confusion of values, &c.

the crucified body of Christ:

> Voici l'Homme, ô mes yeux, quel objet déplorable! . . .
> Ces cheveux, l'ornement de son chef vénérable,
> Sanglantés, hérissés, par ce couronnement,
> Embrouillés dans ces joncs, servent indignement
> A son têt ulcéré d'une haie exécrable.
>
> Ses yeux, tantôt si beaux, rebattus, renfoncés,[1]

the Infant Jesus in the manger:

> Behold, a silly tender Babe
> In freezing winter night
> In homely manger trembling lies,[2]

or the picture of 'the seraphical Saint Teresa with a Seraph beside her':

> Painter, what didst thou understand
> To put her dart into his hand!
> See, even the years and size of him
> Showes this the mother Seraphim.[3]

The link between painting and pictorial poetry was further reinforced by the Emblem Books. For if some religious themes can be visualized as *tableaux vivants* (the birth of Christ with the stable, the manger, the shepherds; Magdalene's repentance with a tearful face, hair spread on her shoulders, a background of rocks), for others, such as abstract truths, one has to devise symbols or emblems. Thus purity is visualized as a dove, love as a dart.[4] It is not only the sense of sight which we are invited to apply to the object of our contemplation, but we are summoned to taste the salt of tears, to smell the brimstone of Hell and to feel, like a fire, the love of God.[5] The relation of this poetry to music will be shown later.

So far, objectionable as may be to some readers a sort of poetry

[1] *Les Théorèmes*, I. LXX; Thierry Maulnier, *Poésie du XVIIᵉ siècle*, pp. 34–35.
[2] Southwell, *New Prince, New Pomp*; *Oxford Book of Sixteenth Century Verse*, p. 239.
[3] Crashaw, *The Flaming Heart*; *Works*, ed. L. C. Martin, 1927, p. 324.
[4] This insistence on visualization of religious themes for edifying purposes is a dominant feature in the Jesuit Ignatius Loyola's *Spiritual Exercises* and is also noted by Bremond among prose-writers as well as among poets: see his chapter on Louis Richeome (1544-1626) and his works—*La Peinture spirituelle* and *Les Tableaux sacrés* (the titles are indicative enough).
[5] And as far as the sense of touch is concerned, the lapsing into convenient eroticism is almost inevitable.

which offers itself so patently as a substitute for another art, it
might yet have some value as a vision of life if it managed to draw
from the religious themes which it thus presents to us the moral
drama they include. This is sometimes the case with La Ceppède's
theorems. But, as a rule, in this poetry the emotion does not rise
from a moral drama and is of a special kind which makes baroque
mystical poetry easily recognizable: a strange mixture of crude
pathos and sensuous pleasure. For if we are confronted with the
pitiful wounds of Christ or the tears of converted sinners, we are
at the same time made to derive enjoyment from the loveliness of
Christ's body or the sweetness of tears:

> His cheekes as snowie apples, sop't in wine,
> Had their red roses quencht with lillies white,
> And like to garden strawberries did shine,
> Wash't in a bowl of milke . . .[1]

> Ces yeux . . .
>   /. . sont hélas! deux soleils éclipsés,
> Le corail de sa bouche est ores jaune pâle.
> Les roses et les lys de son teint sont flétris:
> Le reste de son corps est de couleur d'opale.[2]

> Not in the Evenings Eyes
> When they red with weeping are,
>   For the Sun that dyes
> Sits sorrow with a face so faire.
> Nowhere but heere did ever meet
> Sweetnesse so sad, sadnes so sweet.[3]

As can already be seen from these quotations, the metaphors
chosen by the poets are sensuous, decorative, pleasurable as suggesting sweetness and loveliness. After reading a certain number of
poems, the reader becomes obsessed by recurrent metaphors which
are the same whatever the subjects of the poems: lilies and roses,
blood-drops like rubies, tears like pearls, wine and milk, flames
and fountains, silver and gold. Between the reader and the religious themes he is supposed to contemplate is interposed a shim-
mering screen made of one material: a network of recurrent motifs:

[1] Giles Fletcher, *Christ's Victory*; *The Poetical Works of Giles and Phineas
Fletcher*, Cambridge English Classics, 1908, vol. i, p. 42.
[2] *Les Théorèmes*, II. LXXX; Thierry Maulnier, *Poésie du XVIIe siècle*, p. 35.
[3] Crashaw, *The Weeper*; *Works*, ed. L. C. Martin, p. 81.

tears, wounds, flaming hearts, the turtle and the Phœnix, the grave
and the nest, embroidered with precious stones. Such motifs and
metaphors are common to all baroque mystical poets: they are part
of a ritual and not the metaphorical expression of the poet's inner
experience. This makes baroque very different from metaphysical
imagery, and Mr. Warren is right in stating that whereas Donne's
metaphors are abstract and recondite, Crashaw's are sensuous and
external;[1] and that although Herbert uses symbols and emblems,
'Herbert's poems are autobiographical, lyrics born from the wrest-
lings of his soul with God; Crashaw's are devotional and objective'.[2] This characteristic of non-subjectivity is to be found also in
other aspects of baroque poetry.[3] Not only are these symbols
ritualistic, but they are very often interchangeable—tears turn
into pearls, pearls into lilies, lilies into pure innocents. In Southwell's *Saint Peter's Complaint* the Saviour's eyes are compared
(throughout twenty stanzas) to 'sweet volumes', 'blazing comets',
'living mirrors', 'turtle twins all bathed in virgin's milk', and so on
. . . so that the baroque universe becomes a vast system of correspondences and a world of shifting appearances. So is the Shelleyan
universe, where everything is always melting into something else,
or dissolving in correspondences between one sense and another;
but Shelley's poetic world is both fluid and evanescent, whereas
it is the paradoxical quality of the baroque mystical universe to
remain hard and solid although things appear as if they were
melting away; Shelleyan 'faintness' has a liquid or aerial texture,
baroque ecstatic swoons are carved in solid flesh.[4]

One may agree with Mr. Eliot that Crashaw uses his intelligence,
but, as he says, with 'perversity'; and it seems, in his poetry as in
that of Southwell or Fletcher, that the intelligence does not try to
control the endless flow of metaphors and metamorphoses: tears
turn into milk, water into wine, wine into blood, blood into rubies:
'the effect is often that of a phantasmagoria' suffused with cloying
sweetness.

---

[1] A. Warren, op. cit., p. 99. [2] Ibid., p. 112.

[3] I do not agree with Mr. Mincoff who makes *subjectivity* a characteristic of
all baroque literature.

[4] One may add that Shelley found for himself the symbols of his own universe
(the cloud, the sensitive plant, the west wind . . .)—this to defend Shelley a little
against Mr. Eliot's devastating comparison of Shelley and Crashaw. He admires
in Crashaw 'a deliberate perversity of language'; 'there is brainwork in it; but
in the *Skylark* there is no brainwork' ('A Note on Richard Crashaw', in *For
Lancelot Andrewes*).

Whatever the 'brain-work' in it, this poetry presents all the features which tend to bring mental inertia as a response: the process of visualization of certain physical pictures (Teresa in rapture, the crucified Saviour) is bound to create an artificial fixation of attitudes substituted for the moral significance of the religious theme. The incantatory characteristic of certain poems by Crashaw, noted by Mr. Warren,[1] suggests the sort of poetry in which the music of rhythm, assonance, alliteration, and the use of ritualistic imagery will aim at a hypnotic state, both in the poet and in the reader. The use of antithesis:

> Sweetnesse so sad, sadnes so sweet (Crashaw)

and

> Never such age so young, never a child so old (Fletcher),

the 'living death and dying life' of Southwell, the 'flaming fountain' and 'weeping fire' of Crashaw, cannot even surprise by their strangeness,[2] but lull by their unconvincing and mechanical reiteration.

The preceding remarks may seem rather unfair to the baroque mystical poets, and some elaboration is necessary here, the more so as it is well known that though Crashaw almost automatically repels Protestant taste, he has been praised both by the nineteenth-century poet Swinburne and by the twentieth-century critic T. S. Eliot, and somewhat appeals to the present taste for 'quaint' poetry. A fair critic, eschewing the religious approach to the question, would probably first establish some sort of difference between Crashaw's good poems and his bad ones (rejecting perhaps *The Wager* or Christ's wounds and praising the intensity of the *Hymn to St. Teresa*) and would admit that, in a particular kind of poetry, Crashaw may be successful.

Whatever the ultimate aesthetic judgement on these poets, it would be unfair to attribute their distorted vision to the fact that they chose religious themes, deriving from a fully sacramental and supernatural conception of the world. It should rather be attributed to the use they made of the possibilities offered by Catholic hagiography and the ritual of the Church. If, according to the Catholic tradition, the senses and the imagination may contribute

---

[1] A. Warren, op. cit., p. 192.
[2] They belong to the storehouse of Italian poetry. Here, of course, we must note the influence of the earlier petrarchists and of Marino.

to the glory of God, it does not follow that the glory of God and of His saints should contribute towards indulging the most intense cravings of the senses and the imagination.[1] It is in this reversal of values that baroque poetry loses its balance. That is why, instead of giving us the impression of a real supernatural universe, organized according to the logic of Catholic ritual and doctrine, it gives us an unreal unorganic world, in which, moreover, we have the suspicion that we are offered one thing as a substitute for another: the rapture of the saints for the erotic satisfactions of human love, the precious tears of the sinners for the sweet delectations of masochism, the lilies and roses of virtue for the childish delight in tinsel ornaments. Most of the terms used by critics when talking of Crashaw serve to illustrate this distortion: '*perverted* intelligence', says Mr. Eliot; 'in Crashaw the *undeveloped* and the *overripe* seem concurrently present' (Mr. Warren); 'he has a *morbid*, almost *hysterical*, passion about him' (Sir Edmund Gosse).

From these remarks, it is evident that all religious Counter-Reformation poetry is not baroque.[2] The cult of the saints, for instance, may inspire a sort of unsophisticated, naïve, popular poetry such as the poem of le Père Paul de Barry on Mary Magdalene:

> J'ai quitté tous mes promenoirs,
> J'ai cassé tous mes beaux miroirs,
> J'ai rompu mes robes de soie. . . .
> J'ai jeté par la fenêtre
> Toutes mes pommes de senteur
> Et mes fards, pour ne plus paraître
> Belle aux yeux du monde menteur.
> J'ai brûlé tous mes vieux romans
> Et les lettres de mes amants.[3]

It is also evident that the dramatic value of the religious scenes

---

[1] See Bremond's conclusions on the *humanisme dévot*, particularly the lines in which he points out the dangerous use the devout philosophers and poets made of mysticism: 'Ce disant, nous n'oublions pas que le mysticisme conduit trop souvent ces poètes et ces philosophes, soit à des confusions sacrilèges, soit à des rêveries malsaines. L'idéalisme sensuel des uns ajoute comme une perversité nouvelle à la séduction du paganisme, la métaphysique visionnaire des autres s'engage dans les sciences occultes avec une crédulité fervente qui nous déconcerte' (op. cit., vol. i, p. 520).

[2] It is more or less proved by now (cf. in particular Dejob, op. cit.) that the Counter-Reformation and the Council of Trent directly or indirectly influenced all religious poetry of the late sixteenth and early seventeenth centuries.

[3] Quoted by Bremond, op. cit., vol. i, pp. 206–7.

described in baroque poetry will vary a great deal: the dramatic strength of Southwell's *The Burning Babe* or *New Prince, New Pomp* has been rightly pointed out by critics, whereas it is difficult to feel the drama of the Crucifixion in Crashaw's *On the Wounds of our Crucified Lord*:[1]

> O These wakefull wounds of thine!
>   Are they Mouthes? or are they eyes? . . .
> Lo! a mouth, whose full-bloom'd lips
>   At too deare a rate are roses.
> Lo! a blood-shot eye! that weepes
>   And many a cruel tear discloses.

A more delicate problem is that of appreciating to what extent intelligence does or does not control senses and imagination in baroque poetry. There are examples (as in the case of Crashaw's lines just quoted) where the most normal form of intelligence, common sense, does not seem to intervene, and this accounts for the patent extravagances of the worst baroque poetry. There is also (already mentioned twice) the 'brain-work of a perverted intelligence', as T. S. Eliot puts it, or what Swinburne praises in Crashaw: 'the dazzling intricacy and affluence in refinements, the supple and cunning implication, the choiceness and subtlety'.[2] No doubt intelligence, brain-work, may help, and sometimes with a great deal of subtlety, to construct a distorted universe. But this is not the point.

The point is: will a baroque poet sometimes put a check on his sensuous visions, love of decorative imagery, and over-indulged emotions, in order to get at a real problem, thus attaining a sort of equilibrium between the intellectual and emotional requirements of his temperament? If so, his poetry will very often move from the baroque to the metaphysical.

It may already have become apparent that La Ceppède is the kind of poet who can write a thoroughly baroque poem[3] but can also write metaphysical poetry. With him what seems a typically baroque theme—the red cloak put over Christ's shoulders—becomes the ground for metaphysical poetry.[4]

[1] *Works*, ed. L. C. Martin, p. 99.
[2] Quoted in the introduction by H. C. Beeching to the *Poems of Richard Crashaw*, ed. by J. R. Tutin, p. 1.
[3] See above, pp. 79, 80.
[4] See above, Ch. IV.

Inside one and the same poem—Malherbe's *Les Larmes de Saint Pierre*—we find baroque poetry:

> Les arcs qui de plus pres sa poitrine joignirent,
> Les traits qui plus avant dans le sein l'atteignirent,
> Ce fut quand du Sauveur il se veid regardé:
> Les yeux furent les arcs, les œillades les fleches
> Qui percerent son ame, et remplirent de bresches
> Le rampart qu'il avoit si laschement gardé[1]

(where Malherbe indulges in an orgy of conventional metaphors, which suggest the ritual dart of love, together with the emblem of a soul as a citadel); we find also the lines on Christ's footsteps, commented upon[2] as being metaphysical poetry.

2

The Apocalyptic

There were other religious themes which appealed to the sensibility of the age; among them was the Day of Judgement, when our miraculous globe dissolves into ashes and the Trumpet of Doom calls souls to final separation. In the contemplation of the end of the world such a sensibility could find the most desperate expression of its terror of a universe which in some of its aspects was disintegrating. Exacerbated terror and emphasis on disintegration are bound to distort a poet's vision, and in fact with such a subject another aspect of the baroque appears: a marked taste for the colossal, the limitless, and the cosmic.

One immediately remembers—and this may corroborate the remark made at the end of the last section—that this particular baroque theme inspired a well-known metaphysical sonnet of Donne:

> At the round earths imagin'd corners, blow
> Your trumpets, Angells . . . .[3]

If we compare this sonnet with d'Aubigné's lines on the resurrection of the dead:

> La terre ouvre son sein, du ventre des tombeaux
> Naissent des enterrés les visages nouveaux: . . .
> Ici un arbre sent des bras de sa racine
> Grouiller un chef vivant, sortir une poictrine;

[1] *Les Poésies de M. de Malherbe*, ed. Lavaud, vol. i, p. 10.
[2] See above, Ch. IV.
[3] *Poems*, ed. Grierson, p. 296.

Là l'eau trouble bouillonne . . . .
Comme un nageur venant du profond de son plonge,
Tous sortent de la mort comme l'on sort d'un songe[1]—

we have, clearly, the same theme treated in two very different
ways. Without launching into a minute analysis of Donne's sonnet,
it is easy to point out the strength of thought, translated in subtle
ways by syntax and rhythm; his sonnet is intellectual, passionate,
personal, and abstract. D'Aubigné uses the theme to give a picture,
non-subjective and concrete, without any argumentation whatever.
Donne is concerned with his own relationship with God, and the
baroque theme of the Day of Judgement is for him just a starting-
point. For d'Aubigné, the treatment is baroque as well as the
theme: he tries to make the reader visualize what the Day of Doom
will be like and to rouse in him a sort of supernatural terror both
of judgement and of the cosmic catastrophe. So does John Davies
of Hereford who, thinking of the end of the world coming through
the Plague, depicts the ominous premonitory signs of the *Triumph
of Death*:

> The heav'nly Coape was now ore-canopide,
> Neere each ones Zenith (as his sense suppos'd)
> With ominous impressions, strangely died;
> And like a Canopie at toppe it closed,
> As if it had presag'd the Judge was nie,
> To sit in Judgement his last doome to give,
> And caus'd his cloth of State t'adorne the Skie.[2]

In fact, the final tragedy of the last Judgement, the irrevocable
sentence pronounced by God, can only appeal to baroque sensibility if preceded by disorder on a colossal scale, by the total
upsetting of nature. D'Aubigné, Saint-Amant, Théophile de Viau
have all described the destruction of the cosmos, the death of the
sun and of the moon:

> Le soleil vest de noir le bel or de ses feux,
> Le bel œil de ce monde est privé de ses yeux; . . .

> La lune perd l'argent de son teint clair et blanc,
> La lune tourne en haut son visage de sang;
> Toute estoile se meurt . . . .

[1] *Les Tragiques*, ed. A. Garnier and J. Plattard, 1932, vol. iv, p. 159.
[2] *Humours Heaven on Earth* (1603); *Complete Works*, ed. Grosart, vol. i, p. 45.

> Tout se cache de peur: le feu s'enfuit dans l'air,
> L'air en l'eau, l'eau en terre . . .[1]

Here is Saint-Amant's vision:

> Les estoiles tombent des cieux,
> Les flâmes devorent la terre . . .
> La mer brule comme eau de vie,
> L'air n'est plus que souffre allumé,
> Et l'astre dont l'aube est suivie
> Est par soy-mesme consumé. . . .
> L'unique oyseau meurt pour tousjours, . . .
> Tout est destruit, et la Mort mesme
> Se voit contrainte de mourir[2]—

and Théophile de Viau, after a similar description, adds encouragingly:

> Et ce grand desordre du monde
> Peut-estre arrivera demain.[3]

In spite of the resemblances between d'Aubigné's and Saint-Amant's pictures of the end of the world, some important differences in mood and tone must be noted here. D'Aubigné is highly serious about the catastrophe he describes, the tone is threateningly solemn: his enemies (the lines are taken from *Les Tragiques*, a poem of violence and vengeance) must realize that the wrath of God is terrible and that they will be swept off like chaff in the midst of these formidable events. Saint-Amant and Théophile, both free-thinkers, are not much interested in divine wrath.[4] The rhythm in Saint-Amant's lines is light, almost pleasantly jig-like. The theme obviously appeals to his fancy, as picturesque. It seems that this theme had become so familiar to poets as to be a decorative motif.

[1] D'Aubigné, *Les Tragiques*, ed. Garnier and Plattard, vol. iv, pp. 177–8.

[2] Saint-Amant, *Œuvres poétiques*, ed. L. Vérane, 1930, p. 22. The idea of the death of death, found in Saint-Amant, seems to crown the cataclysm with a paradoxical bitter consolation. It is to be found also in Donne: 'And death shall be no more; death, thou shalt die' (op. cit., p. 297). But that is no comfort to those in Hell:

> Que la mort, direz-vous, estoit un doux plaisir!
> La mort morte ne peut vous tuer, vous saisir . . .
> Criez aprés l'enfer: de l'enfer il ne sort
> Que l'eternelle soif de l'impossible mort.

(D'Aubigné, op. cit., vol. iv, pp. 183–4.)

[3] Théophile, *Œuvres poétiques*, ed. R. Lefèvre, 1926, p. 210.

[4] Saint-Amant's poem is addressed to a bishop, but the pious tone and references to God are not very convincing.

If we consider with what almost savage rage (in the case of d'Aubigné) and cynical, malignant enjoyment (in Saint-Amant and Théophile) the baroque poets contemplate the destruction of the cosmos, we are bound to think of those poets who, with patience and love, tried to build up the same cosmos into something harmonious and eternal,[1] and thus we measure the gap between the optimism of the Renaissance and the pessimism of the late Renaissance.

3

The Macabre and the Morbid

During the late Renaissance the theme of death assumed once more a prevailing importance, under its most gruesome shape, that of the macabre; once more, because one thinks of the morbid obsession with death in the French art and poetry of the fifteenth century.[2] During the Renaissance, when man was temporarily cured of this pathological fixation on the physical facts of death, the theme of death was treated abstractly and elegantly:

> Pour obseques reçoy mes larmes et mes pleurs,
> Ce vase plein de laict, ce panier plein de fleurs,
> Afin que vif, ou mort, ton corps ne soit que roses.[3]

The theme of death is not in itself baroque (no more than it is in itself metaphysical, as previously noted).[4] It becomes baroque when its treatment indicates some distortion and lack of balance. The distortion begins with death becoming an obsession, and more especially with the poet's deriving some unwholesome satisfaction from brooding upon what in death is physically repulsive.

At the end of the sixteenth century, and the beginning of the seventeenth, a second *Danse macabre* passed over Europe. The skeleton became a familiar adjunct to mortuary monuments (for

---

[1] See above, Ch. III, 2.

[2] Cf. Villon and other fifteenth-century poets, more particularly Pierre de Nesson, 'le poète de la Mort' (*Les Vigiles de Job*). See P. Champion, *Histoire poétique du XVᵉ siècle*, 1923. The existence of the *Danse macabre* in the fifteenth century (not only in France but in Italy, in Germany, in England), the fact that death was then the main subject for poets, painters, and sculptors in France at least, are so well known that one is extremely surprised to read in an article on 'Death and the Baroque', by Mr. Aldous Huxley (*Horizon*, Apr. 1949, p. 281) that there was no skeleton in art or poetry in the Middle Ages and that one has to wait until the middle of the sixteenth century for a fashionable death's head.

[3] Ronsard, 'Comme on voit sur la branche . . .'.

[4] See above, Ch. IV.

instance Bernini's statue of Alexander VII) and a familiar compa-
nion of the poet's love (Donne's shroud and his 'bracelet of bright
haire about the bone'). Poets did not hesitate to use realistic words:

> Et quel bien de la Mort? ou la vermine ronge
> Tous ces *nerfs*, tous ces *os*, ou l'Ame se depart
> De ceste *orde charongne* . . . .[1]

We know the taste for the macabre that permeated the Jacobean
drama (Shakespeare, Webster, Tourneur, Ford . . .). M. Lebègue
notes the same taste in the French drama of the same period.[2]

In French lyrical poetry, d'Aubigné did not think of a shroud,
but decorated his bedroom with bones and paid his courtship to a
skeleton:

> Le lieu de mon repos est une chambre peinte
> De mil os blanchissans et de testes de mortz . . .

> Je mire en adorant dans une anathomye
> Le portrait de Diane entre les os . . . .

> Dans le cors de la mort j'ai enfermé ma vie
> Et ma beauté paroist horrible dans les os . . . .[3]

He takes a morbid pleasure in the most gruesome aspects of
nature:

> En ce qui est hideux je cherche mon confort[4]

and in what can conjure up the idea of death:

> J'ayme à voir de beautez la branche deschargee
> A fouller le feuillage estendu par l'effort
> D'Autonne, sans espoir leur couleur orangee
> Me donne pour plaisir l'ymage de la mort.[4]

The macabre is also to be found in Saint-Amant; but there
again, as when the poet deals with the theme of the end of the
world, death and decay have become decorative and entertaining:

> Que j'ayme à voir la décadence
> De ces vieux chasteaux ruinez, . . .

> Les sorciers y font leur sabat
> Les demons follets s'y retirent, . . .

[1] Sponde, ed. Boase, p. 243.
[2] R. Lebègue, 'Le Théâtre baroque en France', *Bibliothèque d'humanisme et
renaissance*, 1942, p. 182.
[3] A. d'Aubigné, *Le Printemps — Stances*; *Œuvres complètes*, ed. Réaume et
de Caussade, vol. iii, p. 69.   [4] Ibid., p. 70.

L'orfraye, avèc des cris funebres,
Mortels augures des destins,
Fait rire et dancer les lutins
Dans ces lieux remplis de tenebres.
Sous un chevron de bois maudit
Y branle le squelette horrible
D'un pauvre amant qui se pendit.[1]

Saint-Amant's goblins and witches are not very dangerous. They have, by the time when he is writing, lost their power. It is not so in d'Aubigné or in Sir John Davies of Hereford. In them the theme of death is closely and seriously linked with that of Hell, of blood-curdling fiends, and black witchcraft.

Baroque sensibility, because it goes beyond the normal in every direction, is bound to present us with strong contrasts. As a counterpart to Crashaw's rosy vision of sweet raptures (or Giles Fletcher's description of Paradise[2]), we have the nightmare of John Davies of Hereford's Dantesque description of Hell; Dantesque is perhaps not the right word since it emphasizes the grotesque horrors which were part of the crude medieval theology. Davies's universe is that of his contemporary the younger Breughel. Here is his description of the House of Time:

The Roofe whereof, with Sculles is seelèd quite;
Whereon (in frets) hang shin-bones here and there:
The walls are hung with Mantles of the Night;
Which, all with vermine vile, imbrod'red were.[3]

He describes the dance of worms and the dance of the evil spirits. The poem seethes with toads, vipers, snakes, cobwebs, spiders, and hellhounds, and horrible and odd visions such as:

And frozen harts do float in sulphred streames

---

[1] Saint-Amant, *La Solitude*; *Œuvres*, p. 5. Compare with the taste for melancholy atmosphere to be found, with softer accents, in English seventeenth-century lyrics:

Fountain heads, and pathless Groves,
Places which pale passion loves:
Moon-light walks, when all the Fowls
Are warmly hous'd, save Bats and Owls;
A mid-night Bell, a parting groan,
These are the sounds we feed upon

(John Fletcher, 1579–1625, from *The Nice Valour*, Act III, Sc. ii; *The Oxford Book of Seventeenth Century Verse*, p. 201).

[2] *Poetical Works*, pp. 83–87.

[3] *Humours Heaven on Earth*; *Complete Works*, vol. i, p. 18.

or a

Goblin, grisly grim,
. . . fishing for a Soule.[1]

Agrippa d'Aubigné's Hell is a complex one. In *Les Tragiques* he gives a traditional description of Hell, not grotesque, but solemnly terrifying. There are churchyards, witches, and evil spirits in his universe.[2] But still more important is the inner Hell raging within him: in politics, religion, or love, he displays the same violence, wild rage for vengeance, raving imaginings of what could bring destruction on his enemies, on his unfaithful Diane, on the whole world, and on himself. This is how, once dead, he means to terrify Diane:

Je briseray, la nuit, les rideaux de sa couche
Assiegeant des trois Seurs infernales son lit,
Portant le feu, la plainte et le sang en ma bouche: . . .
Aux plus subtils demons des regions hautaynes,
Je presterai mon cors pour leur faire vestir,
Pasle, deffiguré, vray miroir de mes peines.[3]

Violence of feeling coupled with extraordinarily powerful imagination, without any control by reason, and a determination to admit of no balance or measure, make of d'Aubigné a thoroughly baroque poet; the distorted universe he expresses in his poetry has two main features.

First, d'Aubigné sees most things, abstract or concrete, as red;[4] red being, of course, closely associated with blood.

Je suis le champ *sanglant*, où la pudeur hostile
Vomit le meurtre *rouge*, et la scythique horreur
Qui saccage le *sang* . . . .

Votre blanc en plaisir teint ma *rouge* douleur.

Tes lèvres de *rubis* . . . l'*incarnat* de ta bouche.

Avecq' le *sang*, l'ame *rouge* ravie.

---

[1] Ibid., p. 21.

[2] See d'Aubigné's strange poem on the killing of a witch and the post-mortem, in *La Sorcière*, and also the lines in which he imagines himself being tempted by an evil spirit:

En bouc et en barbet, en facynant ma veue,
Au lit de mon repos, il viendra m'assaillir.
Neuf goutes de pur sang naistront sur ma serviette.

(*Le Printemps — Stances*; *Œuvres complètes*, vol. iii, p. 72.)   [3] Ibid., p. 79.

[4] In his excellent article on d'Aubigné (*Génies de France*, 1942, pp. 68–87), M. Raymond also has noted d'Aubigné's obsession with blood and with the colour red.

Rougir de mon *sang* chault l'yvoire de ses doigtz.[1]

Et pour moi, dieu secret, *rougit* la jalousie.

Mes yeux enflés de pleurs regardent mes rideaux / *Cramoysir*.

. . . ta *rouge* arrogance.[2]

The other feature of this universe is the colossal proportions of everything in it. Petrarchan poets, before d'Aubigné, had shed torrents of tears, had burnt in flames which were more scorching than the hottest sun, and had died a hundred deaths. But their fine hyperboles looked unconvincing and slightly ridiculous because usually merely conventional and out of proportion with the thinness of the subject. D'Aubigné's hyperboles are more extravagant than those of any of the petrarchists, but they are on the same scale as his feelings. As a lover, he does not moan, he roars; as a human being, he is not an ordinary man but a giant. The process of magnification is to be found everywhere in his poetry. He never counts but by hundreds and thousands:

Mille nymphes des bois (*Hec.* xlvii)

Mille baisers perdus, *mille* et *mille* faveurs (ibid. lviii).

Mille corbeaux pillards (ibid. xcv).[3]

The earth is too small for him; most of the time he is angrily striding across interplanetary space and the conventional pathetic fallacy assumes in his poetry cosmic proportions:

Milles oiseaux de nuit, mille chansons mortelles
M'environnent, vollans par ordre sur mon front:
Que l'air en contrepoix fasché de mes querelles
Soit noircy de hiboux et de corbeaux en ront,
Les herbes secheront soubs mes pas, à la veuë
Des miserables yeux dont les tristes regars
Feront tomber les fleurs et cacher dans la nue
La lune et le soleil et les astres espars.[4]

It is not my purpose to examine why d'Aubigné is a good baroque poet. But at this stage I should like to stress how some of the baroque characteristics in him serve the genre he had chosen in

[1] A. d'Aubigné, *Le Printemps — l'Hécatombe à Diane*, ed. B. Gagnebin, 1948, pp. 24, 59, 42, 31.
[2] *Le Printemps — Stances*; *Œuvres complètes*, ed. Réaume et de Caussade, vol. iii, pp. 82, 83, 92.
[3] *Le Printemps — l'Hécatombe à Diane*, ed. Gagnebin, pp. 66, 79, 117.
[4] *Le Printemps — Stances*; *Œuvres*, ed. Réaume et de Caussade, vol. iii, p. 71.

writing the *Tragiques*. His process of magnification was in keeping
with the very essence of the epic. His wild flights into Heaven and
Hell gave the supernatural background. Even the single-minded-
ness of purpose which, as we shall see, often characterizes the
baroque poet suited the violent simplicity of the epic. And one of
the most interesting and original aspects of his poetry is that he
should also have turned his personal love-story into an epic.

4

The Myopic and Disconnected Vision

A sensibility which is not controlled by reason can shift very
quickly from one extreme to the other. After the cosmic universe
of d'Aubigné, the baroque presents us with the diminutive world
of Théophile, Saint-Amant, and Tristan.

These three poets of the first half of the seventeenth century are
usually grouped under the heading of *poètes libertins*. Their simi-
larities and their differences would constitute an important study
in itself. Here they interest us by one characteristic they have
in common: their landscape painting. Feeling for nature is by no
means necessarily baroque[1] (no more than it is essentially romantic) and becomes material for baroque poetry in the same way as
other themes already mentioned: when distortion and lack of
proportion stand out as the main features of such poetry.

It has been noted, in the chapter on scientific poetry, how in
certain poets a taste for minute description of a definite object in
nature was taking the place of Ronsard's praises of nature as a harmonious whole, with her eternal laws ruling in magnificent hierarchy
both the hawthorn and the stars.[2]

Théophile, Saint-Amant, and Tristan consider nature as a succession of landscapes to be enjoyed for their own sake and depicted
with some precision; and precision for them consists in putting the
stress on concrete details in a landscape. Théophile's description
of winter includes a heron hidden among the rushes, a silent bird on
a stripped branch, a tortoise and snails creeping among icicles:

> La tortue et les limaçons
> Trainent leurs pas par les glaçons;[3]

[1] Although some critics, M. Lebègue for instance, put it among baroque
characteristics.
[2] See above, Ch. III.   [3] *Contre l'Hiver; Œuvres*, p. 25.

and when he is describing the morning, he notes the gesture of the
housewife fastening the hemp on her distaff:

> Presse le chanvre qu'elle attache
> A sa quenouille de roseau.[1]

Tristan, in his poem on Orpheus, lingers over his enumeration
of trees and animals and mentions 'la longue pane rousse [du cas-
tor]', 'l'escurieu sautelant', 'le gris argenté [du tigre]'.[2]

Saint-Amant points out a nest floating on the surface of the sea,
a fish, a sea-shell, a glow-worm.

As a rule, the poet selects a detail in a landscape, cuts it off from
the rest, analyses it, and tries on it all sorts of clever associations,
taking it as a starting-point for his reveries:[3]

> Je reviens au chasteau, resvant,
> Sous la faveur d'un ver qui brille
> Ou plustost d'un astre vivant. . . .

> O feu qui, tousjours allumé,
> Brusles sans estre consumé!
> Belle escarboucle qui chemines,
> Ton éclat me plaist beaucoup mieux
> Que celuy qu'on tire des mines,
> Afin d'ensorceler nos yeux![4]

The second noticeable aspect of their technique in landscape
painting is to pass from one object to another without supplying
the connexion, so that we have at times the same impression as
the one we have in front of an impressionist picture in which the
painter proceeded by dots. M. Adam has noted this *pointillisme* as
a characteristic of Théophile's style: the jerkiness of the rhythm, the
cumulative effect of minute details, the disorderly enumeration.[5]

Théophile does not deny the discontinuity and the characteristic
of freakish *rêverie* in his poetry:

> Je ne veux point unir le fil de mon subject:
> Diversement, je laisse et reprends mon objet. . . .

---

[1] *Le Matin*; ibid., p. 31.

[2] Tristan L'Hermite, *Les Amours et autres poésies choisies*, ed. P. Camo, 1925,
p. 149.

[3] This, according to M. Adam, is due to the influence of Marino; Benedetto
Croce has noted in Marino and his disciples 'l'audace et l'extravagance de l'ob-
servation myope et l'exactitude à la rendre'. Cf. Adam, *Théophile de Viau*, p. 447.

[4] Saint-Amant, *Le Contemplateur*; *Œuvres*, p. 16.

[5] Adam, *Théophile de Viau*, pp. 44–45.

Je veux faire des vers qui ne soient pas contraincts,
Promener mon esprit par de petits desseins,
Chercher des lieux secrets où rien ne me deplaise,
Mediter à loisir, resver tout à mon aise,
Employer toute une heure à me mirer dans l'eau,
Ouyr, comme en songeant, la course d'un ruisseau,
Escrire dans les bois, m'interrompre, me taire.[1]

Saint-Amant's attitude is exactly the same:

Je ne cherche que les deserts
Où, resvant tout seul, je m'amuse, . . .[2]

Poems like Saint-Amant's *Le Contemplateur* or *La Solitude* are indeed *fantasques tableaux*, playful daydreams connected only by the whims of the poet's fancy. He seizes on an aspect of things which happens to suit his mood and to offer lovely and picturesque images, mythological or other, then drops it and takes up another. The poems are composed of a succession of small pictures, each stanza generally starting with the grammatical link of a vague conjunction: 'Puis . . . Là . . . Là . . . Tantôt . . . Tantôt . . .' He discourses with Thetis on fish and sea-monsters, dreams about the Flood, looks at a dove, wonders at the tide, ponders on the marvellous invention of compasses, conjures up the Spirit of the Sea crowned with coral branches and girded with pearls, picks up a sea-shell, admires a glow-worm, shoots rabbits and cormorants . . . and ends with a picture of the end of the world.[3]

The tone and rhythm remain the same whatever the object of his description is; and by juxtaposing the Day of Judgement or a vast expanse of sea with a glow-worm or a fish, he obtains a result which is the opposite of the enlargement we found in d'Aubigné: everything is reduced to the diminutive proportions of the glow-worm and the waves of the sea do not appear to be bigger than the scales of a fish.

---

[1] *Elégie*; Œuvres, pp. 75–76.
[2] *Le Contemplateur*; Œuvres, p. 8. The same attitude is to be found in Tristan:
Et n'aime que la solitude.
Nul plaisir ne peut me toucher
Fors celui de m'aller coucher
Sur le gazon d'une falaise,
Où mon œil se laissant charmer
Me laisse rêver à mon aise.
(*La Mer*; *Les Amours*, p. 215.)
[3] *Le Contemplateur*; Œuvres, pp. 10–23.

Saint-Amant's seascape would deserve a more detailed commentary. Let us quote, as a further illustration of the above remark, the picture of the storm (the sea has previously in the poem been visualized as ridden by hairy Tritons blowing into their conch-shells and will next be contemplated as a mirror for the sun):

> Tantost, elle estale en ses bords,
> Que l'ire de Neptune outrage,
> Des gens noyez, des monstres morts,
> Des vaisseaux brisez du naufrage,
> Des diamans, de l'ambre gris,
> Et mille autres choses de pris.[1]

The tritons, the violence of the storm, the tragedy of drowned people, and ambergris are on the same level, just as, in *Le Contemplateur*, the mythological evocation of the sea-god is on the same level as the apparition of Christ on the Day of Judgement:

> Espouvantable et magnifique
> JESUS au milieu du soleil.[2]

In Théophile this diminutive vision takes very often the form of a special tenderness for what in nature serves his *pointillisme*: the flakes of snow, the drops of water, the notes of the nightingale; and perhaps what he says of this bird could describe his own song:

> Comme en la terre et par le Ciel
> Des petites mouches errantes
> Meslent, pour composer leur miel,
> Mille matieres differentes,
> Formant ses airs, qui sont ces fruits
> L'oyseau digere mille bruits
> En une seule melodie.[3]

On the other hand, Tristan's pictures of imaginary parks suggest the clever and dainty minuteness of Chinese gardens:

> D'un côté l'on y void une *petite* Mer, . . .

> Aux niches de rocher qui sont aux environs
> On voit toujours mouvoir de *petits* personnages;
> Icy des charpentiers, et là des forgerons. . . .[4]

---

[1] *La Solitude*; *Œuvres*, p. 7.
[2] *Le Contemplateur*; ibid., p. 20.
[3] *La Maison de Silvie*; ibid., pp. 201–2.
[4] *Les Plaintes d'Acante*; *Les Amours*, p. 106.

> Avec autant de soin ces autres Jardiniers
> Plantent aussi pour leur usage,
> Une *grande* forest de *petits* Citronniers.[1]

Myopic and disconnected vision is the most striking aspect of these poets' universe. It has other characteristics. As we read the lyrics of these three poets, their baroque landscape takes more definite shape and colour; for, in spite of its kaleidoscopic variety, it includes the same recurrent decorative motifs: Tritons, shells, waterfowl and rushes, grottoes, the Naiad, the poppy. It has a sort of glittering solidity which reminds us of Crashaw's universe, the facets of the piecemeal composition being the more sparkling as a great number of the metaphors are borrowed from jewellery and precious metals: the sea is green enamel and cut jasper, with diamonds at the crest of the waves, pearls and coral roll in the foreground of seascapes, the stream is silver or crystal, and the light of the sun draws over the sky and the water rings of pure gold and flashing purple.[2] Nature is thus made tame and ornate, infinitely artificial, an object of luxury. I suggested the Chinese garden; in a similar way, fish, sea-gods, and naiads appear as if seen through the glass of a goldfish bowl.[3] Therefore, quite naturally, the so-called wilderness of Théophile and Saint-Amant will become Tristan's *La Maison d'Astrée*. The decorative motifs of their landscapes will not only adorn seventeenth-century gardens but

---

[1] *La Maison d'Astrée*, ibid., p. 247.

[2] Mais les flots de vert émaillez
Qui semblent des Jaspes taillez;
S'entredérobent son [the sun's] visage;
Et par de petits tremblements
Font voir au lieu de son Image
Mille pointes de diamants.
  (Tristan, *La Mer*; ibid., pp. 216–17.)

Ces atomes de feu qui sur la neige brillent,
Ces estincelles d'or, d'azur et de cristal
Dont l'hyver, au soleil, d'un lustre oriental
Pare ses cheveux blancs . . . .
  (Saint-Amant, *L'Hyver des Alpes*; *Œuvres*, p. 142.)

Les poissons dorment asseurez,
D'un mur de glace remparez, . . .
Enchassez en l'argent de l'onde.
  (Théophile, *Contre l'Hiver*; *Œuvres*, p. 26.)

[3] Les Tritons, en la regardant
Au travers leurs vitres liquides
  (Théophile, *La Maison de Silvie*, Ode II; *Œuvres*, p. 169).

influence the decoration of houses, furniture, and plate. But before
reaching the stage of massive rigidity, in which a motionless sun
turns into a gilt woodcarving and the shell, losing its iridescence,
affixes its seal on silver spoons, the universe of Théophile, of Saint-
Amant, and of Tristan is expressed in their poetry as a moving
picture, a very delicate interplay of sensations and images which
softens the hard sparkling of too many jewels. It may be the interplay of visual and auditory sensations:

> J'escoute, à demy transporté,
> Le bruit des ailes du Silence
> Qui vole dans l'obscurité[1]

or the interplay of amorous and sensuous delights in woman's
beauty with those in nature, so that the naiad's serenade in her
crystal dwelling, the caressing waters, the fluid hair of a woman,
the whiteness of hands, the teasing fragility of snow, the games
of love and those of fancy are all made of the same delicate and
transparent substance:

> Approche, approche, ma Dryade, . . .
> Preste-moy ton sein pour y boire
> Des odeurs qui m'embasmeront;
> Ainsi mes sens se pasmeront
> Dans les lacs de tes bras d'yvoire.
>
> Je baigneray mes mains folastres
> Dans les ondes de tes cheveux.[2]
>
> Fay moy boire au creux de tes mains
> Si l'eau n'en dissoust point la neige.[3]

But what, above all, gives to this landscape a particular shim-
mering and dream-like quality is the constant fluctuation of light
and shade which plays on it:

> L'onde lutte avec les cailloux
> Et la lumière avecque l'ombre.[4]
>
> Nous font voir des montagnes d'ombre
> Avec des sources de clarté.[5]

[1] Saint-Amant, *Le Contemplateur*; *Œuvres*, p. 17.
[2] Théophile, *La Solitude*; *Œuvres*, pp. 36–37.
[3] Tristan, *Le Promenoir des Deux Amans*; *Les Amours*, p. 53.
[4] Ibid., p. 50.   [5] *La Mer*; ibid., p. 217.

Flowers, sun, and stars alike play with their own reflection in the water:

> L'ombre de cette fleur vermeille,
> Et celle de ces joncs pendants
> Paraissent être là-dedans
> Les songes de l'eau qui sommeille.[1]

> Tantost, la plus claire du monde,
> Elle semble un miroir flottant, . . .
> Le soleil s'y fait si bien voir, . . .
> Et d'abord il semble à nos yeux
> Qu'il s'est laissé tomber des cieux.[2]

> Par fois, dans une claire nuit, . . .
> Diane quitte son Berger
> Et s'en va là-dedans nager
> Avecques ses estoilles nuës.

> Les ondes, qui leur font l'amour,
> Se refrisent sur leurs espaulles,
> Et font danser tout à l'entour
> L'ombre des roseaux et des saules.[3]

Whatever the extreme delightfulness of this poetry, it is difficult to deny that everything which constitutes the reality of the world for man—nature, love, religious beliefs—has been dislocated and disorganized, not even by the personal experience the poet has of love or religion (as was the case with d'Aubigné) but, one would almost say, for fun, for a lovely game of fancy and sensuality.

My analysis has to stop here, but one may wonder if the note of deliberate irresponsibility, of delightful gratuitousness, in some of Théophile's and Saint-Amant's poetry was not a great asset, as far as the artistic result was concerned. Their way of coming almost irrelevantly upon a delicate flower or a moonbeam gives a magic touch to the isolated object; their apparently careless grasp of the concrete world can seize the most fleeting impression. Théophile Gautier, who rediscovered these poets and appreciated their art so much that he contrived at times to rival them, found it difficult to achieve their successful blend of light transparence and jewelled richness.

[1] *Le Promenoir*; ibid., p. 50.
[2] Saint-Amant, *La Solitude*; *Œuvres*, pp. 7–8.
[3] Théophile, *La Maison de Silvie*, Ode III; *Œuvres*, p. 175.

5

The Absurd

It is not surprising to see that the disjunction could go one step farther and present us with a mad universe.

M. Lebègue in his article on 'Le Théâtre baroque en France' has noted the extraordinary number of grotesque, extravagant, and mad characters in early seventeenth-century dramatic production:

Ce goût de l'absurde et de la fantaisie déréglée apparaît dans les ballets de la cour de l'époque, dont plusieurs semblent sortis de l'imagination d'un dadaïste ou d'un aliéné.[1]

In the field of poetry there is one outstanding example of the absurd, and one wonders why there is no other: at least I have not been able to find any other among French or English poetry of that period. Whether an isolated case or not, the following *Ode* by Théophile will show to what extreme a poet's fancy could carry his chaotic vision of the world:

> Ce ruisseau remonte en sa source;
> Un bœuf gravit sur un clocher;
> Le sang coule de ce rocher;
> Un aspic s'accouple d'une ourse;
> Sur le haut d'une vieille tour
> Un serpent deschire un vautour;
> Le feu brusle dedans la glace;
> Le Soleil est devenu noir;
> Je voy la Lune qui va cheoir;
> Cet arbre est sorty de sa place.[2]

6

Conclusion on Baroque Poetry

These different aspects of baroque in poetry have illustrated the definition proposed—baroque as a distorted vision of the universe, distorted through imagination and sensibility. After a survey of what aspects this distortion can assume, a few remarks may be added to the definition.

[1] R. Lebègue, *Bibliothèque d'humanisme et renaissance*, 1942, p. 182.
[2] Théophile, *Ode*; *Œuvres*, p. 94. Some time after this present work had been written, I was glad to see that M. A.-M. Schmidt had found other examples of the absurd in early seventeenth-century poetry and that he also considered it as a feature of the baroque (see in *Trivium*, vol. iv, Year VII, M. Schmidt's article 'Constantes baroques dans la littérature française').

Baroque poetry is mostly descriptive, and this stresses its close link with the visual arts. The point has been made clear as far as mystical poetry is concerned.[1] The study of poets like Sir John Davies suggests the names of Hieronymus Bosch or Breughel. One might liken d'Aubigné's works to huge frescoes. As for Théophile, Saint-Amant, and Tristan, they themselves use the words *tableau* or *peinture* when describing their own poetry:

> Recoy ce fantasque *tableau*
> Fait d'une *peinture* vivante.
> > (Saint-Amant)

> N'est ce pas un des beaux sujets
> Que puisse prendre la *peinture*?
> (Tristan, describing the sea.)

It is also a kind of poetry which, if taken as a whole, offers the most violent contrasts, for, as has been noted previously, baroque imagination will go to extremes: religious mysticism (Crashaw) and the playful scepticism of the *libertins* (Saint-Amant, Théophile); the magnified universe of d'Aubigné and the microscopic world of Tristan and Saint-Amant; the sweet rosy heavens of Fletcher and the murky Hell of Davies of Hereford.

In all these aspects a strong appeal is made to the senses, either pleasurable (Crashaw, Théophile, Saint-Amant) or revolting (d'Aubigné, Davies of Hereford). In all these aspects, too, imagination unleashed gets the better of reason and logic.

One may also see more clearly why the names of later literary movements or schools of poetry have been mentioned by some critics in connexion with these poets.[2]

As a rule baroque poetry either shuns the themes of antiquity, or, as is the case with Saint-Amant and Théophile, uses mythology merely as picturesque and amusing decoration, which may account for its being considered as the opposite of Classicism. We shall see, in fact, that seventeenth-century Classicism took a great deal from the baroque.

It is easy to see why d'Aubigné's lines on Autumn:

> J'ayme à voir de beautez la branche deschargee . . .,

quoted above, would suggest a romantic attitude to nature and why Théophile's absurd ode would conjure up the word Surrealism. Such connexions are, no doubt, interesting.

[1] See above, pp. 78–79.   [2] See Ch. I.

But, as this chapter and the preceding one have attempted to prove, the term baroque can, to the exclusion of any other, be applied to certain poems of certain poets, to characterize and label a sensibility peculiar to the late Renaissance, thus avoiding the confusion between baroque and metaphysical. It is perhaps not unnecessary to repeat here that metaphysical poetry may obviously (as in Herbert's case) have nothing to do with that distortion of the universe which I call baroque; or that metaphysical poetry may, on the contrary, result from the intelligence mastering the reactions of a baroque sensibility (as is very often the case with Donne[1] or with La Ceppède).

But we have also to keep in mind that some of the poets studied in this chapter, as for example Tristan or Saint-Amant, have been called précieux and that no definition of the baroque will be entirely satisfactory so long as there is not a clear-cut distinction between the two words baroque and précieux.

[1] It would, of course, be a study in itself to examine to what extent Donne wrote baroque poetry, and to what extent purely metaphysical.

VII

THE QUESTION OF THE TERM PRÉCIEUX

THE difficulties which arise from any attempt at finding a criterion for the précieux are very much of the same kind as those one has met with in the question of the term baroque. The problem is perhaps even more complicated as instead of one term we are confronted by three: *précieux, préciosité, une précieuse*. The documentation on the subject is considerable and the results attained by critics or historians not easy to sum up. And yet the first necessary step must be to separate what can be considered as already adequately defined from what is still controversial.

A rough division may be made between two aspects of the problem: *la préciosité*, as a social and literary movement, taking place in France, say between 1588 and 1665,[1] marked by a refinement of manners and language, extending at times to the excessive and the ridiculous, and associated with the Hôtel de Madame de Rambouillet; and *la poésie précieuse*, as a kind of poetry not limited to the seventeenth century, which would offer particular characteristics of refinement.

Concerning seventeenth-century French préciosité, we possess a vast amount of historical documentation and valuable criticism, which does not leave a wide margin for further researches or controversy: the social background of the movement is well known,[2] the language of préciosité has been carefully studied;[3] the analysis has gone farther than manners and language as the interest of the critics has been focused more and more on a certain conception of life and especially of love which was peculiar to the women called précieuses.[4] As far as literature proper is concerned, both Brunot

[1] These are the dates generally given in the textbooks of literature. But M. Adam, in his article 'Baroque et Préciosité' in the *Revue des sciences humaines*, July–Dec. 1949, as well as in the paper he read at the Deuxième Congrès des Études Françaises (Paris, Sept. 1950), limits this movement to the period 1654–60.

[2] The staple book on this point is: M. Magendie, *La Politesse mondaine en France de 1600 à 1660*, 1926. See also E. Magne, *Voiture et l'Hôtel de Rambouillet*, 1929, and G. Mongrédien, *Les Précieux et les précieuses*, 1939.

[3] One must start, of course, with A. Baudeau de Somaize, *Le Dictionnaire des Précieuses*, ed. C.-M. Livet, 1856; and the best analysis of précieux language is to be found in F. Brunot, *Histoire de la langue française des origines à 1900*, 1909–30, vol. iii, ch. ix.

[4] See the seventeenth-century psychological study of the précieuses in the

and M. Mornet[1] have studied, at least on the linguistic and historical side, the relationships between préciosité and Classicism; and the debt of classicist writers to préciosité is fully acknowledged. On the other hand the question of préciosité in seventeenth-century poetry is not yet satisfactorily settled. Although poets like Voiture, Malleville, Benserade have been the object of particular studies, it seems that the analytical approach has not made any definite advances lately and that Faguet's *Précieux et Burlesques*,[2] of 1927, is not outdistanced by M. Bray's chapter on the seventeenth-century précieux poets.[3] Neither Faguet, nor M. Bray, nor M. Thierry Maulnier[4] can solve for us the problem of knowing whether, let us say, Tristan is a baroque or a précieux poet.

This last point is closely linked with the second aspect of the précieux: the précieux as a kind of literature (prose as well as poetry) which can be found at any time and in any country. It is obvious that if we do not know exactly why Tristan is a précieux poet, it will be even more difficult to apply, by analogy, the term to Baudelaire or Mallarmé. Yet for almost a century now, the word has been used to characterize poets or prose-writers other than seventeenth-century writers: Sainte-Beuve applied it to Marivaux,[5] Thibaudet to Mallarmé,[6] Madame Magny to Giraudoux,[7] and each time the critic has given a definition of the précieux as a general term.

What would, perhaps, sum up the present state of knowledge concerning the précieux more fully than can be done in this study is M. Bray's book *La Préciosité et les Précieux, de Thibaut de Champagne à Giraudoux*. The author offers us both historical and analytical considerations on précieux characteristics; he is con-

---

Abbé de Pure, *La Précieuse ou le Mystère des Ruelles*, ed. E. Magne, 1938. See also F. Baumal, *Le Féminisme au temps de Molière*, 1926; Jacques Debu-Bridel, 'La Préciosité, conception héroïque de la vie', *Revue de France*, 15 Sept. 1938; O. Nadal, *Le Sentiment de l'Amour dans l'œuvre de Pierre Corneille*, 1948; R. Bray, *La Préciosité et les précieux*, 1948, ch. iii, 'L'Amour précieux'.

[1] D. Mornet, *Histoire de la littérature française classique*, 1942, ch. ii.

[2] E. Faguet, *Histoire de la poésie française de la Renaissance au Romantisme*, 1923–7; vol. iii, *précieux et Burlesques*.

[3] R. Bray, op. cit., ch. v.

[4] See section 1 in Thierry Maulnier's introduction to *Poètes précieux et baroques*.

[5] Sainte-Beuve, *Causeries du Lundi*, 3e éd., vol. ix, 'Marivaux' (pp. 342–63).

[6] A. Thibaudet, *La Poésie de Stéphane Mallarmé*, 1926.

[7] C.-E. Magny, *Précieux Giraudoux*, 1945.

cerned both with a general definition of the précieux and a chronological study of the different aspects of préciosité in the course of
the history of French literature. This work is extremely valuable for
the problem of terminology which constitutes the basis of this study,
not only because it is a handy compendium of what the historians
of seventeenth-century préciosité have amassed little by little, but
also because, in his attempt to characterize the different kinds of
précieux in poetry, M. Bray brings together most of the critical
attitudes towards précieux poetry which have been suggested before him.

The fact that M. Bray gives several definitions of the précieux
(*précieux de relation, précieux de figuration, précieux de création*)
illustrates the particular difficulty encountered by all the critics
before him; this evasive term escapes the strict limits of one general
definition. Already in the seventeenth century the Abbé de Pure,
speaking of *la précieuse*, had confessed: 'La Pretieuse de soy n'a
point de définition; les termes sont trop grossiers pour bien exprimer vne chose si spirituelle.'[1] And it seems, indeed, that when
dealing with the précieux, the critics behave as if they were handling a delicate china cup or approaching a bluebird on tiptoe; as
if also the gross boldness of attempting a definition should be dis-
guised, in order to be forgiven, by subtle nuances and witty para-
phrases, to such an extent that one wonders if the critic who writes
about the précieux does not become, *ipso facto*, a précieux himself.[2]
Whereas, in the case of the baroque, critics have looked for a concise formula—such as the baroque as the art of the Counter-
Reformation—in the case of the précieux they have, as a rule,
circled round their object, noting characteristics, making one
daring step forward in asserting, for instance, that préciosité should
not be assimilated to *la galanterie*,[3] but immediately after retreating
two steps backward in suggesting that it is *un jeu*[4] (which incidentally, in M. Bray's case, contradicts a previous statement on préciosité as a moral phenomenon).[5]

The result is that, as a rule, we are given not one definition
but a string of characteristics which, if they can in most cases be

---

[1] Abbé de Pure, op. cit., vol. i, p. 67.

[2] To this effect of mimetism we owe Faguet's brilliant introductory pages in
his *Précieux et Burlesques*, Thibaudet's chapter on Mallarmé as a précieux, and
probably a great many of Thierry Maulnier's sparkling sentences in his introduction to his anthology.   [3] Bray, op. cit., p. 177.

[4] Ibid., p. 180.   [5] Ibid., p. 165.

applied to the précieux, might apply as well to other kinds of poetry. In fact, when we are given one definition such as Thibaudet's: 'L'obscurité de propos délibéré, la tendance à remplacer dans l'expression un système de clarté directe par un jeu de lumière réfléchie, s'appelle la préciosité',[1] the definition seems to cover the whole of French poetry, or at least leaves out very little (the direct outbursts of feeling of the Romantic poets, or the philosophical poems of Sully Prudhomme).[2] M. Bray may, with great care, distinguish between one kind of préciosité and another, but it is none the less obvious that he extends the scope of the term as widely as possible and includes as précieux Scève,[3] the baroque,[4] Donne,[5] to say nothing of later poets (Baudelaire and Mallarmé). And when, in his conclusion, he turns from the analysis of the different poets in order to synthesize their common characteristics, one wonders whether the names adduced by M. Bray can be said to conform unconditionally to his ultimate definition:

Le jeu inutile et sans cause d'un oisif à l'esprit agile et à l'imagination féconde, hanté par l'ange du bizarre, riche de culture, se plaisant dans une création de luxe qui traduit par des gestes arbitraires une exigence interne de distinction, voilà comment nous apparaît l'art précieux.[6]

It is not proposed here to discuss why it seems impossible to accept the application of such a definition to Donne or Scève. The preceding chapters will have made it clear that metaphysical poetry cannot be considered as pure luxury or arbitrary gestures. Nor does it appear necessary to explain at length how dangerously precarious is the criterion of *jeu inutile* or of *esprit agile et imagination féconde*. As a matter of fact, M. Bray's definition includes characteristics of the précieux which nobody has ever denied—luxury, distinction, and culture. On the other hand, *l'ange du bizarre* seems more appropriate to the baroque than to the précieux, and stands as a

---

[1] Thibaudet, op. cit., p. 73.

[2] Which Thibaudet realizes perfectly: '. . . Jusqu'à Lamartine, je crois qu'il n'existe pas, hormis quelques sonnets de Louise Labé et *La Belle Vieille* de Maynard, une pièce de lyrisme amoureux qui ne soit une œuvre de préciosité' (op. cit., p. 76).

[3] Op. cit., pp. 60–66.

[4] 'La Préciosité de 1600 est un phénomène baroque' (ibid., p. 87).

[5] 'J. Donne . . . est un adversaire du pétrarquisme platonicien . . . et pourtant c'est un grand précieux. Sa subtilité se déploie non dans le style mais dans la pensée. Il aime les idées inattendues, les rapprochements incongrus, les hyperboles stupéfiantes' (ibid., p. 89).

[6] Ibid., p. 396.

warning that here the distinction we want to make between the two terms is dismissed altogether.

We may also observe that, in the revaluation of the term which has taken place lately, critics have shown a strong tendency to stress the *creative* side of the précieux, viewing the précieux writer as a man who attempts, through his refined conceits, to give a metaphysical explanation of the universe.[1] This seems to prove how badly we need the term metaphysical poetry in French terminology. For lack of it critics have resorted to précieux, and it seems an untenable position that the latter term should at the same time characterize drawing-room madrigals and verse in which a poet has endeavoured with all seriousness to express the essential problems of man's destiny.

It may appear by now rather obvious that the question of finding a criterion for précieux poetry is an even more thorny problem than that of the baroque. One cannot dismiss the characteristics of the précieux which are usually pointed out by critics: most of them are reasonably accurate. The difficulty is that none of them provides us with a safe criterion. Précieux poets make a great use of the conceit, of the *pointe*? Certainly, but so do all the poets of the Renaissance and the late Renaissance. Précieux poets are witty? Yes, but this is both too limited and too broad a definition: précieux poetry is not merely wit, and wit itself can be of so many species as to include metaphysical wit as well. Précieux poets are men of culture? So are most poets: would one call Milton or Mr. T. S. Eliot précieux? and so on. These and other similar assertions concerning the précieux are right but lead nowhere. In fact we are embarrassed by an excess of possible criteria, all,

---

[1] 'Préciosité de création, avons-nous dit: en effet elle vise à donner à la création poétique une démarche particulière. Il ne s'agit plus d'exprimer des idées et des sentiments, ni de reproduire le réel, mais de créer un monde à soi, selon sa propre exigence' (Bray, ibid., p. 391).

'La préciosité n'est autre chose que la volonté de faire que toute chose signifie, qu'elle soit différente d'elle-même: elle est *l'Altérité* installée dans le monde . . . Elle nous crée un univers de reflets et de perspectives où chaque objet est miroir du Tout . . .' (C.-E. Magny, op. cit., p. 47).

'Il n'est pas difficile, une fois découverte l'exigence métaphysique qui est au principe de la préciosité . . .' (ibid., p. 48).

In fact what Madame Magny says of the metaphysical précieux would be a good account of metaphysical poetry; and at the same time she is aware of the difference between a conceit bearing on the essential and one bearing on the accidental. (See, pp. 43–44, her distinction between real préciosité and the concetto.)

or almost all, having some value, and yet not only is there not one of them that can suffice to distinguish précieux poetry from other kinds of verse, but even the various lists of them as they appear in the critics mentioned in the preceding pages do not enable us to separate a précieux from a baroque or a metaphysical poet.

Considering that most of the difficulties in the use of the term come from its scope having been too much widened, what is proposed in the following pages is to limit the implications of the word, choosing among the characteristics enumerated those which are the most specific and keeping close to the recognized features of seventeenth-century préciosité.

In the first place, I should like to put the stress, even if somewhat heavily, on what M. Bray calls *la préciosité de relation*, which rests on social relationships and supposes the existence of a closed society, although I would not add with M. Bray that the only closed society is the court or the drawing-room.

In my view, précieux poetry is exclusively a kind of poetry in which the use of a very refined language, of elaborate imagery, and of clever conceits has no other aim than to afford a delicate intellectual pleasure to a certain number of over-sophisticated people of a definite period, and the intellectual pleasure derived from it will depend much upon the code of behaviour, the tastes, and the degree of culture of a particular set of people.

Thus, to give an immediate example before developing this definition, there is the famous conceit in Molière's *Le Misanthrope*:

> Belle Philis, on desespère,
> Alors qu'on espère toujours —

which supposes, if it is to be fully appreciated, that you are an *habitué* of Madame de Rambouillet's Blue Room. You have to accept the Hôtel de Rambouillet code of the perfect lover for whom courtship is long expectancy and almost hopeless waiting, to find pleasure in the pun on the word *espère* (meaning at the same time to wait, to expect, and to hope).

The first condition of précieux poetry is the existence of a somewhat organized group of people who insist on not being mistaken for the common herd; perhaps today we should call them highbrows. The seventeenth-century précieuses consciously differentiated themselves from other people by their language, manners, and tastes, which gave to their way of expressing themselves a semi-hermetic quality:

Elles sont encore fortement persuadées qu'une pensée ne vaut rien lorsqu'elle est entendue de tout le monde . . . qu'une précieuse parle autrement que le peuple, afin que ses pensées ne soient entendues que de ceux qui ont des clartés au-dessus du vulgaire; et c'est à ce dessein qu'elles font tous leurs efforts pour détruire le vieux langage, et qu'elles en ont fait un, non seulement qui est nouveau, mais encore qui leur est particulier.[1]

It is a well-known fact that any group of people having a certain number of things in common tends to adopt a language of its own. So long as this language is used for practical purposes (as is the case with schoolboys' slang or thieves' jargon where it is primarily an instrument of self-defence) it does not lead, of course, to any préciosité. Préciosité begins with the quest for an aesthetic pleasure originating in those particularities of expression. (If Villon was ever précieux it was when he wrote his *Ballades* in Coquillard slang.) Half the pleasure is naturally to share it with the other people of the group. (Unfortunately we shall never know if Villon's disreputable friends appreciated the poetic use he made of their language.) In this way an Oxford or Cambridge circumstantial poem or High Table joke might be précieux (although Universities and their vernacular have been created for practical purposes) when in order to be appreciated in terms of aesthetics it necessitates a knowledge of academic life, vocabulary, and tastes.

The subjects which will appeal to précieux writers will necessarily be of a kind that will interest the other people of the group. As the taste of all small societies tends to the topical and timely,[2] we must expect précieux poetry to be constituted mainly of circumstantial poems. And, in fact, we notice that a great deal of seventeenth-century poetry is composed of poems either of *galanterie* (which is the inevitable topic in any civilized group of men and women; and also we know how the précieuses enjoyed any ratiocination on the subject of love), or written with the specific purpose of paying a compliment to a definite person, or composed about a definite incident. Thus *La Guirlande de Julie* (composed by the best writers of the Hôtel de Rambouillet: Chapelain, Malleville,

[1] Somaize, *Dictionnaire des Précieuses*, Maxime VII, vol. i, p. 158.
[2] See Maxime V of the Précieuses: 'faire plus d'état du présent que du passé ni que de l'avenir' (ibid., p. 158).

Scudéry) was a present of the Duc de Montausier to Julie d'Angennes. This is the most obvious example, but some titles of poems of the same period will illustrate the topical aspect of précieux poetry: *A la petite chienne de Madame la Comtesse de Fiesque* (Benserade), *Stances à une demoiselle qui avait les manches de sa chemise retroussées et sales* (Voiture), *A un Grand qui s'était moqué d'un ruban gris et vert* (Sarrasin), *Madrigal à une Dame qui lui reprochait d'être trop longtemps à la campagne* (Charleval). . . .

Because précieux poetry will often take as its subjects minor incidents, it would be tempting to agree with M. Bray that one element of the précieux 'c'est la petitesse . . . la préciosité a sa place à Lilliput, non à Brobdingnag . . . un art de myope'.[1] But I should not altogether agree. The précieux universe is small inasmuch as it is limited to the interests and vocabulary of a group, but in the absolute it is neither small nor large, but exactly on the same scale as the group. There is no reason to deny that, were there a circle of highbrows at Brobdingnag (and why not?), they would write a sort of précieux poetry which would reflect a gigantic universe.

A more delicate question is that of précieux metaphors. Every critic who has commented on précieux poetry has pointed out the fact that this poetry was an orgy of metaphors. It is not true of all the précieux poets (as will be seen later), but it is true as a rule that précieux poets will prefer the metaphorical mode of communication to the direct expression of a fact, idea, or feeling. This is perfectly in keeping with the definition proposed: the précieux cannot use direct speech, because they want to be understood only by those of their own set. There is another reason: the importance of social relationships, with which this poetry is closely connected. The social code of manners and, incidentally, the social code of morals forbid the direct and plain expression of one's feelings or ideas. Madame de Rambouillet taught the inmates of her Hôtel this reserve, this courteous disinclination to be expansive, and in the précieuses it was not only a question of manners but one of morals:

Le quatrième point est de donner plus à l'imagination à l'égard des plaisirs qu'à la vérité, et cela par ce principe de morale que l'imagination ne peut pécher réellement. (Maxime IV.)[2]

---

[1] Bray, op. cit., p. 393.   [2] Somaize, *Dictionnaire des Précieuses*, p. 157.

Therefore metaphors in précieux poetry will play the part of conventions: they must be such as can be grasped by all the people belonging to the group, they must also be such as will be accepted by the group as conforming to their standards of good taste (i.e. within the code of manners and ethics of the group). Inevitably, therefore, all the précieux poetry of a given period offers the unmistakable feature of monotony. All the petrarchist sonneteers seem alike, because they have adopted the set of metaphors and themes of the fourteenth- and fifteenth-century Italian courts; for the same reason the reading of seventeenth-century poets like Voiture, Malleville, Benserade gives the impression of rereading the same poem over and over again. This criticism is, of course, rather unfair to those poets: they were doing their best to be clever and original, but they had to conform to the conventions. And when the conventions are not those of the literature of a whole country at a certain period but those of a restricted group, they are bound to be overwhelming.

If we consider which metaphors (or which themes) a given set of précieux will adopt, we notice that they are usually of two kinds. They may be borrowed from objects familiar to the group. Thus the first précieux poets, the poets of the 'Cours d'Amour', being under the sign of chivalry, created the conventional imagery of battles, shafts, besieged hearts. . . . In the same way terms belonging to fencing, venery, chess, music, cards will be used by the précieux.[1] As M. Mornet noticed, there is specialization within préciosité, and he gives a very interesting example of *préciosité grammairienne* in the second half of the seventeenth century.[2] The second kind of themes and metaphors to be found in précieux poets does not necessarily belong to their environment and is borrowed from other poets who were not précieux but who are

[1] See Brunot, op. cit., ch. ix, p. 340.

[2] From le Père Pierre de Saint-Louis's *Madeleine* (a poem which M. Mornet gives as an instance of the survival of préciosité at the end of the seventeenth century; the poem had four editions, 1668, 1694, 1700, 1714).

> Ce qui la fait trembler pour son *grammairien*
> C'est de voir, par un *cas*, du tout déraisonnable
> Que son amour lui rend la mort *indéclinable*,
> Et, qu'*actif* comme il est, aussi bien qu'*excessi*.
> Il le rend à ce point d'impassible *passif*.
>
> . . . Pendant qu'elle s'occupe à punir le forfait
> De son temps *prétérit* qui ne fut qu'*imparfait*, . . .
>
> (Mornet, op. cit., p. 91).

imitated because they happen to suit the taste of the group. The
first poet who thought of praising the woman he loved by saying
that she was more beautiful than the rising sun (and it would be
rather difficult to name him) was probably not a précieux, unless,
which is unlikely, he and his lady belonged to a society of astrono-
mers. But the hundred and more sonnets, songs, and madrigals
written on this theme are précieux: the theme happened to suit a
certain attitude to woman, characteristic both of Petrarchism and
of the précieuses, and was adopted with enthusiasm.

Here we see one of the limitations of précieux poetry: the poet
will not choose the metaphors which suit best the feelings or ideas
he wishes to express; he can only choose within the narrow limits
of objects which are part of the life of his group, or else, not invent
new metaphors, but borrow from a store which has the approval
of the group. From the seventeenth-century précieux poets we can
gauge how much of Petrarchism and how much of mythology had
been absorbed (or rejected) by refined circles; we can also see
clearly how the highbrow circles in Ronsard's time could absorb
a great deal of mythology, whereas in the early seventeenth century
préciosité worked in the direction of restraint, and too much
mythology would have been bad taste. Précieux poetry gives us
the lowest common denominator of the literary tastes in the most
sophisticated circles in a given period.

If, leaving the question of imagery proper, which will be illustrated in the next chapter, we come to the arrangement of words in
general, to those devices such as antitheses, hyperboles, riddles,
pointes, periphrases which characterize précieux poetry, we find
that all the critics, except perhaps Faguet, account for them by the
précieux's quest for the unexpected and the quaint.[1]

Une formule précieuse, même sous la forme ancestrale d'une devi-
nette, découvre et fixe entre deux objets des analogies inattendues.[2]

M. Bray, speaking of Donne as précieux, writes:

Il aime les idées inattendues, les rapprochements incongrus, les
hyperboles stupéfiantes,[3]

and at the end of his book, when summing up the characteristics
of the précieux poet:

Il [the précieux poet] . . . établit des rapports inattendus entre des

[1] It may be recalled here that this particular feature has also been attributed
to the baroque poets by M. Lebègue (see above, Ch. V).
[2] Thibaudet, op. cit., p. 75.   [3] Op. cit., p. 89.

objets fort éloignés l'un de l'autre . . . Il vise à la surprise, aussi bien la sienne propre que celle des autres. C'est pour cela qu'il aime la nouveauté; le jamais vu, l'inouï, l'inédit lui est particulièrement cher. Il se nourrit d'originalité.[1]

It seems scarcely necessary to point out that the unexpected connexion between two things is not a criterion of the précieux: the startling surrealist conceit 'le ciel est bleu comme une orange' (and nothing can be more unexpected than the second term of the comparison) would not be called précieux by anybody. But I would even go so far as to say that what precisely characterizes any précieux connexion between two things is that such a connexion is thoroughly expected.[2] Faguet, in his valuable introduction to *Précieux et Burlesques*, realized that although the précieux poets were using devices, such as antitheses and paradoxical metaphors, generally connected with effects of surprise, the result was not to confront the reader with the unexpected, and he offered this explanation:

Dès qu'on s'attend à l'imprévu, tout, même ce qui est vraiment nouveau, paraît quelque chose qui était facile à prévoir.[3]

But this explanation, although subtle, is even too much of a concession to the would-be unexpected quality of précieux poetry. I should rather agree with a remark he makes earlier about the précieux's use of the periphrasis:

La périphrase consiste à faire trouver au lecteur le mot propre qu'on évite, précisément pour qu'il le trouve.[4]

In fact all the devices of précieux poetry are precisely worked out so as to provide the reader with what he expects, and the intellectual pleasure he will experience is not that of the discovery of something new, but the conceited delight of finding that, thanks to his knowledge of the conventions of his group, he has been able to recognize something familiar to him; or, if the feeling or idea expressed is not familiar to him, he will be reassured by the conventional medium through which it is offered to him. If unexpected, out-of-the-way, queer, *inouï*, the conceit would shock,

---

[1] Ibid., pp. 393–4.

[2] M. Bray admits that Desportes's metaphors are somewhat too obvious (p. 83), but considers them as only a debased form of préciosité.

[3] p. 13.   [4] Ibid.

would disturb the pattern of conventions which holds together the members of the group. As will be seen in the next chapter, précieux antitheses, conceits, and *pointes finales* have the marked characteristic of inevitability.

Here again the limitations of précieux poetry appear glaring. The précieux poet must not be more subtle than the average man of his group. Indeed, if we sum up the conventions to which this poet must conform—he must choose a subject which will interest his group, be sufficiently obscure to be appreciated only by his group and yet clear enough not to puzzle unpleasantly any one in the group, deal with a restricted number of metaphors with a sure instinct for what must be avoided as bad taste—then one may admire the *tour de force* aspect of certain précieux poems.

The question of the sincerity of the poet has very often been discussed in relation to précieux poetry.[1] It is undeniable that part of précieux poetry will take the form of mere drawing-room entertainment—tournaments where poets, vying in précieux nimbleness of mind (which is the quick and clever connecting of two familiar propositions or themes), will write without putting their own feelings or thoughts into their verse. But it is not necessarily so, and within the limits of *bon ton*, a poet can very well translate into a précieux poem feelings or thoughts which are both highly serious and sincere. A précieux love-poem does not necessarily imply that the poet is only paying the lip-service of a gallant madrigal to a lady. He may be genuinely in love, and it is not preposterous to suppose that he will like to add to the avowal of his love the present of a delicate intellectual treat in keeping with his social group, which the lady, belonging to the same group, will enjoy. But this is in reality a point which can lead only to theoretical possibilities. We are accustomed to test the sincerity of a poem by the value of the personal experience it expresses and we have no other means of testing this value than by a rather negative process, by realizing 'the absence of any apparent attempt on the part of the artist to work effects upon the readers which do not work for himself'.[2] In précieux poetry the attempt on the part of the artist to work effects which will produce the same stock response

---

[1] See M. Bray, discussing Faguet's and Lanson's points of view (ch. v): 'Voilà qui nous incline à contester que le sentiment soit aussi dédaigné par les précieux que le prétend Faguet.' Yet M. Bray concludes: 'cet art est un jeu.'

[2] I. A. Richards, *Principles of Literary Criticism*, 1947, p. 271.

in any member of the group, is not only so apparent, but also so much an intrinsic quality of this poetry that it will automatically make us suspicious and it will be impossible to distinguish, by internal evidence, the précieux poem which is the expression of a sincere feeling from that which is a mere entertainment, because in both cases, to conform to the conditions of précieux poetry, the poet will have to resort to the same artificial devices. One might perhaps deduce from this that a poet who has an important individual experience to impart will not choose to write précieux poetry, which would necessarily stifle his creative power.

It is easy to see the relation between préciosité and snobbery and one would readily subscribe to Brunot's opinion that

> La Préciosité a des racines lointaines, pour la raison que gorriers, affétés, précieux, incroyables, dandys, gens select . . . se tendent la main à travers les siècles, que leurs tendances générales se ressemblent, si leurs goûts passagers diffèrent, et que leur niveau d'esprit est en somme à peu près constant.[1]

It is also easy to perceive that précieux literature plays an important part in the evolution of the language. This part is both destructive and positive. Précieux poetry kills all the metaphors it uses because it turns them into the conventions of a group; but a great many of the conventions of the group fall very soon into common use, cease to be précieux and contribute to enriching the vocabulary of a country. (The influence of the seventeenth-century précieuses on the evolution of the French language is a well-acknowledged fact;[2] this point will be discussed in the next chapter.)

As for précieux poetry, it cannot be overlooked or dismissed with scorn, if one is interested in the evolution of poetry, as it reflects this evolution in the literary tastes of the sophisticated sets.

I said previously that it gives us the measure of the literary tastes of a given period, but here an important reservation has to be made. Précieux literature only reflects the literary tendencies of its age in so far as those tendencies are compatible with its essential aim: to form a polite society, in which the blessings of culture and civilization can be enjoyed without the intrusion of

---

[1] Op. cit., ch. ix, p. 66.   [2] See Brunot and Mornet, op. cit.

the most troublesome problems of the age. A précieux society does not fight for any creed, political, religious, or literary, but it stands in firm opposition to everything that menaces the vested interests of civilization. This characteristic has been too much overlooked and critics have suggested that the ideal atmosphere for préciosité was a period of peace, order, and high civilization in a country.[1] But when such a stage of civilization is reached, préciosité, I think, has no longer any reason to exist and merges into the general trends of civilization. In fact the précieux *côteries* we know of stand out against a background of wars and unrest: the 'Cours d'Amour' against the barbarism of the Middle Ages, Charles d'Orléans' court at Blois against the Hundred Years War, Desportes and the *mignons* of Henri III against the Religious Wars, Madame de Rambouillet's Blue Room against the grossness of the court of Henri IV and the political commotions of the early seventeenth century. While part of the literature of these periods expresses the upsetting problems of the time, the précieux writer refuses to be upset, and plays in the first place for self-protection and safety. In that respect he is an escapist. Charles d'Orléans, to take an example outside the period studied in this work, offers a striking instance of such a position adopted by the précieux artist. Judged by his poetry, he ignored the tragic problems of his own life and those of his time, and took refuge either in the acceptance of a golden imprisonment or later, in his refined court at Blois, exploiting the wealth of courtly wit and culture. Nobody could possibly deduce from his poetry that the main theme of French fifteenth-century lyrics was death; whereas Pierre de Nesson, who led a comparatively happy life at the court of the Duc de Berry, and had no murdered father to avenge or any direct responsibility in the fate of France, expressed a painfully sharp insight into the agonizing atmosphere of the country. This tends to prove that the précieux poet either chooses to be conditioned by his environment or instinctively seeks the congenial environment, the closed précieux group where he can take refuge. But to call him escapist is only partly true, as the word implies too much of a negative quality: the précieux poet does not escape into a dream-world of his own or an imaginary *jardin secret*. His positive achievement is to shelter the delicate flowers of civilization from the rough winds of tempestuous times: his hot-house is not

[1] See Bray, op. cit., ch. i, p. 19.

his private property, it belongs to the tradition of culture. Unselfish in a way, he puts aside his own problems as well as those of his age to share with his group a salvaged common heritage, and stands like an impersonal landmark of what he considers, and partly justifiably, to be, at a given period, the highest possible degree of civilization.

VIII

SOME ASPECTS OF PRÉCIEUX POETRY

I

Précieux Prosody and Précieux Language

PRÉCIEUX poets have been depicted in the preceding chapter as the guardians of the storehouse of culture, enjoying it within a limited set of people and playing for safety against the odds of troublesome problems.

Did they find themselves safe enough in turning their attention to the technique of versification and to an interest in the language of poetry for its own sake?

In the sixteenth and seventeenth centuries précieux poets seem to have experienced a particular delight in the possibilities offered by French scansion. They did not create any new form of verse but made the most either of the Grands Rhétoriqueurs tradition or of the Italian borrowings. In that respect a chronological study of the précieux poets would tell us which poetic form was the prevalent fashion at the Court of Henri III or at the Hôtel de Rambouillet. This has been carried out in all the works concerned mainly or partly with the evolution of French prosody.[1] But, more than the variations of the sonnet-form or the reintroduction of the madrigal, what is striking is the fact that précieux poets of the sixteenth and seventeenth centuries resorted again and again to the same tricks of prosody, as if by the first half of the sixteenth century a stock of technical devices had been gathered together which was destined to be enjoyed and handled in every possible way by the précieux poets for more than a century. There is in this clever handling of versification for versification's sake, not only the fun of the game (although some précieux *bouts-rimés* or riddles are mere drawing-room games), but also the sophisticated delight of the gourmet before some rare dish cooked according to the best recipes, and the conceited satisfaction of *la difficulté vaincue*, increased by the knowledge that the members of the group know their cookery-book and also are experts in the sort of difficulties to be overcome.

[1] See H. Vaganay, *Le Sonnet en Italie et en France au XVIème siècle*, 1903; J. Vianey, op. cit.; H. P. Thieme, *Essai sur l'histoire du vers français*, 1916.

Let us take as an example the possibilities offered by rhyme. Marot is well known for his extraordinary cleverness in playing with rhymes:

(*rimes annexées*)   Dieu gard ma Maistresse et regente,
                Gente de corps et de façon.
                Son cœur . . .

(*rimes couronnées*)   La blanche colombelle belle
                Souvent je voys priant criant.

(*rimes enchaînées*)   Dieu des amans, de mort me garde,
                Me gardant donne moy bonheur,
                Et me le donnant prens ta darde.[1]

A century later précieux poets find the same pleasure in playing with these fanciful rhymes:

Tourment sans passion, passion sans pointure,
Pointure sans douleur, douleur sans sentiment,
Sentiment sans vigueur, vigueur sans mouvement . . .[2]

Even in English poetry, where rhyme has not the same appeal, we find this kind of précieux rhyming: for instance, Sidney's

---

[1] Clément Marot, *Œuvres complètes*, ed. A. Grenier, vol. i, p. 452. See in Sebillet (*Art poétique français*, ed. Félix Gaiffe, 1932) other examples of Marot's extreme variety in the use of rhymes. Marot is thus a précieux poet, in so far as he is the sophisticated court poet. He is not only a précieux poet, because part of his verse reveals other sides of him, particularly a good-natured humour which owes nothing to courtly witticism and can even go against the précieux conventions (see for instance his humoristic treatment of the conventional pathetic fallacy in his *Complainte pour la mort de Madame Louise de Savoie*). This shows that, when dealing with a précieux poet, it is important to see clearly to what extent he has yielded to the précieux set he belongs to and to what extent he has freed himself from their conventions in order to express his personality. It is, for instance, rather surprising to discover that Voiture, the typical précieux poet, the lap-dog of the précieuses, had in him a vein of straightforward 'narquois' humour which did not derive from the Hôtel de Rambouillet and was rather similar to that of Marot (whom he admired). See, for instance, this song:

Les Demoiselles de ce temps
Ont depuis peu beaucoup d'amans.
On dit qu'il n'en manque à personne;
L'année est bonne . . .

(*Les Œuvres de Monsieur de Voiture*, 1734, vol. ii, pp. 134–5), which recalls the unsophisticated bantering tone of Marot:

Mes damoyselles
Bonnes et belles,
Je vous envoye
Mon feu de joye . . .

(op. cit., vol. i, p. 254).

[2] Quoted by Bray, op. cit., p. 186.

sonnet already quoted in Chapter II, in which every line ends alter-
nately with the words *day* and *night*:

> Now that of absence the most irksome night
> With darkest shade doth ouercome my day;
> Since Stella's eyes, wont to giue me my day,
> Leauing my hemisphere, leaue me in night;
> Each day seemes long, and longs for long-staid night;
> The night, as tedious, wooes th'approach of day: . . . [1]

The précieux writers' interest in language is one of the characteristics of préciosité which has been most closely gone into, as far
as the seventeenth century is concerned.[2] This interest in language
is due to various causes, all of them in keeping with the definition
of the précieux which has been proposed: the précieux must have
a language of their own; the possibilities of language just like
those of versification are part of the artistic pleasurable treasures
of which the précieux circles consider themselves the true benefi-
ciaries; and also the formation of a polite society implies a right of
search into vocabulary and the power to legislate on the uses of
words. If one considers the first reason for their interest in language
—the wish to have a jargon belonging to themselves only—one
might infer that, where language is concerned, the précieux will
have some creative power. But in fact that creative power works
within extremely narrow limitations.

Although the question of the précieuses' neologisms is controversial,[3] it seems reasonable to agree with Brunot, who considers
the list of words coined by the seventeenth-century précieux salons
to be a very short one.[4] On the other hand part of their treatment
of vocabulary consists in discerning the crude or low, in fact any
words which appear to them incompatible with refined society.
Their positive contribution to the language rests mainly on their
marked preference for certain words or on their habit of replacing
a word by a periphrasis. The words they relished were either
vague words such as *air, bel air, bon air, un je ne sais quoi*; or useless
words: *ma chère, car enfin, à n'en point mentir*, &c.; or exaggerated
words: *furieux, furieusement, du dernier bien, ravissant*.[5] This ten-

[1] *Astrophel and Stella*, Sonnet LXXXIX; *Complete Poems*, ed. Grosart, vol. i,
p. 116.
[2] See the works of Brunot, Mornet, and Bray, already mentioned.
[3] See Bray, op. cit., pp. 170–1, for a summary of this controversy.
[4] Op. cit., vol. ii, ch. ix.
[5] See the works by Brunot, Somaize, and Bray, already mentioned.

dency is that of people for whom language is not a creative instrument destined to grasp reality with accuracy and vigour. Useless words, vagueness of expression, and overstatement are rather a sign of impotence.[1]

If we come to the periphrases invented by the précieuses, it is undeniable that replacing a familiar word such as *fauteuil* by *les commodités de la conversation* may certainly have achieved one of the précieux aims—that of having a jargon of their own—and accounts for their reputation for obscurity,[2] due to an 'alliance de certains mots qui ne se rencontrent ensemble que dans leur bouche'.[3] The question of this *alliance de mots* particular to the précieuses has a certain bearing on the question of précieux poetry, as it gives us a good illustration of the value and uses the précieux attached to metaphors. C. L. Livet highly praises the précieuses: 'combien de mots nouveaux et nécessaires, de tours hardis et heureux, de métaphores énergiques, elles laisseront à la langue'.[4] But even if we agree with him about a certain number of expressions which have enriched the French language,[5] on the other hand the reading of the *Dictionnaire des Précieuses* does not confirm the eulogy of *tours hardis* and *métaphores énergiques*, nor does it suggest anything bold, vigorous, and pithy. The metaphors mentioned by Somaize are worked out by the précieuses according to a very limited number of mechanical devices, and, as a rule, operate in the sense of the dislocation of the language and the weakening of the expression. Either a quality belonging to an object stands for that object itself (death is *la Toute-Puissante*, fire *l'élément combustible*, a business man *un inquiet* . . .); or the object is replaced by one of its uses (a broom is *l'instrument de la propreté*—obviously that would apply as well to a duster, or a bath). Even more mechanical is the

---

[1] It is interesting to note here (the point will be developed later) that this précieux emphatic vocabulary (*furieux, horrible, ingrat, cruauté, rigueur* . . .), which is overstatement with the précieux, will be understatement in Racine.

[2] 'L'on a vu, il n'y a pas long-temps, un cercle de personnes des deux sexes, liées ensemble par la conversation et par un commerce d'esprit; ils laissoient au vulgaire l'art de parler d'une manière intelligible; une chose dite entr'eux peu clairement, en entraînoit une autre encore plus obscure, sur laquelle on enchérissoit par de vraies énigmes, toujours suivies de longs applaudissements: par tout ce qu'ils appelloient délicatesse, sentiments, tour et finesse d'expression, ils étoient enfin parvenus à n'être plus entendus, et à ne s'entendre pas eux-mêmes' (*Les Caractères de La Bruyère*, 1763, vol. i, pp. 227–8).

[3] Ibid., p. 203.

[4] *Dictionnaire des Précieuses*, Préface, p. xxviij.

[5] Such as *rire d'intelligence, faire des avances, sécheresse de la conversation*, &c.

device which consists in replacing the word by its mythological equivalent (a bed is *l'empire de Morphée*, the fire-place *l'empire de Vulcain*, tears *les perles d'Iris*, a fan *un Zéphire*, to swim *visiter les Naïades*...). There is not much invention either in following the logic of language: we speak of the *bras* of an arm-chair; let us carry the metaphor a step further and we obtain the précieux periphrasis for 'please sit down': 'contentez, s'il vous plaît, l'envie que ce siège a de vous *embrasser*'. Nor can one see any creative improvement in replacing the word *j'aime* by an overstatement *j'ai un furieux tendre*, nor will the qualities of beauty be made clearer or more striking if, instead of *elle est belle*, we are given two vague adjectives *elle est dans son bel aimable*. And let us add that sometimes the so-called *alliance de mots* is nothing but a lengthy periphrasis, destined to avoid the use of one word: instead of 'la chaise empêche que l'on ne se crotte', 'la chaise est un admirable retranchement contre les insultes de la boue et du mauvais temps'.

These general considerations on versification and language serve to emphasize the précieux's interest in technical problems, their delight in playing a difficult game according to conventional rules (prowesses of prosody), and their wish to be appreciated or understood only by those who had adopted the same rhetoric of language. This conventional rhetoric of language is, as we have seen, a mutilation of reality (either by refusing low words or by reducing an object to one of its qualities) or a failure (perhaps wilful) to grasp it (refuge into vagueness), and suggests the mechanical working of formal logic. These characteristics will appear more clearly if, leaving aside the question of the précieuses' conversational style, we come to précieux poetry proper.

2

The Rhetoric of Préciosité

Everybody agrees on the fact that précieux poetry displays an excessive use of all such rhetorical figures as metaphors, hyperboles, antitheses, periphrases, &c. As has been said in the preceding chapter, a poet is not précieux because he makes use of them, nor would even an excessive use of them be in itself a précieux characteristic. Such figures of speech become précieux when they work according to the formal pattern of a conventional rhetoric, outside reality.

I do not propose to cover the whole field of précieux rhetoric, but a few examples will illustrate the *formal* aspect of it. One of the most mechanical devices of précieux rhetoric consists in adopting a comparison (taken from the common stock of literature) and either drawing from it all the logical consequences or simply splitting it into fractions. Thus in Sidney's Sonnet XLIX:

> I on my horse, and Loue on me, doth trie
> Our horsmanships, while by strange worke I proue
> A horsman to my horse, a horse to Loue,
> And now man's wrongs in me, poor beast! descrie.
> The raines wherewith my rider doth me tie
> Are humbled thoughts, which bit of reuerence moue,
> Curb'd-in with feare, but with guilt bosse aboue
> Of hope, which makes it seeme faire to the eye:
> The wand is will; thou, Fancie, saddle art,
> Girt fast by Memorie; and while I spurre
> My horse, he spurres with sharpe desire my hart;
> He sits me fast, howeuer I do sturre;
> And now hath made me to his hand so right,
> That in the manage my selfe take delight.[1]

Once the premisses are given (Love is a horseman to me) the deductions follow almost automatically (the reins are humble thoughts, the wand is will, the saddle fancy, &c.).[2]

As a rule the choice of the comparison is more or less indifferent to the poet, as he will select it from a set of accepted ones; the same comparison will be used over and over again by different poets or even by the same poet, and will be used to express different feelings or moods; so that the achievement of the précieux poet will lie, not in creating the right metaphor to express a feeling, but in developing a stock comparison in keeping with the feeling without destroying the conventional pattern.

Here are two poems, one by Charles d'Orléans and the other by Desportes (chosen on purpose with a century and half between them, to show, in passing, how very difficult it would be to establish a chronology of précieux themes), in which the same conventional

---

[1] Sidney, *Complete Poems*, p. 68.

[2] Such a device would certainly fall under Dr. Johnson's condemnation: 'Thus all the power of description is destroyed by a scrupulous enumeration; and the force of metaphors is lost when the mind by the mention of particulars is turned more upon the original than the secondary sense, more upon that from which the illustration is drawn than that to which it is applied.' (*Lives of the English Poets*, vol. i, p. 45.)

comparison (the heart as a besieged citadel) is developed with great care for adjusting the allegory to the mood:

> Rafraîchissez le châtel de mon cœur
> D'aucuns vivres de Joyeuse Plaisance,
> Car Faux Danger, avec son alliance,
> L'a assiégé, tout entour, de Douleur.
>
> Se ne voulez le siège sans longueur
> Tantôt lever ou rompre par puissance,
> Rafraîchissez le châtel de mon cœur
> D'aucuns vivres de Joyeuse Plaisance.
>
> Ne souffrez pas que Danger soit seigneur
> En conquêtant sous son obéissance
> Ce que tenez en votre gouvernance:
> Avancez-vous et gardez votre honneur,
> Rafraîchissez le châtel de mon cœur.[1]

> La garnison d'Ennuis qu'Amour fait demeurer
> En mon cœur pour sa garde, est si grande et si forte
> Qu'il ne faut avoir peur qu'un seul Soupir en sorte,
> Ni qu'il puisse en ses maux seulement respirer.
>
> Si quelque heureux Plaisir se veut avanturer
> D'approcher de mon cœur, afin qu'il le conforte,
> Il esprouve à son dam qu'il se faut retirer;
> Car s'il veut passer outre, on le tue à la porte.
>
> Le Desespoir sanglant, capitaine inhumain,
> Sans jamais se lasser, tient les clefs en la main,
> Et ne fait rien entrer que du parti contraire.
>
> Tous Pensers gracieux il en a sçeu bannir;
> Mes esprits seulement n'oseraient s'y tenir,
> S'ils n'étaient affligez et comblez de miseres.[2]

The atmosphere is slightly different: Charles d'Orléans expresses a request for relief and Desportes a mood of despondency, but in both cases the feeling is a straightforward and simple one, so that the pattern of one developed comparison can fit it perfectly. Moods and attitudes expressed by précieux poetry must have this

---

[1] Bray, *Anthologie de la poésie précieuse*, p. 29.
[2] Desportes, *Cléonice*, XLVIII; *Œuvres*, ed. A. Michiels, 1858, p. 202.

quality of lending themselves to ready-made imagery. If ready-made imagery does not fit the attitude, we rightly suspect irony and puzzling contradictions; thus Scève uses the conventional imagery of the loveliness of dawn which does not fit his morning thoughts,[1] or Sponde destroys the value of accepted metaphors by contrasting them with brutal reality.[2] Scève and Sponde are both trying to express the complexity one of a mood, the other of an attitude towards death. Neither Charles d'Orléans nor Desportes is concerned with exhausting either the feeling of starvation or the state of discouragement of an ill-treated lover. The relationship between metaphor and content makes clear the attitude of the précieux poet towards the reality he wishes to express in his poetry. I would not say that his metaphor is only ornamental (although it is obviously destined to give pleasure, but the criterion of the pleasurable in general would apply to more than one kind of poetry), but that, instead of bringing out the complexity or contradictions of a given experience (as metaphysical poetry does) or distorting and upsetting reality (as is the case with baroque metaphors), it reduces experience to a single item which falls under acknowledged and well-classified categories.

Classifying moods or feelings is a means of taking the disquieting element out of them. This explains why fifteenth-century préciosité adopted allegories, why Sidney used the stiff personifications of Virtue, Reason, Love, Beauty. It explains also in what consists the highly-praised faculty of psychological analysis attributed to the early seventeenth-century précieuses. Their subtle research into the complexities of love was in fact a work of over-simplification: the 'Carte de Tendre' is not a synthesis of the experiences of a lover, it is a convenient card-index cabinet. The method is the same as the one to be found in the précieuses' codifying of the language: to select one quality (among the hundred included by an object or an experience) and to give it the full value of an absolute statement.

Allegories, personification of abstract qualities, developed comparisons represent the first stage in that task of *taming* reality undertaken by the précieux. In the final stage, metaphors are no longer needed for this purpose, and partly disappear from the rhetoric of précieux poetry. A poet like Tristan can safely write on *les vains efforts, les justes reproches, les fâcheux obstacles, le dépit*

[1] See above, Ch. II.   [2] See above, Ch. IV.

salutaire[1] without resorting to allegory or protective imagery: these moods are stamped with their identification marks.

Another rhetorical device used by the précieux poets is antithesis. Antithesis is usually considered as causing a shock of surprise. In fact, the shock occurs only if we are made to realize an antithetical relation of which we were unaware. This does not happen easily, as our mind has a natural tendency to think of an object as antithetical to another: we think of *white* as opposed to *black*, of *day* as opposed to *night*. It is sometimes part of the internal logic of the language (thus *pardonable*, for instance, will suggest *unpardonable*) or part of an accepted logical order of things (*night* is the absence of *day*light). Précieux antitheses do not upset us because they are precisely of this kind; they work as mechanically as the working of our automatic associations of ideas, and the pleasure we can derive from finding them in a poem is the pleasure one experiences in watching a well-known mechanism:

> Amour au même instant m'aiguillonne et m'arrête,
> M'assure et me fait peur, m'ard et me va glaçant,
> Me pourchasse et me fuit, me rend faible et puissant,
> Me fait victorieux et marche sur ma tête. . . .[2]

The précieux antithesis acts on us as a spring-release and starts our mind on a familiar mental groove which reassuringly takes us away from the implications of whatever content the poem is supposed to have. In its simple and crude form (the putting together of two contradictory qualities) antithesis will never give a shock. The successful antithesis—the one which confronts us with the unexpected—is worked out in a complex way, and, instead of relying on the automatic response, requires from the reader a firm grasp of the situation involved: thus in Scève's *dizain* quoted in Chapter II, the antithesis:

> Tu me seras la Myrrhe incorruptible
> Contre les vers de ma mortalité[3]

draws its power from various components: from the association of the image (*Myrrhe*), the concrete word (*vers*), and the abstract quality (*mortalité*), from the contrast in rhythm and diction between these two last lines and the beginning of the *dizain* and

---

[1] *Les Amours.*
[2] Desportes, *Les Amours d'Hippolyte*, XXVII; *Œuvres*, p. 132.
[3] See above, Ch. II, p. 19.

from the sense of the whole poem. I would almost say that the only antitheses which shock occur either in the form of a metaphysical conceit or in some form of dramatic irony.

The précieux's use of hyperbole is even more characteristic of their wish to escape not only the complexity of reality but reality itself. I said that when précieux poets adopted the idea that their mistress was more beautiful than the rising sun, they did so because it fitted a certain attitude to woman which was part of their code of manners. They adopted it also because it was so removed from any real fact that nobody would consider it as a serious statement, unless the context, so to speak, should prove it to be so; and far from this being the case, in a précieux poem the context brings out the unreality of the hyperbole:

> Mais, dès que de vous je m'approche,
> Mon cœur *se gelle* et *devient roche*;
> Devant vos attraits gracieux
> Je pers esprit, voix et haleine;
> Et, voulant vous conter ma peine,
> Je ne sçay parler que des yeux.[1]

These lines suggest arch and graceful courtship; the tone is the false bashfulness of the lover who is already expecting success from adroit ogling, so that the heart which *se gelle et devient roche* belongs to a range of experience which is extremely remote from the content of the poem.

Sometimes we need not even examine the context of the poem to measure the gap between the hyperbole and the feeling expressed: in the famous Job sonnet, by Benserade, the statement that the lover's sufferings are worse than Job's is ludicrous enough in itself without necessitating any further examination of the poem.

The characteristic of the *gratuitousness* of the hyperbole, when used by précieux poets, is moreover stressed by the fact that their hyperbolical metaphors are interchangeable, and the poet is no more attached to the one than to the other:

> Ce ne sont pas des yeux, ce sont plutôt des dieux:
> Ils ont dessus les rois la puissance absolue.
> Dieux? non, ce sont des cieux: ils ont la couleur bleue
> Et le mouvement prompt comme celui des cieux.

[1] Desportes, *Œuvres*, p. 150.

> Cieux? non, mais deux soleils clairement radieux,
> Dont les rayons brillants nous offusquent la vue.
> Soleils? non, mais éclairs . . .[1]

As they do with all other rhetorical devices, précieux poets destroy the potential value of a hyperbole, either by the process of enumeration (as in the lines just quoted), or by improving upon the hyperbole in a sort of crescendo:

> J'ai langui malheureux quatre longues journées
> Sans voir les deux beaux yeux de celle à qui je suis;
> Hélas! non quatre jours, mais plutost quatre nuits
> Sans clarté, sans liesse, à mon mal ordonnées.
> Qu'ay-je dit? quatre nuits, mais plutost quatre années,
> Toutes pleines d'horreur, de soucis et d'ennuis
> Ou quatre mille morts, que souffrir je ne puis.[2]

If we remember at this stage that Scève also used a hyperbole on the same theme of absence:

> Asses plus long qu'un Siecle Platonique
> Me fut le moys, que sans toy suis esté[3]

in one of the *dizains* analysed in Chapter II, and that this *dizain* can be considered as being metaphysical poetry, we are bound to see that the use of hyperbole is not a monopoly of précieux poetry. But in Scève the magnifying of duration, translated by the hyperbole, is relevant to the problem of absence which is treated in the *dizain* as a serious metaphysical problem; and the complexity of the hyperbole, with the two meanings attached to *siècle platonique*, makes it even more relevant: as a matter of fact it was the only hyperbolical metaphor possible, as it was the only one which could convey in one single expression the stretching of time and the physical separation of the lovers.

(A more complicated use of hyperbole in metaphysical poetry may be found in the well-known poem of Marvell, *Definition of Love*, in which throughout the poem the most hyperbolical statements of the poet about his love are used to express a contradiction inherent in his love, without the poet losing his grasp on the connotations imparted by the hyperboles.)

---

[1] Laugier de Porchères, *Sur les yeux de Madame la Duchesse de Beaufort*; Bray, *Anthologie de la poésie précieuse*, p. 64.
[2] Desportes, *Les Amours d'Hippolyte*, XXII; *Œuvres*, p. 130.
[3] *Délie, Dizain* CCCLXVII; *Œuvres poétiques*, p. 127.

The baroque poet, too, will use hyperboles, but there also it will
be possible to distinguish them from the précieux hyperboles. It
has already been noted that d'Aubigné uses exactly the same hyperbolical metaphors as the petrarchan précieux, but, whereas we are
not moved by floods of tears and a hundred deaths in Desportes,
d'Aubigné's hyperboles are upsetting; with him the context tells us
that such hyperboles are on the same level as his feelings.[1]

Hyperboles, in either metaphysical or baroque poetry, are disquieting: in metaphysical poetry, because the poet uses them as a
sort of test of reality (working at times like a *reductio ad absurdum*[2])
and we are made to face contradictions; in baroque poetry, because
we have to take the hyperboles at their face value. But in précieux
poetry they are gratuitous and their function is precisely to mini-
mize the importance of the feeling or idea they characterize, by
taking it as far as possible from the field of actual experience. The
same remark would apply to the use of overstatement which has
been mentioned as typical of the précieuses' language.

It is necessary to say a few words about the so-called startling
pointe finale of a précieux poem. Nothing is less unexpected and
startling than the last *trait* or *chute* which ends the précieux poem.
The whole sonnet or madrigal tends towards its ineluctable coming.
It has already been noted how in Sidney's sonnets the working of
formal logic brought necessarily the last statement of a poem;[3]
sometimes it is not even the pattern of formal logic but a sort of
merely verbal logic which will lead to an inescapable final pun:

> . . . Rich in the treasure of deserv'd renowne,
> Rich in the riches of a royall hart,
> Rich in those gifts which giue th'eternall crowne;
> Who, though most rich in these and euery part
> Which make the patents of true worldly blisse,
> Hath no misfortune but that Rich she is.[4]

(Sidney's Stella was married to a man called Rich.)

The same expectedness is to be found in the following sonnet
by Voiture:

> Des portes du matin l'Amante de Cephale,
> Ses roses épandoient dans le milieu des Airs;

---

[1] See above, Ch. VI.

[2] A good illustration of this may be found in Marvell's *To his Coy Mistress*, in
which the hyperbolical duration of conventional courtship is confronted with
the actual time.   [3] See above, Ch. II.

[4] Sidney, *Complete Poems*, vol. i, p. 54 (Sonnet XXXVII).

K

Et jettoit sous les Cieux nouvellement ouverts,
Ces traits d'or et d'azur qu'en naissant elle étale.

Quand la Nymphe divine, à mon repos fatale,
Apparut et brilla de tant d'attraits divers,
Qu'il sembloit qu'elle seule éclairoit l'Univers,
Et remplissoit de feux la rive orientale.

Le Soleil se hâtant pour la gloire des Cieux,
Vint opposer sa flâme à l'éclat de ses yeux,
Et prit tous les rayons dont l'Olympe se dore,

L'onde, la terre, et l'air s'allumaient à l'entour:
Mais auprès de Philis on le prit pour l'Aurore,
Et l'on crut que Philis étoit l'Astre du Jour.[1]

The whole tenor of the sonnet is to prepare us for the idea that
Philis could be mistaken for the rising sun: accordingly we have in
the first part a picture of dawn, in the second Philis presented in
such a way that one might almost say the poet is altogether giving
the game away with the line 'Qu'il sembloit qu'elle seule éclairoit
l'Univers', the third part brings the rivalry of the sun, and the
fourth the inevitable triumph of Philis.

It may be recalled here that in Scève's metaphysical poems, the
last image, which could as well be called *pointe finale*, has on the
contrary a startling quality, that of a sudden jump into a field of
imagery which transcends the content of the *dizain*.[2]

3

The Red Herring of Petrarchism

This analysis (by no means exhaustive) of précieux rhetoric was
meant to point out clearly that précieux poetry does not differ
from metaphysical or baroque poetry by its imagery or its rhetorical devices, but by the use it makes of that imagery and those
figures of speech. There does not exist in itself what we could call
a précieux image. It is the function of the device in a given poem
which enables us to decide whether it is précieux or not.

A great deal of confusion has arisen from giving to certain
images or certain rhetorical devices a value in the absolute, and
labelling as petrarchan any poem in which the use of certain

[1] *Œuvres*, vol. ii, p. 111.   [2] See above, Ch. II.

decorative images, of hyperboles and antitheses, reminds the critic of the Italian poets who used them too. This over-simplification is the more dangerous in that petrarchan is considered as synonymous with précieux: 'L'histoire de la Préciosité au XVIème siècle est à peu près celle du Pétrarquisme', says M. Bray.[1]

At the beginning of the comparison between Sidney and Scève, after an acknowledgment of the two poets' debts to the Italians, the question of their Petrarchism was set aside as being irrelevant to the point at issue, although it may appear now, in the light of the preceding section, that if Sidney was in no way a forerunner of the metaphysical poets, it was precisely because he was a typical précieux poet and his préciosité owed a great deal to his Italian models.

But it is time now to settle the question of the relation between Petrarchism and préciosité. In fact Petrarchism is the red herring of sixteenth-century poetry, for the excellent reason that all sixteenth-century poetry bears the stamp of Italian influence or imitation, either at first or second hand. Vianey's book, *Le Pétrarquisme en France*, extremely interesting as a study of the Italian sources of French sixteenth-century poems, shows how easily all the production of lyrical poetry of the age may be dragged under the heading of petrarchan. Nobody could possibly deny or even reduce the importance of Italian influence. But at this stage of the present study it is obvious that we cannot take Petrarchism as a synonym for sixteenth-century préciosité, since this would make the latter term cover the whole bulk of sixteenth-century poetry.

M. Bray's statement is true in a way: all précieux poetry in the sixteenth century is in some respect petrarchan, but the reverse is not true; poets have been influenced by Italian models and have produced a kind of poetry which was not précieux.

Italian poetry was fashionable in all the sophisticated groups to be found in the sixteenth century, and rightly enough, as the Italian courts of the fourteenth and fifteenth centuries, following the tradition of the French *Cours d'Amour*, had set brilliant examples of that escapism into the refinement of culture which is the essence of préciosité. It has already been stressed that précieux poetry borrows from others what fits its purpose: that, in the sixteenth century, it should take up the conventions of Petrarchism was therefore inevitable. Précieux literature is an art not of production

[1] Op. cit., p. 67.

but of consumption: the précieux consumer was to feed, from the time of Marguerite de Navarre to that of Madame de Rambouillet, on that petrarchan tradition which was in fact the epitome of what, in the cultural riches of Europe, was safe from any political, religious, or social problems.

Most of the sixteenth-century poets who were in contact with the sophisticated groups yielded for various reasons (flattery to noblemen or madrigals to ladies) to petrarchan-précieux conventions: certain poems of Ronsard (those written for the enjoyment of the court) and some *dizains* of Scève are petrarchan-précieux. Here is an illustration taken from Scève's *Délie*:

> Si en ton lieu j'estois, ô doulce Mort,
> Tu ne serois de ta faulx dessaisie.
> O fol, l'esprit de ta vie est jà mort.
> Comment? je voy. Ta force elle à saisie.
> Je parle aumoins. Ce n'est que phrenesie.
> Vivray je donc tousjours? non: lon termine
> Ailleurs ta fin. Et ou? Plus n'examine.
> Car tu vivras sans Cœur, sans Corps, sans Ame,
> En ceste mort plus, que vie, benigne,
> Puis que tel est le vouloir de ta Dame.[1]

There is nothing more here than the conventional petrarchan dialogue developing the conventional idea that the lover is sentenced by his lady to a sort of death-in-life. But, as we have seen, Scève can also turn the petrarchan dialectic to the grasping of metaphysical problems and then he ceases to be précieux.

We saw also how Sponde could work out an effect of dramatic irony by contrasting comfortable and conventional petrarchan images with unpleasant reality, and how in the seventeenth century Marvell made an ironical use of an assumed petrarchan courtship to stress the devouring power of time (*To his Coy Mistress*).

Even when a poet seems to adopt, not only the images and devices of the petrarchists, but a petrarchan theme cut off from reality, his treatment of the theme is sometimes not altogether précieux. If we compare, among the innumerable sonnets written on the theme of 'La Belle Matineuse', two poems which have been quoted in the course of this work: Du Bellay's 'Déjà la nuit en son parc amassait . . .'[2] and Voiture's 'Des portes du matin . . .',[3] we

---

[1] *Délie, Dizain* LXXI; *Œuvres poétiques*, p. 28.
[2] See above, p. 27.   [3] See above, p. 129.

see that although the subject-matter of Du Bellay is as conventional as Voiture's (it is the same), Du Bellay is creating a world of delicately mixed images, which is his own poetic vision and not the précieux closed universe, whereas in Voiture all the images are straightforwardly conventional, so conventional that they do not suggest any poetic universe, but act as mere abstract signs.

Let us also recall that d'Aubigné's hyperboles, certainly of petrarchan origin, are baroque and not précieux.

4
Relationships between Metaphysical, Baroque, and Précieux Poetry

This section is really nothing more than a parenthesis, as by now it must appear very clearly that although metaphysical, baroque, and précieux poetry can be distinguished from one another, their relationships are very intricate.

Précieux elements may become baroque (as they do in d'Aubigné) or metaphysical (as they do in Scève). They may also become classical. Racine's well-known conceit, in *Andromaque*:

Brûlé de plus de feux que je n'en allumai[1]

is considered as a précieux *pointe*, and indeed it reflects the diction of the précieux and their ingenious punning. If the line occurred in Desportes or Benserade, I would agree to call it précieux. But, as it is, we have to take it very seriously. That Pyrrhus is *brûlé de feux* is not an exaggerated statement; his moral sense and sense of honour are obliterated by his devouring love for Andromaque; he has become a blackmailer and a perjurer; nor are the *feux allumés dans Troie* simply a convenient reminder of Pyrrhus's warlike exploits. In a précieux poem the line would probably suggest that even a victorious warrior could lose in the battle with love—which would be a gallant platitude. In Racine the line sums up the inextricable situation of Pyrrhus as he sees it: the fires of Troy and those of his love are inextricably united, since he would never have loved Andromaque if it had not been for the Trojan war, and hopelessly antagonistic. There is also in the line a subtle

[1] A subtle analysis of this line, seen from a point of view somewhat different from my own, is to be found in Professor R. C. Knight's article 'Brûlé de plus de feux' in *Studies . . . presented to R. L. G. Ritchie*, Cambridge, 1949.

psychological indication: Pyrrhus is a man who thinks in terms of give and take, and who, somewhat naïvely, cannot help thinking (establishing a false comparison) that the suffering he undergoes because of his love amounts to more than a burned city and that he is accordingly in some way now even with Andromaque. Thus when we come to analyse this so-called précieux *pointe*, we find that the hyperbolical metaphor is very different in its function from a précieux conceit. That Racine took the idea of the play on words from the précieux is irrelevant. In fact Racine's diction is in many respects that of the précieux poets, but it works in an almost opposite sense. As already suggested in a footnote, such words as *feux, cruel, tendre, horrible*, which are overstatements with the précieux, become with Racine the instruments of his well-known restraint in expression. To seize the total implication of Racine's lines, one has to perform the inverse process to that of the précieux and restore the words to their full meaning.

The baroque constituents can become metaphysical as we have seen in Donne or La Ceppède. They can also become précieux, when a baroque theme is adopted by the sophisticated groups. This transition from the baroque to the précieux is particularly interesting to watch in the *libertin* poets and especially in Tristan. We saw how the baroque landscape was tamed into a garden. The following sonnet will illustrate how one of the most disturbing baroque themes, the theme of the macabre, could be turned into a harmless madrigal:

A des Cimetières

Sejour melancholique, où les ombres dolentes
Se pleignent chaque Nuit de leur aversité
Et murmurent tousjours de la necessité
Qui les contraint d'errer par les tombes relantes.

Ossemens entassez, et vous, pierres parlantes
Qui conservez les noms à la Postérité,
Representans la vie et sa fragilité
Pour censurer l'orgueil des Ames insolentes.

Tombeaux, pasles tesmoins de la rigueur du Sort
Où je viens en secret entretenir la Mort
D'une amour que je voy si mal recompensée.

Vous donnez de la crainte et de l'horreur à tous;
Mais le plus doux objet qui s'ofre à ma pensée
Est beaucoup plus funeste et plus triste que vous.[1]

5

The Question of 'Wit'

Concerning the relationships of the three different sorts of poetry dealt with in this study, another question arises: that of their respective share in 'wit'. Wit is a word much used in relation to the metaphysical poets,[2] and précieux poets are supposed to be witty. The word is not to be taken in its vague sense of a clever way of bringing together unexpectedly two things hitherto unconnected, because this would serve as a definition of any far-fetched metaphor, of the conceit, and might apply to all the poets of the period; on the other hand, wit must not be restricted to the faculty of producing mere verbal witticisms.

I shall adopt the meaning modern English critics have given it in connexion with metaphysical and Augustan poetry, although I propose to enlarge the definition, so as to cover more than metaphysical poetry.

As far as poetry goes, the word implies the poet's faculty of seeing and expressing the discrepancy between the images he uses or the statements he makes, and reality. In his attitude towards this discrepancy the poet can be either serious, or simply amused.

That metaphysical wit is of the serious kind has been so much stressed by twentieth-century critics in England that one only needs to refer to Mr. T. S. Eliot's essay on Marvell:[3] 'this alliance of levity and seriousness (by which the seriousness is intensified) is a characteristic of the sort of wit we are trying to identify.' Yet not all metaphysical poets have wit, or shall we say that the 'metaphysical' quality may not be found in its complete wholeness in some poets (and this would perfectly fit the case of the French poets mentioned in this work as metaphysical, who, as we saw, were lacking in one or other characteristic of true metaphysical

---

[1] Tristan, *Les Amours*, p. 12.

[2] A study of metaphysical wit would have to start with Cowley's *Ode to Wit* and would include a large bibliography. The question of wit being a side-issue in the present study, I shall only mention, as sufficient for the elucidation of the term, T. S. Eliot's essay on 'Andrew Marvell' (in *Selected Essays*) and F. R. Leavis's 'The Line of Wit' (in *Revaluations*).

[3] *Selected Essays*, pp. 278–90.

poetry). However, Scève and La Ceppède have no wit, because
the sphere of their poetry is too far removed from the common
field of experience; they are aware of contradictions and discrepancy, but inside a sphere which, in the case of La Ceppède,
is the universe of religious mysteries, and in the case of Scève is
closed by the boundaries of a diction which is too aloof to include
the shift of tone necessary to produce wit. But Sponde's dramatic
irony is worked through wit and precisely by his shift from conventional imagery to gruesome realistic words.

One sees immediately that wit is not to be found in purely baroque
poetry; I say purely baroque, to reserve the border-line cases of
poets like Tristan or Théophile. Wit implies a sense of proportion
which is not to be found in the baroque poets. They do not appear
to be conscious of the fantastic nature of their distorted universe;
the intense monotone of their poetry indicates clearly that they
never shift their observation-post. As a general rule indeed, whenever the world of imagination is accepted by the poet with an
intense fervour discarding all the elements of reality which might
contradict it, wit becomes impossible. And what is true of the
baroque would also be true of the romantic poets.

Wit in précieux poetry is a more complicated question. Here
the discrepancy between the larger field of actual experience and
the limited précieux world is the basic principle on which this kind
of poetry rests; and of course any précieux poet is conscious of it.
But will he express that consciousness? Never, if the discrepancy
is serious enough to be disturbing. If he did, he would become a
metaphysical poet, and there may be cases in which the degree
of seriousness in the poet's attitude to discrepancy, or the degree of
seriousness of the discrepancy, will be the only test to differentiate
metaphysical from précieux wit. But he may quite possibly give
expression to that consciousness if the discrepancy is amusing.
This is not very frequent because, as a rule, the précieux poet will
prefer to ignore the discrepancy altogether.

But, if we examine the lines by Desportes already quoted[1]—

> En voulant vous conter ma peine
> Je ne sçay que parler des yeux —

the last two lines, and the tone especially, imply that the poet is
not taken in by what he expresses in the previous lines, and that

[1] See above, p. 127.

he does not expect the lady to believe him either, but that he relies much more on an eloquent appealing glance. There is here a sort of complicity, suggesting: 'This is all very well, but I know better and so do you.'

A very similar example can be found in the following sonnet by Benserade:

> Beaux yeux dont l'atteinte profonde
> Trouble des cœurs incessamment
> Le doux repos, qui ne se fonde
> Que sur un si doux mouvement; . . .
>
> Beaux yeux qui sur les cœurs avez
> Tant de puissance et qui savez
> Si bien jouer de la prunelle;
>
> Beaux yeux, divin charme des sens,
> Votre amour est en sentinelle
> Pour attraper tous les passants.[1]

The first stanzas express the convention of Beauty's overwhelming power (here Beauty is the beauty of the eyes), but the 'et qui savez si bien jouer de la prunelle' suggests that the loveliness of the eyes rests perhaps more in the arch and provocative glances of the lady (a fact which belongs to the field of actual experience) than on the supremacy of Beauty; and the conventional picture of *l'Amour en embuscade* is debased into female wiles familiarly expressed as *attraper tous les passants*. Faint as it is, this is an attempt at expressing the divergence between the convention and reality.

Another way in précieux poetry of expressing this awareness of the conventional quality of imagery is to exaggerate part of it so as to make it appear ludicrous. Thus Tristan, taking up the theme of 'La Belle Matineuse' (like so many!), wrote a sonnet which is similar to those of Voiture or Malleville, except when we come to the last tercet:

> Et tandis que de honte il [the sun] étoit tout vermeil;
> En versant quelques pleurs, il passa pour l'Aurore,
> Et Philis en riant passa pour le Soleil.[2]

Whereas in the usual 'Belle Matineuse' sonnet, the defeat of the sun is indicated within the relatively sober limits of personification

[1] Bray, *Anthologie de la poésie précieuse*, p. 128.
[2] *Les Amours*, p. 177.

(he sometimes hides in the sea for shame), Tristan has developed the embarrassment and annoyance of the sun to such an extent that we suspect a tongue-in-the-cheek attitude in 'En versant quelques pleurs il passa pour l'Aurore'.

As a rule, we do not find very often in précieux poetry those neat shifts of tone which characterize wit; it is more a question of undertones. Moreover, few précieux poets seem to have tried to use the possibilities of such undertones. We shall have to wait for La Fontaine if we want to find a poet who, while using précieux conventions in a way not very different from the early seventeenth-century poets, achieved the 'tough reasonableness beneath the slight lyric grace', which is, according to Mr. T. S. Eliot,[1] the essence of wit.

6

The Evolution of Précieux Poetry

A chronological study of précieux poetry in the sixteenth and seventeenth centuries is an uneasy and unrewarding task. The examples given in the preceding pages show that the themes, imagery, and prosody of précieux poetry did not change much in the course of these two centuries. The précieux poets are not so fond of *nouveauté* as one might think; they are, on the contrary, essentially conservative, even retrograde.[2]

Yet one can perceive in the evolution of the poetry written by précieux writers their slow digestion of Petrarchism and the assimilation of certain new currents in poetry at large.

The somewhat rigid petrarchan formal logic, so strongly articulated in Scève's précieux *dizains* (and in Sidney), will become more supple in Desportes, and almost invisible in Voiture.

Although allegories are still to be found occasionally in Voiture,[3] as has already been said, this crude form of taming reality will be

---

[1] 'Andrew Marvell', in *Selected Essays*.
[2] 'Le succès de Desportes marque moins un progrès qu'un recul d'un demi-siècle' (J. Lavaud, *Philippe Desportes*, 1936, p. 498).
[3] . . . Le Repentir et la Peur au teint blême,
    Les prompts Souhaits, et les violens Désirs,
    La Fausse Joye, et les vains Déplaisirs,
    Les tristes Soins, et les Inquiétudes,
    Les longs Regrets amis des Solitudes,
    Les doux Espoirs, les bizarres Pensers;
    Les courts Dépits, et les Soupirs legers. . . .
(Voiture, op. cit., vol. ii, p. 86.)

replaced by the abstract indication of classified moods (Tristan). As précieux poetry does not create new metaphors and kills those it borrows from others, the normal evolution will be towards the abstract and, in fact, the poetry of Benserade and Voiture is singularly sober in its use of images.

Of all the Pléiade's innovations, the précieux poets will retain very little; they will discard from their poetic vocabulary all the dialectal words and technical terms by which Ronsard meant to enrich the language and which, obviously, were distasteful to refined circles; they will simplify the mythological world of Ronsard and reduce it to a handful of clichés—*l'Amant de Céphale* for dawn, Penelope as a symbol of constancy, a nymph for a woman, &c.—easily grasped by moderately read people.[1]

They assimilated, as we have seen, a certain amount of the baroque; not its fundamental distortion of vision, but its decorative side, either removing the sting from baroque themes (as in Tristan's sonnet on churchyards) or choosing the aspect of the baroque which was, outwardly at least, the least upsetting. This is the baroque of Théophile and of Saint-Amant. In these poets certain disquieting baroque themes, such as the end of the world, have already become pleasantly innocuous; their 'solitudes' could be turned into well-kept gardens and their jewellery looted in order to adorn the stilted mythological figures of drawing-room madrigals.

Saint-Amant is altogether baroque. Théophile's poetry is either baroque or so personal that it is almost at the opposite extreme to the conventional feelings expressed by the précieux. But Tristan represents a very interesting case of a poet who is sometimes baroque, as in his poem *La Mer*, and most of the time précieux, as in almost all the poems of *Les Amours*. In certain of his poems we can see either the juxtaposition of the baroque and the précieux; *Le Promenoir des Deux Amants*, from which illustrations of baroque poetry have been drawn in Chapter V, ends with four stanzas which are so heavily stamped with the worst kind of conventional Petrarchism that they are usually omitted in anthologies, as

[1] '. . . une incompréhension absolue du sentiment païen de la nature et de la vie qui éclaire presque toute la poésie de Ronsard. Désormais les poètes de salon ne connaîtront qu'une Antiquité morte, un grand corps sans âme; la mythologie les fournira de métonymies, d'allégories, d'images douces et fanées; elle ne sera plus qu'un magasin d'accessoires conventionnels, inventoriés une fois pour toutes à l'usage de la société' (Raymond, *L'Influence de Ronsard*, vol. ii, p. 343).

destroying the delightful delicacy of the poem.[1] In others we can
see their fusion; as in *La Maison d'Astrée*[2] where we witness the
making of a baroque garden.

7

Préciosité in England

In this chapter English poetry has scarcely been mentioned, with
the exception of Sidney. Yet it is obvious that préciosité is not an
essentially French phenomenon and will be found in any country
when the conditions for its existence happen to be fulfilled (as
was the case for the Italian courts in the fourteenth, fifteenth, and
sixteenth centuries). If we survey English literature in the sixteenth
and early seventeenth centuries we find that there is, of course,
précieux poetry, but that it is mainly second-hand and so near the
French précieux that, for instance, Lodge's *Sonnets to Phillis* or
Constable's *Diana* are almost a translation of Desportes into
English.[3]

Sidney is worth mentioning as not being a mere translator.
Inside the précieux group of Lady Pembroke's circle he worked
out his own blend of Petrarchism, French influence, and even
imitation of the Greek lyricists. I have stressed his limitations,
which are those of a précieux poet: but within them he possessed
undeniably that faculty of eclectic discrimination and suppleness

[1] Ah! je n'en puis plus, je me pasme
Mon âme est preste à s'envoler;
Tu viens de me faire avaler
La moitié moins d'eau que de flame.

Ta bouche d'un baiser humide
Pourroit amortir ce grand feu:
De crainte de pecher un peu
N'acheve pas un homicide.

J'aurois plus de bonne fortune
Caressé d'un jeune Soleil
Que celuy qui dans le sommeil
Receut des faveurs de la Lune.

Climeine, ce baiser m'enyvre,
Cet autre me rend tout transi.
Si je ne meurs de celui-cy,
Je ne suis pas digne de vivre.
Les Amours, p. 53.

[2] Ibid., pp. 244–55.

[3] See A. H. Upham, *French Influence in English Literature*, pp. 121–31.

in adapting foreign themes to English diction which represents almost the highest possible creative power in a précieux poet.

The fact that précieux poetry is almost absent in the Elizabethan and Jacobean period is not very surprising if we remember that précieux poetry postulates a closed society which rejects the greater part of reality and takes refuge in limited accepted conventions. What characterized English court lyricists (and the seventeenth-century Cavalier poets are a good illustration) is that they were more ready to absorb than to reject. Elizabethan and Jacobean England is essentially receptive, and more eclectic than critical. Court lyrics remained in the main current of national poetry; the amplification and figures of Elizabethan rhetoric were not restricted to a sophisticated set of people; they were the common property of all poets.

Yet, in the domain of prose, English literature offers us a very good example of préciosité in John Lyly's *Euphues*. Lyly, because of his family,[1] his years spent at Oxford where he belonged to the most sparkling literary set, his position in later life, as a sort of official dramatic entertainer, was a typical courtly writer of the highbrow kind. The study of his style[2] has brought out the fact that Euphuism was based on a very methodical rhetoric similar to that which we found in précieux poetry. Indeed, like any précieux poet, Lyly took the various devices of rhetoric, and relied on the automatic working of antithesis, parallelism, repetition, &c., coupled with a similar use of a traditional resource of the English language: alliteration and assonance. The pattern of this framework is as a rule more elaborate than any of those adopted by précieux poets, but underneath the complexity of the various cogwheels the working of the mechanism is exactly the same. Only long quotations would do full justice to the elaboration of the pattern which works not only in the ordering of a single sentence but in whole paragraphs.

Lyly's imagery conforms also to what we expect from a précieux writer. He is well known for the extravagant use he made of ornamental devices. His analogies and illustrations, strange as they may seem to us, were not of his own invention; he was making

---

[1] A. Feuillerat, *John Lyly*, 1910. See ch. i: 'Une famille d'érudits au XVIème siècle.'

[2] See C. G. Child, *John Lyly and Euphuism*, Leipzig, 1894, and also Feuillerat, op. cit.

use of the stock of learning (historical or mythological persons of the ancient world, natural history, &c.) which was accessible to the cultured man of his environment; what appear to us the wildest statements ('the Snayle that crept out of hir shell was turned eft soones into a Toad, and therby was forced to make a stoole to sit on'[1]) were part of the accepted legends to be found in all the books of reference of the time. It was a sort of erudite préciosité, the erudition being more superficial than real.[2] The vogue of Euphuism in England is held to have lasted from 1579 to 1590, and Professor J. D. Wilson remarks that Lyly and his imitators or co-creators belong to the same University coterie of Euphuists. As a matter of fact, the sentences which Professor Wilson borrows from a Spanish courtier speaking of the poet in general, and which he applies to the Oxford Euphuists, come very near the definition of préciosité proposed in this work:

. . . a very lofty and fine discretion . . . and finally he must be of gentle birth, courteous and sedate, polished, humorous, polite, witty and have in his composition honey, and sugar, and salt, and a good presence and a witty manner of reasoning; moreover he must be also a lover and ever make a show and pretence of it.[3]

8

Préciosité persisted in France throughout the seventeenth century, but in the second half its vitality had been absorbed by the classicists, according to the law mentioned at the end of the preceding chapter—that préciosité has no reason to exist when a country has reached a certain degree of civilization. At the court of Louis XIV there was no need for any précieux group to fight for refinement. Refinement was the *mot d'ordre* of the Court and the Court was France. Only by-products of préciosité could survive for some time.

[1] Lyly, quoted by Feuillerat, op. cit., p. 421.
[2] See Feuillerat, op. cit., p. 423.
[3] J. Dover Wilson, *John Lyly*, 1905, p. 49.

IX

THE COMING OF FRENCH CLASSICISM

THE quest for metaphysical, baroque, and précieux poetry in the French literature of the late Renaissance has led us rather far into the seventeenth century. At the time when poets like Tristan or Malleville wrote their verse, Malherbe had already come and his reform taken place. The classical age was about to begin and, with it, literature would no longer present those aspects of poetry which have been studied in the preceding chapters.

The classicists' regulations concerning poetry (such as later on were to be codified by Boileau), or even the earlier reform by Malherbe, did not come as a sudden shock. The traditional conception of the evolution of French poetry has a strong tendency to stress the antagonism between Malherbe and Boileau on the one hand, and sixteenth-century poetry on the other. It is undoubtedly tempting to adopt this point of view, which, as a matter of fact, was the position adopted by the seventeenth century itself when it passed condemnation on the preceding age, and haughtily refused to be indebted to it. Indeed, the present study seems to confirm such a view, as obviously all the kinds of poetry I have dealt with up to now are those to be rejected by Classicism. But in order to follow the trends of metaphysical, baroque, and even précieux poetry, it has been necessary to leave aside a certain number of other trends which must now be taken into account. The ultimate checking of a possible metaphysical line, the dismissal of baroque poetry, or the assimilation of préciosité would otherwise appear in a simplified perspective, as crude arbitrary gestures on the part of the classicists. In fact the last chapter has already suggested that clear-cut distinctions are not incompatible with an acknowledgement of the supple evolution of poetry, and that the transition between one category and another may be a matter of nice differences; the more so in the case of the late Renaissance since the disintegration of the Pléiade's ideal made it possible for all kinds of poetry to coexist.

The failure of metaphysical and baroque poetry will appear more clearly if we take a bird's-eye view of the coexistent trends of poetry which were destined to contribute to the formation of

French classical poetry. The points I shall make below do not amount to more than a mere sketch of the late sixteenth- and early seventeenth-century aspects of poetry which bridge the gap between Ronsard[1] and La Fontaine; but to submit such a sketch may be the only way of re-placing the metaphysical, baroque, and précieux poets in their true perspective in the evolution of French poetry.

I

The Line of Grace and Harmony

Ronsard's interest in verbal music has already been mentioned. Everybody agrees on the melodious quality of his best-known lines, and when we look closely at them we realize how skilful and varied is the pattern of pauses, stresses, alliterations, and vowel-sounds within the scheme of regularity. Let us just recall the extreme skill of pauses and stresses in

> Quand vous serez bien vieille /, au soir / à la chandelle /
> Assise auprès du feu /, devidant et filant /,
> Direz /, chantant mes vers, / en vous esmerveillant . . .;

the imitative music of

> Tu deviendras campagne, et en lieu de tes bois,
> Dont l'ombrage incertain lentement se remue,
> Tu sentiras le soc, le coutre, et la charrue:
> Tu perdras ton silence et, haletants d'effroy,
> Ni Satyres ni Pans ne viendront plus chez toy . . .;[2]

or the inimitable lilt of

> La Grace dans sa feuille, et l'amour se repose,
> Embasmant les jardins et les arbres d'odeur . . . .[3]

We saw how the supple and harmonious rhythm of Ronsard was fragmented and hardened by poets such as Du Bartas, Du Perron, or Sponde. To grace and melody some had preferred the strength

---

[1] It is perhaps not unnecessary to stress, at this point, that in the following pages, references to Ronsard are taking into account only the main trends of his poetry. A certain simplification, compulsory here, has meant that I could not point out some interesting minor baroque tendencies in Ronsard; I should like to mention, for those interested in the versatility and complexity of sixteenth-century poetry, an article by M. Raymond, 'Classique et Baroque dans l'œuvre de Ronsard' (*Concinnitas. Beiträge zum Problem des Klassischen*, June 1944).

[2] *Œuvres complètes*, ed. Laumonier, 1914–19, vol. iv, p. 144.

[3] Sonnet, 'Comme on voit sur la branche . . .', ibid., vol. i, p. 216.

of a stiff monotonous rhetorical pattern, others the rugged rhythm
of direct speech.[1]

Yet immediately after Ronsard there were poets who remained
faithful to the *jugement de l'oreille* as Ronsard puts it. In that
respect Desportes carried on the graceful smoothness of the Ronsardian rhythm almost to the point of enervating the line with too
many soft vowel-sounds.[2] Desportes went farther than Ronsard
in that direction because, cut off from the concrete world and
having no explosion of strong personal feelings to express in his
poetry (he was a précieux), he specialized in a *molle douceur* (and
accordingly avoided overlapping and hiatus in order to reach a
kind of undulating regularity) which could translate admirably the
toneless, shadowy, and graceful tenor of his themes:

> Autour des corps, qu'une mort avancée
> Par violance a privez du beau jour,
> Les ombres vont, et font maint et maint tour,
> Aimans encor leur depoüille laissée.
>
> Au lieu cruel, où j'eu l'âme blessée
> Et fu meurtri par les flèches d'Amour,
> J'erre, je tourne et retourne à l'entour,
> Ombre maudite, errante et déchassée.
>
> Legers esprits, plus que moy fortunez,
> Comme il vous plaist vous allez et venez
> Au lieu qui clost votre dépouille aimée.
>
> Vous la voyez, vous la pouvez toucher,
> Où, las! je crains seulement d'approcher
> L'endroit qui tient ma richesse enfermée.[3]

The gently elegiac note, the suggestion of ritual dance in which
shadows scarcely touch the ground, the plaintive sweetness so
elegantly worked out, show that Desportes could make the most
of the musical possibilities of French prosody.

---

[1] See above, Chs. III and IV.

[2] M. Raymond notes in Desportes 'la multiplication des voyelles claires et des
nasales', especially in the following sonnet:

> O Nuict! jalouse Nuict, contre moy conjurée,
> Qui renflammes le ciel de nouvelle clarté,
> T'ay-je donc aujourd'huy tant de fois désirée,
> Pour estre si contraire à ma félicité? . . .
>
> (Raymond, *L'Influence de Ronsard*, vol. ii, p. 107.)

[3] Desportes, *Les Amours d'Hippolyte*, LVII; *Œuvres*, p. 154.

L

A minor poet, Jean de Lingendes (1565-95),[1] may serve as
another illustration. M. Valéry Larbaud has closely studied the
prosody of his poem *Changements de la Bergère Iris* and come to
the conclusion that Jean de Lingendes's work was prosodically (and
grammatically) perfect. There is no substance in the poem: the
bucolic trend in Ronsard has already become the conventional
pastoral; but the poet achieves a blend of sensuous suggestions
and elegantly subdued feelings which works out almost entirely
through the ear of the reader, to such an extent that, as M. Valéry
Larbaud remarks, the melody and rhythm of Lingendes's stanzas
are dangerously catching:

> Doux baiser, le plus doux vray'ment
> Que jamais receut un amant,
> Jugez de sa douceur extreme,
> Et de quelle sorte il me pleut,
> Puis que ceste bouche qui l'eut
> Ne le peut pas dire elle mesme.

> Doux baiser si doux en effet
> Que le plaisir en fut parfait,
> Car l'amour qui me le fit prendre,
> Iris y semblant incliner,
> Lui-mesme me le fit donner,
> Et luy-mesme me le fit rendre.

> Mon esprit se vint rendre alors
> Enchanté sur ces rouges bors,
> Ma vie, en ceste douce envie
> Pour ma passion appaiser,
> N'estant plus pour tout qu'un baiser,
> Mais un baiser qui fut ma vie.

> Ainsi par ce baiser rendu,
> Ayant dans sa bouche perdu
> Mon ame en ces douceurs charmee,
> Je perdis la memoire aussi
> De n'avoir jamais plus soucy
> De chose auparavant aimee.[2]

---

[1] Jean de Lingendes has been rediscovered by M. Valéry Larbaud (*Ce vice
impuni, la lecture . . . Domaine Français,* 1941, pp. 110-31).

[2] De Lingendes, *Œuvres poétiques,* ed. E. T. Griffiths, 1916, pp. 33-34.

The flowing quality of this line of melody is also to be found later in Racan:

> Et vous, eaux qui dormez sur des lits de pavots,
> Vous qui toujours suivez vous-mêmes fugitives . . .[1]

and the highest achievement of that musical fluidity, which fits so well languid moods and sobbing undertones, will be Racine's

> Ariane, ma sœur, de quel amour blessée
> Vous mourûtes aux bords où vous fûtes laissée.

Strangely enough one of the rhythmical experiments which had broken the supple metre of Ronsard, the stiff rhetoric of Du Perron or Bertaut, came to be reconciled to melody through Malherbe. For while he approved of the strength of the well-balanced anti-thesis (exactly separated by the pause after the sixth syllable in the alexandrine) and the firmly rhetorical pattern:

> N'esperons plus, mon ame, aux promesses du monde;
> Sa lumiere est un verre, et sa faveur une onde,
> Que tousjours quelque vent empesche de calmer;
> Quittons ses vanitez, lassons nous de les suivre:
> C'est Dieu qui nous faict vivre
> C'est Dieu qu'il faut aimer . . . ;[2]

at the same time he could adopt the caressing rhythm and delicate interplay of vowel-sounds which we noted in Desportes:

> Beauté, mon beau souci, de qui l'ame incertaine
> A comme l'Ocean son flus et son reflus.[3]

The rhetorical stiffness will still linger on, in Corneille's drama-tic verse mainly; but with Racine and La Fontaine the perfect blend of strength and supple musicality will be reached.

The Ronsardian line of poetry had not lost much in this evolu-tion.[4] The loss was almost entirely on the side of the poetry which tried to use the abrupt rhythms of direct speech.

---

[1] In his *Odes sacrées*, quoted by V. Larbaud, op. cit., p. 148.
[2] *Poésies*, vol. i, p. 7.
[3] *Dessein de quitter une Dame qui ne le contentoit que de promesses*, ibid., vol. ii, p. 198.
[4] Except perhaps some strong run-on lines and the possibility of making subtle hiatus: 'Mais batt*ue ou* de pl*uie ou* d'excessive ardeur' (Ronsard, op. cit., vol. i, p. 216).

2

The Quest for Clarity

Whatever the obscurity to be found in the Pléiade poets, it is more than counterbalanced by their desire for clarity; the more so as they had to struggle against a double tradition of obscurity: that of the Rhétoriqueurs and that of the Hellenic oracular tradition. It is true that they may at times have the obscurity of précieux poetry (those of their productions which were written in praise of a monarch or of a nobleman may include allusions which only the group of courtiers could grasp) and also that they are not interested in grammatical and syntactical clarity as Malherbe will be, but then we have to keep in mind that the French language was still immature. However, their poetry evolved, as we have seen, towards a more limpid form of poetic expression. The erudition of their earlier work (which denoted a marked disdain for the common reader) gave place to an increasing recognition of the necessity for stylistic clarity. Du Bellay attacked Scève's obscurity and Ronsard passed censure on Du Bartas's *La Semaine* on the ground of the chaotic structure and indistinct meaning of the poem.

If we compare Du Bellay's *Regrets* with his earlier work *L'Olive*, there is no possible doubt as to which is the more difficult of the two works. As for Ronsard, we saw also how he proceeded from the complexity, mixed imagery, and ambiguities of the sonnets to Cassandre to the easily grasped similes of his last sonnets, how the difficult mythology of his first odes or sonnets was replaced by a sober use of current mythological figures.[1] A sonnet to Cassandre was a complicated intellectual synthesis of a lover's mood or an elaborate mythological representation of it; a sonnet to Marie or to Hélène is the simple expression of a very simple mood.

With Desportes, who went back to the petrarchan rhetoric of love, we might expect a kind of poetry expressing complex psychology. In fact, however, his sonnets to Diane (and even more so his *Stances* and *Complaintes*) are long-drawn-out explanations of the lover's feelings. He takes pains to analyse, to simplify, to expound. His syntax displays a tendency to multiply the number of the conjunctions destined to aid explanation: *c'est que, or, donc si,*

---

[1] See for instance in the sonnet to Marie ('Comme on voit sur la branche') the restrained use of mythology: *La Parque, le ciel jaloux, les pleurs de l'aube, la Grâce, l'Amour.*

mais plutôt. He seems constantly afraid of not being understood by his reader, and M. Bray has very rightly noted that when he ventures on a comparison such as

> Amour a mis mon cœur comme un rocher à l'onde,
> Comme enclume au marteau, comme une tour au vent
> Et comme l'or au feu . . .

he begins by specifying the action of water, then of the hammer, of the wind and of fire, and then, in case we have still failed to see the point, explains that

> L'onde c'est ton orgueil; le marteau mon tourment;
> Le vent, ta volonté tournant légèrement.[1]

Malherbe will, of course, condemn as absurd some of the extravagant metaphors of Desportes. Some are indeed absurd, as far as common sense is concerned, but they have a sort of linear logic within them and they are not difficult to follow.

Once Malherbe has added common sense, that is, reason, to logic and simplicity, the classical ideal of clarity will be complete.

Here once more the losses are not on the side of the Ronsardian line. The criterion of common sense will rule out baroque poetry; that of clarity, all difficult poetry, including primarily metaphysical poetry and also précieux poetry (let us remember that one of the main reasons for the attack of the classicists against the précieux, as is clearly formulated by La Bruyère at the end of the century,[2] was their obscurity).

3

The Triumph of the Commonplace

It was stressed, in the section concerning Ronsard's poetry,[3] that the criteria of delightfulness and of aptness were bound to limit the choice of subjects 'not to those which were vitally important in the poet's own experience or in the experience of his age, but to those which lent themselves to classical allusions and references to delightful things (the perfect blend of nature and learning)—that is a certain number of commonplaces' such as the passing of time, the transitory quality of youth, love in general, death, &c. . . . There is little doubt that the Pléiade poets were more interested in the generally true or the classically true than in

---

[1] Bray, *La Préciosité et les Précieux*, pp. 83–84.
[2] See above, Ch. VIII, p. 121, n. 2.   [3] See above, Ch. III, pp. 26–31.

the truth of a personal experience.[1] Whenever they completed the hedonistic side of their poetry by the utilitarian one (their recurrent use of the word *doux-utile* was a tacit recognition of their Horatian conception of poetry) the ethical aim of their verse could only be to show eternal truth.[2]

In the late Renaissance the problems of the age became so acute that they partly swept away the possibility of a kind of poetry destined to please, except of course in the précieux. Metaphysical poetry such as La Ceppède's and Sponde's (or Donne's and Herbert's) is neither hedonistic nor utilitarian (even when religious): it expresses the personal problems of both an intelligence and a sensibility struggling to obtain a coherent grasp on a situation implying metaphysical difficulties. Baroque poetry distorts any subject it touches, so that it would be difficult to apply the epithet 'commonplace' to themes which are outside the range of common experience. After all, the touchstone of a good commonplace in literature is the amount of verisimilitude it affords. Précieux poetry has little concern for truth, either general or particular, or for verisimilitude, and if we speak of its commonplaces it is in a very restricted sense, meaning only the conventional themes of a group of précieux people.

The many-sided pessimism of the late Renaissance, coming after the radiant optimism of the mid-sixteenth century, had produced a violent swing of the pendulum in the evolution of French poetry, but by the beginning of the seventeenth century some poets were already showing signs of a sort of balance and worldly wisdom.

There is no need here to dwell on the two precursors of Malherbe, the official poets at the court of Henri III and Henri IV, Bertaut and Du Perron. Let us simply recall that Bertaut was considered by Ronsard a good poet but *un poète trop sage*,[3] and

[1] Even what may seem personal poetry, Du Bellay's *Regrets*, relies more on general truths applicable to his own case than on the sounding of his own experience.

[2] Des poetiques espris
L'utile et douce escriture
Comprent ce qui est compris
Au ciel et en la Nature.
    (Du Bellay, *Ode au Seigneur des Essars*; *Œuvres poétiques*, vol. iv, p. 174.)

[3] Mon oncle [Desportes] m'a conté que, monstrant à Ronsard
Tes vers estincelans et de lumière et d'art,
Il ne sceut que reprendre en ton apprentissage
Sinon qu'il te jugeoit pour un poëte trop sage.
    (Régnier, *Satyre V*; *Œuvres*, ed. P. Poitevin, p. 58.)

followed Desportes in his regularity of diction and of prosody; and that Du Perron would allow only what he called *les métaphores universelles*:

Pour l'élocution [speaking of Du Bartas] elle est impertinente en ses métaphores, qui pour la plupart ne se doivent prendre que des choses universelles ou si communes qu'elles aient passé comme de l'espèce au genre, comme le Soleil; mais lui au lieu de dire les Coursiers d'Eole, il dira ses postillons et descend toujours du genre à l'espèce, qui est une chose fort vicieuse (*Perroniana*)[1]—

thus limiting the field of imagery to metaphors related to some general truth commonly accepted. This limitation upon imagery is in itself significant. But it is even more significant to watch the poet setting limits to himself in his exploration of experience.

Here is again the theme of the end of the world as treated this time by Maynard:

> Le Temps amènera la fin de toutes choses;
>   Et ce beau ciel, ce lambris azuré,
> Ce théâtre, où l'aurore épanche tant de roses,
>   Sera brûlé des feux dont il est éclairé.
>
>   Le grand astre qui l'embellit
>   Fera sa tombe de son lit;
>   L'air ne formera plus ni grêles, ni tonnerres;
>   Et l'univers qui, dans son large tour,
>   Voit courir tant de mers et fleurir tant de terres,
>   Sans savoir où tomber, tombera quelque jour.
>
>   (*A Alcippe*)[2]

The theme is familiar to us and the comparison between these lines and those which Donne, d'Aubigné, Saint-Amant, or Théophile devoted to it brings out the particular tone of this poem. Maynard is not experiencing any urgent desire to settle his accounts with God (like Donne), nor is he visualizing, awe-struck, with eyes wide open, the apocalyptic catastrophe in all its terrible vividness (like d'Aubigné), nor grinning at the picturesque dislocation of the universe (like Saint-Amant or Théophile).

There is no concrete description in Maynard; even the images are clichés with very little evocative power ('lambris azuré', 'aurore

---

[1] Quoted by Raymond, *L'Influence de Ronsard*, vol. ii, p. 290.
[2] A. Dorchain, *Les Chefs-d'œuvre lyriques de Malherbe et de l'école classique*, 1921, vol. i, pp. 44–45.

épanche tant de roses'), the conceits verge upon abstraction ('fera
sa tombe de son lit', 'brûlé des feux dont il est éclairé'). The rhythm
is slow, peaceful. Both the abstraction and the quiet steadiness
of the pace ensure an impression of reassuring remoteness; there
is not the slightest suggestion that, as Théophile puts it:

> ce grand désordre du monde
> Peut-être arrivera demain.

No mention of angels blowing trumpets, no apparition of Christ.
The thought is philosophical, not religious. The end of the world
is considered by Maynard as the ancients or Ronsard would have
considered it. The first line quoted gives the tone and meaning of
the passage: 'Le Temps amènera la fin de toutes choses', a serene
statement of a general truth, acknowledged and accepted, belonging to the domain of abstraction and to the field of those commonplaces which are convenient subjects for philosophical meditations
and objurgatory verse. Maynard's poem is concerned with teaching
his friend a wise attitude towards life and death. It is, of its kind,
a very beautiful poem, striking by a sort of noble fullness and
haughty restraint. It expresses the pagan attitude to the inevitable
catastrophe, an attitude which will be that of the classicists and
which was that of Ronsard, and it is indeed significant that the
sober and impressive finality of the last line comes from Ronsard
through Bertaut:

> qu'à la fin la mort toutes choses emmeine
> Et que mesme le ciel, qui fait mourir les Rois
> Et perir un chacun, perira quelquefois.
> (Ronsard, Tombeau de Charles IX)[1]

> Mais encor ce grand Tout, ce grand Tout que tu vois
> Qui ne scait où tomber, tombera quelquefois.
> (Bertaut, Elégie Funèbre)[2]

The early seventeenth-century man goes back to the philosophy
of the ancients, but not with the enthusiasm and pride of the
humanist Ronsard. No danger of Towers of Babel this time. Man
is still the centre of the universe but has accepted his limitations,
so that the sobered humanist becomes a moralist. We often think
of a moralist as a prose-writer, but the equivalent of moralism is

---

[1] *Œuvres complètes*, ed. Laumonier, 1914–19, vol. v, p. 245.
[2] Bertaut, *Œuvres poétiques*, ed. A. Chenevière, 1891, p. 126.

in poetry that kind of meditative and oratorical verse which starts with Malherbe and his disciples and which takes as its subject of meditation philosophical commonplaces. The attitude is that of gravity and restraint, so that the same images which in some baroque poets are delightful and picturesque, assume in these poets a dignified grandeur,

> Et l'on verra bientôt naître du sein de l'Onde
> La première clarté de mon dernier Soleil.
>
> (MAYNARD)[1]

Moralism is anti-metaphysical. It resolves the conflict between humanism and religion (having rejected devout humanism) by separating religious creed from rationalistic truth and works out a peaceful coexistence of both. The result, as far as poetry is concerned, is that the poet will no longer express metaphysical difficulties in his verse. Characteristically enough, there is no echo of Montaigne's thought in the meditative-oratorical poetry of the early seventeenth century. His humble and intimate revolt against the limitations of man's earthly domain was too unsafe a basis for moralism. For their philosophical themes, poets went to the serene stoicism and solid argumentation of Du Vair's *Traité de la constance et consolation* and *Traité de l'éloquence française*.[2] Malherbe's philosophical banalities included in the *Consolation à Monsieur Du Perier* are entirely similar to those expressed by Du Vair in the first book of his *Traité de la constance et consolation*.[3]

Therefore, it is not surprising that the theme of death will undergo a change from what it was in metaphysical or baroque poetry. Here is Malherbe on the transitory glory of monarchs:

> Ont-ils rendu l'esprit, ce n'est plus que poussière
> Que ceste majesté si pompeuse et si fière
> Dont l'esclat orgueilleux estonne l'Univers,
> Et dans ces grands tombeaux où leurs ames hautaines
>> Font encore les vaines
>> Ils sont mangez des vers.[4]

The commonplace (*sic transit . . .*) is expressed with magnificent power. The abrupt concreteness of the last line contrasting with the fullness of movement and lofty images of the two preceding

---

[1] Thierry Maulnier, *Poésie du XVIIᵉ siècle*, p. 145.

[2] See in Brunot, *La Doctrine de Malherbe*, 1891, the great influence of Du Vair on his contemporaries, and more particularly on Malherbe, pp. 59–72.

[3] Ibid., pp. 68–69.   [4] Vol. i, pp. 7–8.

lines, shows the transition from Sponde to Classicism. This stanza is
perhaps more perfect than anything Sponde could have written and
still retains in the last three lines something of the dramatic irony
which constitutes Sponde's achievement. But such dramatic accents
will become rarer and rarer and the theme of death will assume the
gentle melancholy and elegiac elegance it had in Ronsard:

> Puis nous treuvons la Mort qui met nos corps en cendre.

> Le Temps qui sans repos, va d'un pas si leger,
> Emporte avecque luy toutes les belles choses:
> C'est pour nous avertir de le bien mesnager
> Et faire des bouquets en la saison des roses.[1]

(These lines are by the versatile Tristan who, when he is neither
baroque nor précieux, is already a classicist poet.)

Another consequence of moralism is that religious poetry still
produces beautiful poems when merely laudatory (as in the religious verse of Corneille and Racine) but becomes less and less
capable of expressing the dramatic struggle of a soul towards God.[2]
Gradually, in fact, these poets give up the attempt to express a
personal experience. As a rule the classicist writer, even when he
expresses some dramatic experience, depersonalizes it. But the
classicist's depersonalization should not be assimilated to that of
the précieux writer, who finds in it a form of safety. Some critics
have suggested that the classicists were also playing for safety and
in that case we might be led to this assimilation; but I should not
agree. The classicist leaves outside the domain of literature a
certain number of aspects of reality, such as metaphysical problems, not because he is afraid that they might be disturbing but
because they belong in his mind to a different order of things.
Within the limitations of what he considers to be the proper study
of writers—that is, a man's world limited to man—he will not
shrink from the expression of human experiences which are disturbing enough. He does not escape into a world of formal beauty.

Undoubtedly the classicists went back to the Horatian attitude,
both hedonistic and utilitarian. They all asserted that the first
golden rule was *plaire* and all firmly declared that their works had
an ultimate moral value. We know that this word moral may be

---

[1] Tristan, *Consolation à Idalie*; *Les Amours*, p. 49.
[2] This change in the religious poetry of the seventeenth century was, of course,
a gradual process and would merit a special study.

misleading and certainly does not imply moralizing. What the classicists meant by it was first that they did not want to be reproached for immorality, and also that their work included something that was of use: the knowledge of the human mind. The word 'moral' as we usually understand it is irrelevant in the case of Racine, La Fontaine, or La Rochefoucauld, but the *utile* side is there: in their commonplaces the classicists (I am thinking particularly of Racine or La Rochefoucauld) expressed a lucid, and sometimes very painful and dramatic, vision of human life as it is in the universe, so general and yet so closed, of nature and reason.

4

The Failure of Colloquialism and the Discarding of the Concrete

As has been mentioned, Ronsard was responsible for the principle of poetic diction:[1] 'La Langue prosaïque est ennemie de l'éloquence poétique.' In this respect, on the theoretical side he was already a classicist. On the practical side, it is undeniable that Malherbe censured most of the devices by which Ronsard meant to enrich the poetical instrument: composite words, technical terms, archaisms, dialectal expressions. But Malherbe came when the French language was in a more mature state, and having been enriched by Ronsard, could, by a very normal process, be pruned by Malherbe. In the opposition between Ronsard and Malherbe, the point at issue is not the possibility of employing ordinary speech: they both agreed in repudiating it.

We saw how a strong tendency to colloquialism appeared after Ronsard in those very poets who had endeavoured to break the Ronsardian rhythm; and as a matter of fact, the remarks to be made here are parallel to those made in the first section of this chapter concerning rhythm.

The Ronsardian poetic diction branched out in two directions. His grand style was adopted by Du Bartas without discrimination and came to a dead end. But Du Bartas was in fact taking up the earlier principles of Ronsard and at the same time he was, for instance, making an orgy of composite words:

> . . . torche sainte,
> Chasse-ennuy, chasse-dueil, chasse-nuict, chasse-crainte,[2]

of a kind which Ronsard had given up using.

---

[1] See above, Ch. III.   [2] *Works*, ed. Holmes, vol. ii, p. 212.

Here again the true disciple is Desportes and the evolution is in the direction of purity. Being a précieux poet, Desportes made his choice within the Ronsardian vocabulary and limited himself to the words which could best suit polite society. Characteristically he discarded dialectal expressions, and among technical terms retained mostly terms of venery which were part of the conversation of noblemen. At the same time he increased the proportion of abstract words.

Du Perron's *métaphores universelles* have already been mentioned. Like Desportes's preference for abstract words, Du Perron's statements on general metaphors show how poetic diction was, little by little, not only tending to differentiate itself from prosaic diction but losing touch with the concrete, so that the diction of metaphysical poets like La Ceppède and Sponde, who did not hesitate to use bold concrete words, was bound to be defeated.

Régnier may be thought of as one of the last champions of colloquialism. The conversational tone of his satires,[1] and even of his elegies, the use of everyday familiar expressions:

> Et dans la gallerie encor' que tu lui parles,
> Il te laisse au roy Jean, et s'en court au roy Charles . . .;[2]

the concrete picturesqueness of his images:

> Comme un poète qui prend les vers à la pipée (*Satire* X);[3]

> Son œil tout pénitent ne pleure qu'eau béniste (*Satire* XIII) . . .[4]

link him to Villon and Rabelais. But, as is well known, Régnier stood in opposition to Malherbe and Malherbe won.[5]

Meanwhile the précieuses were influencing the language of poetry in a direction parallel to that of Desportes (himself a précieux poet), Du Perron, and Malherbe, discarding concrete words (considered as low) and bringing into use vague abstract terms.

The last refuge of the concrete was in the baroque universe of the *libertin* poets.

---

[1] Quoi! comment! est-ce ainsi qu'on frappe Despautère.
Quelle incongruïté! Vous mentez par les dents.
Mais vous? . . . Ainsi ces gens, à se picquer ardens,
S'en vindrent du parler à tic tac, torche, lorgne;
Qui casse le museau; qui son rival esborgne; . . .
                    (*Satire X*; *Œuvres*, ed. Poitevin, p. 143).
[2] Ibid., p. 120.   [3] Ibid., p. 119.   [4] Ibid., p. 173.
[5] The colloquialism to be found in the later satirists such as Sigogne or Scarron is stamped with the mark of the *burlesque* and no longer influences the general evolution of lyrical poetry.

The Ronsardian diction had followed a logical evolution but had certainly undergone heavy losses on the side of the concrete. Yet La Fontaine's poetry was to show that there were still for the classicist poet possibilities of recapturing a certain amount of the concreteness of the universe.

5

The Last Flashes of Metaphysical, Baroque, and Précieux Poetry

I shall say very little about the last stages of précieux poetry proper, in the course of the seventeenth century. As has already been suggested, by the second half of the century the précieux element had no longer any important part to play in the field of literature at large. The unit of refinement was no more a précieuse's drawing-room but the Court. The classicists had assimilated a certain amount of the précieux characteristics (in their diction, their rules of *les bienséances*, and their taste for psychological analysis) and were combining these with their own ideal of universal truth. The précieux 'highbrow' had become *l'honnête homme*. Précieux poetry did not disappear altogether, despite the attacks of Molière, Furetière, or La Bruyère; but it was more and more reduced to drawing-room entertainment (*bouts-rimés* especially) and no longer in the current of the evolution of French poetry.[1]

This section will be devoted to a few examples of a kind of poetry which mainly represents the tail-end of the baroque but which offers mixed characteristics—some of them précieux, others classical, and with even a touch of the metaphysical.

Tristan's poetry has been pointed out as typical transition poetry. The lines I shall quote, written by minor poets, are contemporary with the last works of Tristan and Saint-Amant (roughly mid-seventeenth century).

Jean de Bussières's[2] *Les Descriptions poétiques*, as is clearly implied in the title, carried on the descriptive poetry of Théophile and Saint-Amant. The sunrise inspired him with the following lines:

> Un rouge à couleur de rose
> Qui doucement se fait voir
> Insensiblement dispose
> Le Monde à le recevoir.

---

[1] For illustration see in Mornet, *Littérature française classique*, the chapter on 'Permanence de la Préciosité littéraire', pp. 125–45.   [2] 1607–87.

La Nuit de crainte s'envole
Changeant en course ses pas,
Et va sous un autre pôle
Porter l'ombre du trépas.

Dans les replis de ses toiles
Qu'elle resserre en courant
Elle cache les étoiles
Qui la suivent en mourant.[1]

The delicate indication of colour, the graceful personification of night and of the stars, recall the playful and lovely atmosphere which suffuses the baroque landscape of Saint-Amant and Théophile, with perhaps more sophistication ('un rouge à couleur de rose' is a subtle ambiguity on the word *rose*, relying for its effect on the pleasurable suggestion of red roses, and on the pleasing unexpectedness of a red which turns out to be pink). But Jean de Bussières is also a moralist; a similar description of a sunset in another passage is meant this time to be instructive, and is accordingly followed by serious considerations:

·Ce doux repos de la Nature
Me trace une rare peinture
Du repos de l'Eternité,
Où nos âmes, comme autant d'astres,
Libres de tous mortels désastres,
Luiront dans l'Immortalité.[2]

Du Bois Hus's *La Nuit des Nuits*[3] is worth quoting at some length, if we want to judge his use of a baroque landscape:

Le monde change de couleur,
Une générale pâleur
Efface la beauté des plaines
Et les Oiseaux surpris sur les bords des marais,
Courtisans des fontaines,
Se vont mettre à couvert dans le sein des forêts.

---

[1] Thierry Maulnier, *Poètes précieux et baroques*, pp. 215–16.
[2] Ibid.
[3] The exact identity and dates of birth and death of this poet are unknown. *La Nuit des Nuits* together with two other poems was published in 1640. The fragments quoted here are taken from Thierry Maulnier's *Poètes précieux et baroques*, pp. 217–19, and from the anthology edited by Professor Boase for the Department of French Studies of Glasgow University, pp. 34–37.

Quelques brins d'écarlate et d'or
Paraissent attachés encor
A quelque pièce de nuage:
Des restes de rayons peignant tout à l'entour
    Le fond du paysage,
Font un troisième temps qui n'est ni nuit ni jour. . . .

Le Silence vêtu de noir,
Retournant faire son devoir
Vole sur la mer et la terre,
Et l'Océan joyeux de sa tranquillité
    Est un liquide verre
Où la face du Ciel imprime sa beauté.

Le visage du Firmament
Descendu dans cet élément
Y fait voir sa figure peinte,
Les feux du Ciel sans peur nagent dedans la mer
    Et les poissons sans crainte
Glissent parmi ces feux qui semblent les aimer.

Dans le fond de ce grand miroir
La Nature se plaît à voir
L'onde et la flamme si voisines
Et les Astres tombés en ces pays nouveaux,
    Salamandres marines,
Se baignent à plaisir dans le giron des eaux.

L'illustre Déesse des mois
Quittant son arc et son carquois
Descend avec eux dedans l'onde.
Son Croissant est sa Barque, où l'hameçon en main,
    Fait de sa tresse blonde,
Elle pêche à loisir les perles du Jourdain.

Le Ciel en ce soir bienheureux
S'habillant de ses plus beaux feux
Eclate plus que d'ordinaire,
Et la nuit infidèle à son obscurité
    A sur notre hémisphère
Beaucoup moins de noirceur qu'elle n'a de clarté. . . .

Une esclatante Nuit déployant dans les Cieux
    Ses rayonnantes voiles
Pour mieux voir son Amant a pris de nouveaux yeux. . . .

Riche et miràculeuse Nuict
Qui sans bouche et sans aucun bruit
Enfantes pourtant la PAROLE . . . .[1]

We recognize the familiar elements of the baroque landscape: the personification of Silence, the glass-like substance of the sea, the fish and water-fowl, the play of light and shade, and specially the fanciful reflection of the stars in the water, and here these *jeux de miroir* are particularly elaborate. But the poem is more than a delightful conjuring up of unconnected images. Here we find connexion, order, and purpose. Du Bois Hus is describing a very special night: the night Christ was born ('La nuit des Visions Célèbres' as he will say in one of the following stanzas). Of course the poet enjoys the landscape he is painting quite apart from any religious purpose, but nevertheless this landscape is not a mere game of his fancy. He is careful to give a certain structure and connexion to the various parts of the description: the setting of the sun, the twilight, the night, and then the praise of that miraculous Night. He also tries to suggest the particular quality in the atmosphere of the landscape: the silence and the tranquillity of the sea are signs of expectation, the stars are brighter than usual, and the night, instead of its customary darkness, is suffused with a sort of luminosity. Because of the divine quality of that night and the loftiness of the subject, Du Bois Hus's description does not give the impression of a diminutive landscape crammed with minute particulars, or the impression of the foreground artist we so often get with Saint-Amant; the landscape here has depth and vastness.[2] It suggests vistas and a shifting of the angle of vision, perhaps because it is at the same time pagan and Christian, and even more because it is both a general and a localized landscape: the miraculous night is all over the world but more precisely in Palestine,[3] and the poet obtains a very successful effect by blending the pagan and the Christian, the general and the local, in:

Son Croissant est sa Barque, où l'hameçon en main
Fait de sa tresse blonde
Elle pêche à loisir les perles du Jourdain.

[1] To the English reader this poem will naturally recall Milton's *Ode on the Morning of Christ's Nativity*.

[2] Although we may think that the sublime religious feeling in it is translated in too many instances into a sort of précieux religious language of the type 'Pour mieux voir son Amant a pris de nouveaux yeux'. It is even more marked in the stanzas following those quoted here.

[3] Palestine and Bethlehem are mentioned in the following stanzas.

The poem, as I have mentioned in a footnote, is somewhat spoilt by an incapacity on the part of Du Bois Hus for expressing religious emotions otherwise than in précieux conventions. But his treatment of a baroque landscape as a mode of expression for a serious subject can make us realize the possibilities offered by such creation of atmosphere and make us regret that seventeenth-century poets did not take fuller advantage of them.

Du Bois Hus is not the only poet who used the loveliness of the baroque landscape for religious purposes: others, like him, belonging to the last group of choristers of devout humanism, rejoiced in the beauty of the external world, and praised God for it. But, little by little, devout humanism was ousted by a more puritanical attitude towards the enjoyment of the external world, probably due to Jansenist influence. Religion and lyrical poetry became more and more divorced from each other; laudatory religious verse tended to avoid fancy, or the mixture of the pagan and the Christian, as being in bad taste, and general abstract words to designate aspects of nature took the place of landscapes. We may note, in passing, some lines written by one of the last poets of devout humanism, Martial de Brives, from his *Paraphrase sur le Cantique des Trois Enfants* (published 1660):

Benedicite aquae omnes

> Clairs amas des Mers précieuses
> Qui, pendants sur le Firmament,
> Et coulants sans écoulement
> Semblent être judicieuses:
> Eaux assises dessus les feux
> Qui dorent d'un éclat pompeux
> Le front de la Nuit la plus noire;
> Bénissez le Dieu qui remplit
> De tant de lumière et de Gloire
> Comme d'un Sablon d'or votre superbe lit. . . .

Benedicite nives

> Belle soie au Ciel raffinée,
> Neige dont l'air se déchargeant
> Comme d'une toison d'argent . . .[1]

At the same time another poet, Godeau (1605–72), published

---

[1] Martial de Brives has been discovered by M. Marcel Arland, who is re-editing his works. These lines are taken from D. Aury's *Anthologie de la poésie religieuse*, pp. 184 and 187.

M

in the same anthology (*Le Parnasse séraphique*, 1660) a poem on
the same subject: *Benedicite omnia opera domini domino*, but in
Godeau the concrete imagination is already poorer and clichés
belonging to the grand style (*clairs ruisseaux, prés fleuris, beaux
cieux, célestes flambeaux*) curtail the evocative power of the description.[1]

The last poem to be mentioned in this section is another sunset
by Hippolyte de la Mesnardière (?–1663), whose *Poésies* were published in 1656.

Le Soleil Couchant

Le grand Astre va lentement
Vers les saphirs de l'onde amère,
Et Vénus dans l'autre Hémisphère
Donne ordre à leur appartement.

Ces grands rideaux à fond vermeil
Dont l'or pétille dans la Nue
Sont d'une étoffe peu connue
Aux pays où va le Soleil.

La Pourpre qui luit sous ses pas
Et l'air s'écarte en mille pointes
Où parfois deux couleurs sont jointes
Et parfois ne se joignent pas.

Dieux! la merveilleuse clarté!
Alceste, admirez la nuance
De ce jaune-clair qui s'avance
Sous cet incarnat velouté.

L'œillet d'Inde serait ainsi
Dans sa douce et sombre dorure
Si sur les pans de sa bordure
La Rose tranchait le souci. . . .

Voyez ces tirades de feu
Dont le Ciel vers le Nord éclate,
Et dans ces plaines d'écarlate
Ces bois d'amarante et de bleu.

---

[1] Godeau's *Paraphrase du Cantique des Trois Enfants* will be found in D. Aury's
Anthologie de la poésie religieuse, pp. 229–34.

Les Opales du Point du Jour
Et ses Jacinthes sombres-claires
Sont des objets bien plus vulgaires
Que les Rubis de son Retour.

Sa Rondeur croît en descendant:
Telle est la Sphère de notre Ame,
Le cercle infini de sa flamme
S'augmente par notre Occident.

Dans l'air il laisse les couleurs
Qui sont les jasmins et les roses
Et toutes ses Métamorphoses
Sont les germes d'autant de fleurs.[1]

Here we find again the baroque poet's delight in exerting his visual sensibility and in dwelling upon the coloured and varying surface of things. The poem is mostly a study in gradation of colours, and although we recognize the baroque fabric of diamonds, gold, and precious stones, the study in colours is infinitely more sophisticated than anything Théophile or Saint-Amant would have done. In fact, the colouring is too rich: the velvety scarlet, the dark golden sheen of the carnation, the solid blue or amaranth suggest the heavy lusciousness of palace decoration or of hot-house flowers. The transparence of the open air has gone. I would almost say that the poet has reached the boundary between the baroque and the précieux. The sublime beauty of the sunset is translated in terms which can fit a drawing-room atmosphere: the mention of Venus's apartment, the deliberate choice of expensive flowers and of colours such as amaranth or *jaune-clair*, which are those of rich brocade or velvet, are significant. But as we hesitate between the baroque and the précieux we come to the stanza:

Sa Rondeur croît en descendant:
Telle est la Sphère de notre Ame,
Le cercle infini de sa flamme
S'augmente par notre Occident —

which has a true metaphysical ring. The poet refers to a well-known paradoxical feature of the setting sun—that it seems to increase in volume as it sets on the horizon—which inspires him

[1] This extract is taken from Thierry Maulnier's *Poètes précieux et baroques*, pp. 307–9.

with the conceit of the Soul which irradiates more fire as the end of our life draws near. It is strange, in the midst of a baroque land-scape, to light upon a kind of geometric imagery which reminds us of Donne or Marvell.

As with the metaphysical conceit, La Mesnardière's conceit encloses a contradiction. The Soul is both a sphere (that is limited in volume) and an infinite ring of fire. The infinite can be increased, which is mathematically impossible, but the poet accepts the conse-quences of the mathematical absurdity just as he accepts the opti-cal delusion of a larger sun, as the best way of expressing both the limitations of our soul (which matures slowly towards the end of our life) and its limitless possibilities in death.

This strange poem supposes, on the part of the poet, a high degree of sophistication, refined taste, a certain consciousness of his own précieux characteristics, and at the same time the ability to tackle serious problems with vigour. But although the three elements (baroque, précieux, metaphysical) are present, they do not blend, and the poem remains unsatisfactory, in spite of its beauty. It leaves us with the uneasy feeling that, with it, French poetry had reached a stage when the blend was perhaps possible and could have produced some sort of metaphysical poetry like that of Marvell.

In point of fact French poetry was to have its Marvell, but the perfect blend which was to mark in France, as Marvell's poetry did in England, the climax of an evolution, was not made of the same components as we find in La Mesnardière's abortive endeavour.

6

La Fontaine

La Fontaine's poetry lies outside the scope of this study. More-over, the deprecatory cliché 'Everything has been said on La Fon-taine', which no twentieth-century critic ever fails to put forward, stands like a salutary warning to innocent enthusiasm not to cover ground which has been ploughed into innumerable criss-cross ruts.

All I wish to stress here, and very briefly, is that, in spite of the hypothetical possibilities of other kinds of poetry (such as were mentioned at the end of the last section), La Fontaine's verse was the natural outcome of the evolution which the present work has endeavoured to trace. This is not minimizing the genius of this poet; his genius lay in co-ordinating the various trends of poetry which could express the spirit of his age and in bringing this blend to perfection.

Characterizing this perfection is a delicate task and it is easy to go a step too far in one direction or another: to call La Fontaine, for instance, the embodiment of French genius because he was the poet of an age which was, perhaps, the highest point of French civilization: or to think of him as *le fantaisiste*, standing apart from the poetry of his time because he wrote free verse, enjoyed country walks, and was absent-minded; or, on the contrary, because of the extreme refinement of his technique, to put the stress on the artificiality of his poetry.

Rather than the characteristic of *élégance, naturel, génie bien français, humour,* &c., I should like to emphasize the qualities of maturity and balance which mark his poetry.

Maturity has its blessings and also its particular difficulties. One of the blessings is the possibility of profiting from past experiments. La Fontaine's technique is the result of a hundred years of experimentation in French prosody and the climax of that line of grace and harmony mentioned above; his mastery of the alexandrine, in *Adonis* for instance, is comparable to Racine's, and his free verse is the epitome of all the prosodic forms and rhythms tried before him.

Another blessing, which is a mixed one, is to have done with the crude emotions and rash revolts of adolescence and to have established a hierarchy of values based on a clear awareness of limitations. ·

There is no revolt in La Fontaine, no rebellious act against the heritage of former poetry, but a firm attitude of clear-sightedness as to the respective values of what composes the patrimony. He accepts the legacy of the baroque, but not as a possible poetic vision of the universe: unobtrusively, in the wake of Tristan, he breaks the last thread which linked the baroque to poetry by handing it over, definitively, to the visual arts, and there is no ambiguity left. La Fontaine's delight in the baroque is represented only by his faculty of appreciating painting and landscape-gardening.[1]

---

[1] See in *Psyché* the description of a baroque grotto, with the rockery, Tritons, sea-shells, and coral, *Œuvres diverses*, ed. Clarac (Pléiade edition), 1948, pp. 128-9,

He accepts the précieux convention of hyperbolical compliments to women:

> Aminte, c'est à vous que j'offre cet ouvrage;
> Mes chansons et mes vœux, tout vous doit rendre hommage;
> Trop heureux si j'osois conter à l'Univers
> Les tourments infinis que pour vous j'ai soufferts!
> Quand vous me permettrez de chanter votre gloire,
> Quand vos yeux, renommés par plus d'une victoire,
> Me laisseront vanter le pouvoir de leurs traits . . .
>
> (*Adonis*.)[1]

But he knows the relative value of this language, just as he knows the relative value of the mythological universe, the legacy of Ronsard:

> Rien ne manque à Vénus, ni les lis, ni les roses,
> Ni le mélange exquis des plus aimables choses,
> Ni ce charme secret dont l'œil est enchanté,
> Ni la grâce plus belle encor que la beauté.
> Telle on vous voit, Aminte: une glace fidèle
> Vous peut de tous ces traits présenter un modèle;
> Et, s'il falloit juger de l'objet le plus doux,
> Le sort serait douteux entre Vénus et vous.
>
> (*Adonis*.)[2]

La Fontaine knows that he has behind him a long tradition of various pictures of Venus and that a delicate negative approach, *Rien ne manque* underlined with subtle irony, is the only way to conjure up the perfection of her beauty to which he can add only the touch of extreme refinement: *la grâce*. The sudden transition (which is a sort of parenthesis in the telling of the story) *Telle on vous voit, Aminte* . . . indicates that Venus and Aminte have their equal share of tender irony. It is a pleasurable convention that Venus should embody the loveliness of woman, it is also a pleasurable convention that Aminte should be compared to Venus. This tender irony is the form La Fontaine's wit takes in *Adonis*: only a line-by-line analysis would do full justice to the mastery with which he achieves the 'tough reasonableness beneath the slight

and in *Le Songe de Vaux*, the very clear distinction he makes between the different arts:

> J'y fais parler quatre arts fameux dans l'Univers,
> Les palais, les tableaux, les jardins, et les vers.
>
> (Ibid., p. 82.)

[1] Ibid., p. 3.   [2] Ibid., pp. 4–5.

lyric grace' (and to this slight lyric grace we owe some of the most perfect lines in French poetry:

> Jours devenus moments, moments filés de soie . . .
> O vous, tristes plaisirs où leur âme se noie,
> Vains et derniers efforts d'une imparfaite joie,
> Moments pour qui le sort rend leurs vœux superflus,
> Délicieux moments, vous ne reviendrez plus! . . .[1]).

Throughout the poem we are made to realize that we are in a world of conventions, and made to accept these conventions as a means of imparting the sensuous delights of love and its inevitable sufferings.

In the same way mythology will be used in the *Fables*, not only for the fun of providing the mock-heroic, but as a way of bringing everything to the reasonable proportions of a human scale, a result La Fontaine obtains by balancing gods against animals:

> Deux coqs vivaient en paix: une poule survint
> Et voilà la guerre allumée.
> Amour, tu perdis Troie! . . .

Whether it is cocks and hens, or Paris and Helen, it is the same old story, and the poet's attitude to it is neither scornful nor sentimental: it is a blend of sympathy, irony, and tender pity.

This mature sense of the relative value of things is still further marked in La Fontaine's *Fables* by the mixture of colloquialism and poetic diction which produces a constant shifting of tone. It is a way of showing that one must not be deceived by appearances and that whether you look at things in their assumed nobleness and glamour or in their humble everyday reality, the same truth will out.

La Fontaine's observation-post is in the tradition of Théophile's *Solitude* and Saint-Amant's *Contemplateur*:

> Solitude, où je trouve une douceur secrète,
> Lieux que j'aimai toujours . . .;[2]

but the 'Contemplateur' is no longer an idle dreamer, playing with delightful images: he is a moralist. The playful and gratuitous attitude has gone, just as Ronsard's enthusiastic and buoyant *joie*

---

[1] Ibid., pp. 6 and 7.
[2] *Fables, contes et nouvelles*, ed. Pilon, &c. (Pléiade edition), 1948, p. 268.

de vivre has become *La Volupté*, which is its sophisticated and grown-up heir:

> . . . le jeu, l'amour, les livres, la musique
> La ville et la campagne . . .
> Jusqu'au sombre plaisir d'un cœur mélancolique . . .

Maturity implies an awareness of limitations and acceptance of these limitations. La Fontaine cannot go back to feeling for nature as it was expressed in Ronsard: Pan and the nymphs no longer walk the earth and Ronsard's woodlands have become the insipid scenery of the conventional pastoral. On the other hand the baroque landscape has been transformed into something artificial and luxurious. The limitations are so inexorable that it seems almost miraculous that La Fontaine has been able to put trees and streams into his verse. But this achievement bears also the stamp of maturity: the rich colours of the landscape and its heavy jewels are dismissed; from the *libertin* poets (and also from Racan's pastoral atmosphere) La Fontaine retains only the transparence of the open air and of water, in the same way as he has retained only the transparent shadows of the gods and goddesses who peopled Ronsard's landscapes. A fable like *Le Chêne et le Roseau* (the technical accomplishment of which has so often been analysed) is a well-known illustration of La Fontaine's treatment of feeling for nature. The oak has all the majestic beauty Ronsard lent to the trees of 'La Forêt de Gastine'; the delicate loveliness of Théophile's landscape is still there, mixed with suggestions of concrete sensations (the smell of marshlands, the feel of the wind); but the reed is no longer the decorative accessory of the baroque landscape and there is not a single detail which is not directed to the ultimate implication of the poem, the moralist's attitude, the telling of the story as an example to man.

La Fontaine has accepted the moralist's universe, centred on man, limited to man. Within these limitations, his poetry expresses an extreme variety and complexity playing on a refined sensibility. The apparent levity of *Adonis* and the *Fables* must not conceal how serious is the balance between sensibility and awareness of the problem man has to face in his quest for earthly happiness. Valéry, who wrote the best possible commentary on *Adonis*, has rightly dismissed the legendary figure of La Fontaine as a lazy, wool-gathering and lackadaisical personage, and has insisted on his extreme concentration of thought and discipline of sensibility:

Je n'y vois que recherches volontaires, assouplissement des pensées, consentement de l'âme à des gênes exquises et le triomphe perpétuel du sacrifice.[1]

The pendulum of French poetry found there its momentary, precarious equilibrium.

[1] Paul Valéry, 'Au sujet d'*Adonis*', *Variété II*; *Œuvres*, vol. vii, 1937.

CONCLUSION

Having placed the French metaphysical, baroque, and précieux poets in perspective in the evolution of French late Renaissance poetry, I ought to conclude by re-placing French poetry of the late Renaissance in its European framework. But this can only be done as a symbolic gesture: stretching out a hand to the other specialists of comparative literature. We are used by now to thinking in terms of European culture (or at least western European culture) and we agree that the Renaissance and late Renaissance represent, as the historians put it, the Beginning of Modern Times, that is, of the phase when western Europe began to elaborate that blend of Christian and pagan culture which is by now a four-century-old tradition. Not only the literary riches we possess, but our criteria of civilization, our attitude to life, and even our problems have their probable sources in what happened to the 'mind of Europe' at the turning-point of the Renaissance and the late Renaissance. This study has been concerned with one small corner of the mind of Europe in that age: with some aspects of French lyrical poetry, considered, moreover, only in relation to one of the other European literatures, the English. It is therefore offered as a contribution to a vaster work, which would be a synthetic study of European literature in the Renaissance and late Renaissance and which would include primarily common features and particular differences rather than questions of inter-influences which are after all in a way only consequences, since a literature imitates that of another country inasmuch as it has already in it a current of thought or sensibility which that imitation will satisfy. I said that it was rash to hope for a European terminology concerning the poetry of our period. Yet even keeping Gongorism to Spain, Marinism to Italy, and 'Barock' to Germany, one should be able on the one hand to see clearly how far they are synonymous with the terms discussed in this study; or, when, as in the case of the German 'Barock', they are not, to discover on the other hand which components in them may be synonymous with French and English terms. In this way we should be able to perceive, in the field of poetry at least, the general pattern of the great currents which flowed over Europe, and against this general pattern the national characteristics would show more clearly.

As indicated in the Introduction, the guiding principles of this work have been two very simple beliefs: one that comparative literature is a valuable means of appreciating the literature of one's own country both as part of European culture and as having a strong individuality of its own, and the other that one can only compare things which are clearly defined. It remains to sum up the results obtained and discuss their significance both in the parallelism between French and English poetry and in the field of French poetry proper.

I do not propose, in the following generalizations, to dwell on points of comparative literature which have already been studied by critics. Ronsard and Spenser at one end of our period, French seventeenth-century Classicism and Augustan neo-Classicism in England at the other end, have already been emphatically paralleled and rightly enough. What this study would suggest is that the Spenserian and Ronsardian lines of poetry had during the late Renaissance a similar destiny. The influence of both Spenser and Ronsard was in their time overwhelming. We saw how Ronsard checked the Scèvian line of poetry; in Spenser's case, one may venture to say that there were probably in Wyatt's poems some elements of direct and homely speech and conciseness of texture which heralded later poets and which were checked by the deliberate and delicate artistry of Spenser.[1] The late Renaissance broke the Spenserian and Ronsardian lines alike. French and English poets then expressed problems which were the same in France and in England: the same conflicts between Humanism and Christianity; and in the two countries the age was one of political unrest and religious troubles. As there were no philosophers in the sixteenth century to solve the problems, these problems found a convenient channel of expression in poetry (or drama[2]), hence the emergence of baroque and metaphysical poetry in both France and

---

[1] I am thinking here more particularly of a poem like *Remembrance*:
> They flee from me, that sometime did me seek
> With naked foot, stalking in my chamber.
> I have seen them gentle, tame, and meek,
> That now are wild. . . .

(Sir Thomas Wyatt; *Oxford Book of XVIth Century Verse*, p. 51.)

[2] Drama lies outside the scope of this work. Yet let us recall that although nothing in France could match the abundance and the brilliance of the Elizabethan and Jacobean drama, French drama at the same time can humbly offer similar characteristics (see R. Lebègue, 'La Tragédie shakespearienne en France', *Revue des cours et conférences*, June–July 1937).

England. It is true also of the two countries that the early seven-teenth-century philosophers, Bacon and Descartes, rejecting scho-lastic thought which, because it was 'pre-eminently metaphysical, . . . concerned with Being and Essence, Cause and End'[1], was the backbone of metaphysical poetry, were to prove fatal to this kind of poetry.[2]

As a matter of fact, in the late Renaissance, both in England and in France, every kind of poetry was possible; the spiritual conflict which had broken out in Europe had not yet been solved and poetry could express the various tendencies which were working freely. Therefore it is not surprising that baroque and meta-physical poetry should reflect this spiritual conflict in both coun-tries, or that there should be poets escaping into précieux poetry. But what emerges also from this study is that even during this rich chaotic period the reactions of English and French poetry to the same problem were stamped with national characteristics. The preceding chapters must have made it clear that if we consider English and French metaphysical, baroque, and précieux poetry, the share of the baroque is more or less equal in the two coun-tries, but on the other hand English poetry achieved important results with metaphysical poetry whereas in France the stress was on the précieux. It seems that in the late Renaissance the two countries had already made their choice as to the kind of poetry that could fit or not fit the poetic material and racial spirit of each.

What strikes us in Elizabethan and Jacobean poetry is that it is national and eclectic, that it can combine the classical inheritance, love for beauty and music, with a tendency to come nearer to the diction of common life. This, of course, can be illustrated by great names such as Jonson or Donne, but it is even more striking if we think of poets who do not rank among the first, Sir Walter Ralegh for instance, and who reflect the unchecked and disorderly vitality of English poetry: 'an epitome of the eclecticism of the most cultured spirits of the age', says Mr. F. P. Wilson of Ralegh;[3]

[1] Basil Willey, *The Seventeenth Century Background*, 1946, p. 12.

[2] 'The Cartesian spirit made for the sharper separation of the spheres of prose and poetry, and thereby hastened that "dissociation of sensibility" which Mr. Eliot has remarked as having set in after the time of the Metaphysical poets' (ibid., p. 87).

[3] F. P. Wilson, *Elizabethan and Jacobean*, 1946, p. 12. See also Miss Brad-brook's study of Ralegh in *The School of Night*, 1936.

or if we peruse a book of madrigal verse[1] and see how the poets of song-books could be conventional without being précieux, because the conventions of their classical or petrarchan inspiration were tuned to the strains of popular tradition, and how they could preserve a sort of lyricism which was a national quality.

On the French side we notice on the contrary that from Ronsard to La Fontaine certain tendencies are strongly stressed which are very different from those exhibited by English poets: the rejection of colloquialism; a more conscious interest in the principles of art (men like Ronsard or Malherbe were deeply interested in analysing clearly what poetry must be and must not be);[2] the impulse to be civilized at all costs and to escape into précieux circles (none of the followers of Spenser ever became précieux as did Desportes, Ronsard's follower); and the overwhelming delight in pagan themes.

The differences mentioned are already visible even before we reach the mid-seventeenth century, when economic and political differences between France and England might be considered as the determining factor for differences in literature (for while France was enjoying order and refinement under an absolute king, England was undergoing two revolutions).

Before Louis XIV and before the influence of Descartes, French poetry was showing unmistakable signs of finding its congenial atmosphere in pagan antiquity rather than in Christian or national themes. The pagan world was never to any English poet (except much later to Keats) what it was to Ronsard: an attitude to life and a genuine vision of the universe.[3] It is true that later on, with the classicists, we shall not find again in all its freshness, philosophical enthusiasm, and concreteness the pagan universe, but it will be, so to speak, taken for granted. Very early in France, with Maynard and Malherbe, following Ronsard, and also to a certain extent with the *libertin* poets and with the précieux poets, we see

[1] See E. H. Fellowes's anthology *English Madrigal Verse*, 1928, also the critical study by F. Delattre, *La Chanson élisabéthaine*, 1948.

[2] It is a commonly admitted view that English criticism on poetry at the same time is comparatively poor. J. W. H. Atkins in *English Literary Criticism—the Renascence*, 1947, objects to this view, but admits in his conclusion that English criticism of the late sixteenth century was more independent of general principles and yielded more to eclecticism and natural instincts than the French.

[3] French scientific poetry, which is at the bottom a fervent and critical organizing of the world according to humanism, has no equivalent in England except Chapman, and even in Chapman the fervour is more a matter of a deliberate attitude as the eclectic cultured writer than of a genuine belief in the pagan ideal.

the French mind making its choice in the conflicts of the late Renaissance and choosing an attitude which, even when it is not the moralist's attitude, is in any case anti-metaphysical and even *laïque*, thus heralding the divorce between literature and religion which was to be the main feature not only of French classical poetry but of French literature during three centuries.

Whereas English literature produced masterpieces and an important school in metaphysical poetry, and also in the baroque if we consider Elizabethan and Jacobean drama as partaking, within the conventions of drama, of both the metaphysical and the baroque spirit,[1] French literature, as we have seen, offers extremely interesting examples of metaphysical poetry but few of them, and its baroque drama[2] is limited to minor or obscure playwrights.

On the other hand, the aristocratic characteristics of French poetry are marked very strongly, as we have seen from the importance of précieux poetry. This is evident even in a metaphysical poet like Scève. All through the sixteenth and seventeenth centuries French poetry has very little to do with popular tradition.

The obvious explanation for these differences is to be found in the differences between the two languages, and these are well known: the English language, with its variety of stresses, its syncopated rhythm of utterance, its freedom of syntax, its mixture of Latin and Saxon words, its great wealth of synonyms, is more spontaneously poetic, so that poetry can afford to be colloquial and deal with everyday reality, whereas the regular unemphatic flow of the French language needs, in order to become poetic, an artificial system not only of scansion but of themes and even of atmosphere.

It has been said that

Il n'y a presque pas dans le peuple français de poésie diffuse, de puissance de création poétique, de *folk-lore* . . . le paganisme classique offre seul aux poètes français non seulement la sécurité d'une très ancienne consécration littéraire, mais encore sa dignité de religion morte, douée d'un arbitraire adorable . . . [les poètes français] sont unanimes

---

[1] To develop this point fully would require a separate study. Let us only suggest that whereas in poetry the 'reconciliation of opposites', 'the blend of passion and ratiocination', is given in the concentrated form of the metaphysical conceit, in drama the same elements might be expressed by dramatic irony, by reconciliation and opposition in characters, and by other devices pertaining to drama but with the same ultimate result.

[2] See Lebègue, 'Le Théâtre baroque en France'.

dans la volonté de dédaigner les matériaux bruts de l'univers et de ne reconnaître pour leur qu'une substance abstraite et purifiée . . . la poésie française ne se sent à l'aise qu'aux prises avec les thèmes les plus élémentaires. . . .[1]

I should not altogether agree. This kind of voluntarily artificial, pagan poetry, choosing its subjects among commonplaces, shunning the religious and the national themes, came to the fore also because it happened to be the best suited to the moralist's attitude which the French chose to adopt at the end of the sixteenth century. It is thus not so much a question of the genius of the language or of the essence of French poetry as one of a certain choice, by no means necessarily final, made by the French mind at a given time.

It has been pointed out in the course of this study that direct speech and everyday vocabulary were not incompatible with the essence of French poetry, since we have poets like Villon, Sponde, and later Laforgue and Apollinaire. It is a very thin and broken line, but sufficient as an argument, as these poets are by no means minor ones.

The end of the nineteenth century and our present century have witnessed certain revolts against the moralist's attitude to life. The results in poetry have been, as far as we can judge now, either the desperate attempt of Mallarmé, or the dislocation of language in the surrealist poets, or a return to the Villon tradition (Apollinaire and the later Aragon), or an interest in a religious vision of life with Péguy (who went back to the stiff rhetoric of Du Perron) and Claudel. It is not certain that the Ronsard–La Fontaine line of poetry which seems to have steadily proceeded through the various literary movements and reached a sort of climax with Paul Valéry, will have the last word.

An attempt to give very definite meanings to the three words metaphysical, baroque, and précieux, has made it easier, with the help of a denominator common to French and English poetry, to reveal that the two countries had the same possibilities during the chaotic period of the late Renaissance, and therefore to appreciate the choice made by French poetry.

The possibilities offered to the poets of that age and taken by them show plainly the richness, variety, and interest of their poetry without needing any lengthy eulogy. But I hope that even a work deliberately restricted to the question of terminology will

[1] Thierry Maulnier, *Introduction à la poésie française*, pp. 36–50.

suggest the precious contribution of these poets to the treasury of French, and European, poetry: the blend of thought and passionate feeling in the metaphysical poems of Scève, La Ceppède, or Sponde; in the baroque poets either a visionary power or a sense of the lovely concreteness of things which the romantic poets will be at a loss to recover; and even in the précieux poets, all minor authors, the quest for elegance which is not only the best quality of polite society, but an important asset in the refinement of sensibility.

BIBLIOGRAPHY

A STUDY of this kind naturally necessitated consulting a large number of works not all of which proved directly relevant to the issues discussed here. The following bibliography includes only those works actually quoted or referred to above.

I. ANTHOLOGIES

French

ARLAND (M.), *Anthologie de la poésie française*, Paris, 1945.

AURY (D.), *Anthologie de la poésie religieuse française*, Paris, 1943.

BOASE (A. M.), *Department of French Studies, Anthologie I (XVIᵉ–XVIIIᵉ siècles)*, University of Glasgow, s.d.

BRAY (R.), *Anthologie de la poésie précieuse de Thibaut de Champagne à Giraudoux*, Paris, 1946.

DORCHAIN (A.), *Les Chefs-d'œuvre de Malherbe et de l'École classique*, London, 1921.

MAULNIER (T.), *Introduction à la poésie française*, Paris, 1939.

—— *Poésie du XVIIᵉ siècle*, Paris, 1945.

—— and AURY (D.), *Poètes précieux et baroques*, Angers, 1941.

DE LA MAYNARDIÈRE (H.), *Poètes chrétiens du XVIᵉ siècle*, Paris, 1908.

English

CHAMBERS (E. K.), *The Oxford Book of Sixteenth Century Verse*, Oxford, 1945.

FELLOWES (E. H.), *English Madrigal Verse*, Oxford, 1928.

GRIERSON (H. J. C.), *Metaphysical Lyrics and Poems of the Seventeenth Century*, Oxford, 1921.

—— and BULLLOUGH (G.), *The Oxford Book of Seventeenth Century Verse*, Oxford, 1946.

II. WORKS OF THE PERIOD

AUBIGNÉ (A. D'), *Œuvres complètes*, ed. Réaume et de Caussade, Paris, 1873–92.

—— *Les Tragiques*, ed. A. Garnier et J. Plattard, Paris, 1932.

—— *Le Printemps — L'Hécatombe à Diane*, ed. B. Gagnebin, Geneva, 1948.

BERTAUT (J.), *Œuvres poétiques*, ed. Chenevière, Paris, 1891.

CHAPMAN (G.), *The Poems of George Chapman*, ed. Phillis Brooks Bartlett, Oxford, 1941.

COLLETET (G.), *L'Art poétique du Sʳ Colletet*, Paris, 1658.

CRASHAW (R.), *The Poetical Works*, ed. L. C. Martin, Oxford, 1927.

—— *The Poems of Richard Crashaw*, ed. J. R. Tutin, London, s.d.

DAVIES OF HEREFORD (J.), *The Complete Works*, ed. the Rev. A. B. Grosart, Chertsey Worthies Library, 2 vols., 1878.

DESPORTES (P.), *Œuvres de Philippe Desportes*, ed. A. Michiels, Paris, 1858.

DONNE (J.), *The Poems of John Donne*, ed. H. J. C. Grierson London, 1929.

DU BARTAS (G.), *The Works of Guillaume de Salluste, Sieur du Bartas*, ed. U. T. Holmes, J. C. Lyons, R. W. Linker, University of North Carolina Press, 1938.

—— *Du Bartas, poète chrétien*, ed. M. Braspart, Neuchâtel, 1947.

DU BELLAY (J.), *Œuvres poétiques*, ed. H. Chamard, Paris, 1908.

—— *La Deffence et Illustration de la langue francoyse*, ed. H. Chamard, Paris, 1948.

FLETCHER (GILES and PHINEAS), *The Poetical Works of Giles and Phineas Fletcher*, ed. F. S. Boas, Cambridge, 1908.

GREVILLE (F.), *Poems and Dramas of Fulke Greville, First Lord Brooke*, ed. G. Bullough, Edinburgh, 1938.

LA BRUYÈRE (J. DE), *Les Caractères*, Amsterdam, 1763.

LA FONTAINE (J. DE), *Fables, contes et nouvelles*, ed. E. Pilon, R. Groos, J. Schiffrin, Paris, 1948.

—— *Œuvres diverses*, ed. P. Clarac, Paris, 1948.

LINGENDES (J. DE), *Œuvres poétiques*, ed. E. T. Griffiths, Paris, 1916.

LYLY (J.), *Complete Works*, ed. R. W. Bond, Oxford, 1902.

MALHERBE (F. DE), *Les Poésies de M. de Malherbe*, ed. J. Lavaud, Paris, 1936.

MAROT (C.), *Œuvres complètes*, ed. A. Grenier, Paris, s.d.

PELETIER (J.), *Art poétique*, ed. J. Boulanger, Paris, 1930.

PURE (L'ABBÉ M. DE), *La Précieuse ou le Mystère des Ruelles*, ed. E. Magne, Paris, 1938.

REGNIER (M.), *Œuvres*, ed. P. Poitevin, Paris, s.d.

RONSARD (P. DE), *Œuvres complètes*, ed. P. Blanchemain, Paris, 1857.

—— *Œuvres complètes*, ed. P. Laumonier, Paris, 1914–15.

—— *Œuvres complètes*, ed. P. Laumonier, Paris, 1921– .

SAINT-AMANT (M. A. GIRARD DE), *Œuvres poétiques*, ed. L. Vérane, Paris, 1930.

SCÈVE (M.), *Délie*, ed. E. Parturier, 2ᵉ tirage, Paris, 1931.

—— *Œuvres poétiques*, ed. B. Guégan, Paris, 1927.

SEBILLET (T.), *Art poétique français*, ed. F. Gaiffe, Paris, 1932.

SIDNEY (SIR PHILIP), *The Complete Poems of Sir Philip Sidney*, ed. the Rev. A. B. Grosart, London, 1877.

—— *Astrophel and Stella*, ed. C.-M. Garnier, Paris, 1939.

SOMAIZE (A. BAUDEAU DE), *Le Dictionnaire des Précieuses*, ed. C.-M. Livet, Paris, 1856.

SPONDE (J. DE), *L'Œuvre poétique de Jean de Sponde*, ed. M. Arland, Paris, 1945.

—— *Poésies*, ed. A. M. Boase, Geneva, 1949.

TRISTAN L'HERMITE (F.), *Les Amours et autres poésies choisies*, ed. P. Camo, Paris, 1925.

TYARD (PONTUS DE), *Œuvres poétiques*, ed. C. Marty-Laveaux, Paris, 1875.

VOITURE (V. DE), *Les Œuvres de Monsieur de Voiture*, Paris, 1734.

VIAU (THÉOPHILE DE), *Œuvres poétiques*, ed. L.-R. Lefèvre, Paris, 1926.

III. CRITICAL WORKS

ADAM (A.), *Théophile de Viau et la libre pensée française en 1620*, Paris, 1935.

—— *Histoire de la littérature française au XVIIe siècle — l'époque d'Henri IV et de Louis XIII*, Paris, 1948.

—— 'Baroque et Préciosité', *Revue des sciences humaines*, July–Dec. 1949.

ATKINS (J. W. H.), *English Literary Criticism—The Renascence*, London, 1947.

BAUMAL (F.), *Le Féminisme au temps de Molière*, Paris, 1926.

BERTRAND (L.), *La Fin du Classicisme*, Paris, s.d.

BOASE (A. M.), 'Then Malherbe Came', *Criterion*, 1930–1.

—— 'Jean de Sponde, un poète inconnu', *Mesures*, 15 Oct. 1939.

—— 'Poètes anglais et français de l'époque baroque', *Revue des sciences humaines*, July–Dec. 1949.

—— and RUCHON (F.), *La Vie et l'œuvre de Jean de Sponde*, Geneva, 1949.

BRADBROOK (M. C.), *The School of Night, a Study in the Literary Relationships of Sir Walter Ralegh*, Cambridge, 1936.

BRAY (R.), *La Préciosité et les Précieux*, Paris, 1948.

BREMOND (H.), *Histoire littéraire du sentiment religieux en France*, Vol. I: *L'Humanisme dévot*, Paris, 1916.

BRUNOT (F.), *La Doctrine de Malherbe*, Paris, 1891.

—— *Histoire de la langue française des origines à 1900*, Paris, 1909–30.

BUSH (D.), *English Literature in the Earlier Seventeenth Century*, Oxford, 1945.

BUSSON (H.), 'Sur la Philosophie de Ronsard', *Revue des cours et conférences*, 1929–30.

CHAMPION (P.), *Histoire poétique du quinzième siècle*, Paris, 1923.

CHASTEL (A.), 'Sur le baroque français', *Cahiers de la Restauration française, iv*, 1944.

CHILD (C. G.), *John Lyly and Euphuism*, Leipzig, 1894.

CLEMENTS (R. J.), *Critical Theory and Practice of the Pléiade*, Cambridge, Mass., 1942.

DEBU-BRIDEL (J.), 'La Préciosité, conception héroïque de la vie', *Revue de France*, 15 Sept. 1938.

DEJOB (C.), *L'Influence du Concile de Trente sur la littérature et les beaux-arts*, Paris, 1884.

DELATTRE (F.), *La Chanson élisabéthaine*, Paris, 1948.

DRYDEN (J.), *Essays of John Dryden*, ed. W. P. Ker, Oxford, 1900.

ELIOT (T. S.), *For Lancelot Andrewes*, London, 1928.

—— *Selected Essays*, London, 1932.

ELLIS-FERMOR (U. M.), *The Jacobean Drama, an Interpretation*, London, 1936.

FAGUET (E.), *Histoire de la poésie française de la Renaissance au Romantisme*, Paris, 1923–7.

FEUILLERAT (A.), *John Lyly*, Cambridge, 1910.

FREEMAN (R. M.), *English Emblem Books*, London, 1948.

FUSIL (C.-A.), *La Poésie scientifique de 1750 à nos jours*, Paris, 1918.

HUXLEY (A.), 'Death and the Baroque', *Horizon*, April 1949.

JOHNSON (S.), *Lives of the English Poets*, ed. G. Birkbeck Hill, Oxford, 1905.

KNIGHT (R. C.), 'Brûlé de plus de feux . . .', *Studies . . . presented to R. L. G. Ritchie*, Cambridge, 1949.

KOHLER (P.), 'Le Classicisme français et le problème du Baroque', *Lettres de France, Périodes et Problèmes*, Lausanne, 1943.

LARBAUD (V.), *Ce Vice impuni, la lecture — Domaine français*, Paris, 1941.

LAVAUD (J.), *Philippe Desportes, un poète de cour au temps des derniers Valois*, Paris, 1936.

LEAVIS (F. R.), *Revaluations*, London, 1936.

LEBÈGUE (R.), *La Poésie française de 1560 à 1630*, Paris, 1951.

—— 'La Tragédie shakespearienne en France', *Revue des cours et conférences*, June–July 1937.

—— 'Le Théâtre baroque en France', *Bibliothèque d'humanisme et renaissance*, 1942.

—— 'Les Larmes de Saint Pierre, poème baroque', *Revue des sciences humaines*, July–Dec. 1949.

LE BRETON (G.), 'Le Deuxième Congrès des Études Françaises', *Revue d'Histoire littéraire de France*, Oct.–Dec. 1950.

—— 'La Clé des *Chimères*: l'Alchimie', *Fontaine*, 1945.

LENGLEY DUFRESNAY (N.), *L'Histoire de la philosophie hermétique*, Paris, 1742.

LUCAS (F. L.), *Seneca and Elizabethan Tragedy*, Cambridge, 1922.

MAGENDIE (M.), *La Politesse mondaine en France de 1600 à 1660*, Paris, 1926.

MAGNE (E.), *Voiture et l'Hôtel de Rambouillet*, Paris, 1929.

MAGNY (C.-E.), *Précieux Giraudoux*, Paris, 1945.

MAHOOD (M. M.), *Poetry and Humanism*, London, 1950.

MARK (J.), 'The Uses of the Term Baroque', *Modern Language Review*, vol. xxiii, 1938.

MAULNIER (T.), *Langages*, Lausanne, 1946.

MORNET (D.), *Histoire de la littérature française classique (1660–1700)*, Paris, 1942.

NADAL (O.), *Le Sentiment de l'amour dans l'œuvre de Pierre Corneille*, Paris, 1948.

D'ORS (E.), *Du Baroque*, version française de Mme A. Rouardt-Valéry, Paris, 1935.

PURCELL (J. M.), 'Sidney's *Astrophel and Stella* and Greville's *Cælica*', *Publications of the Modern Language Association of America*, vol. l, 1935.

RAINE (K.), 'John Donne and the Baroque Doubt', *Horizon*, July 1943.

RAYMOND (M.), *L'Influence de Ronsard sur la poésie française*, Paris, 1927.

—— *Génies de France*, Neuchâtel, 1942.

—— 'Classique et Baroque dans l'œuvre de Ronsard', *Concinnitas: Beiträge zum Problem des Klassischen*, Basel, June 1944.

—— 'Propositions sur le Baroque et la littérature française', *Revue des sciences humaines*, July–Dec. 1949.

REYNOLD (G. DE), *Le XVIIᵉ Siècle*, Montreal, 1944.

RICHARDS (I. A.), *Principles of Literary Criticism*, London, 1947.

SAINTE-BEUVE (C.-A. DE), *Causeries du Lundi*, 3ᵉ édition, Paris, s.d.

SAULNIER (V.-L.), *Maurice Scève*, Paris, 1948.

SCHMIDT (A.-M.), *La Poésie scientifique en France au seizième siècle*, Paris, 1938.

—— 'Constantes baroques dans la littérature française', *Trivium*, vol. iv, Year VII, Zürich.

SHIPLEY (J. T.), *Dictionary of World Literature*, London, 1945.

SMITH (J. C.), 'On Metaphysical Poetry', *Scrutiny*, Dec. 1933.

STECHOW (W.), 'Definitions of the Baroque in the Visual Arts', *Journal of Aesthetics and Art Criticism*, vol. v, 1946.

STEWART (J.), *Poetry in France and England*, London, 1931.

THIBAUDET (A.), *La Poésie de Stéphane Mallarmé*, Paris, 1926.

TUVE (R.), *Elizabethan and Metaphysical Imagery*, Chicago University Press, 1947.

UPHAM (A. H.), *The French Influence in English Literature*, New York, 1908.

VAGANAY (H.), *Le Sonnet en Italie et en France au XVIᵉ siècle*, Lyon, 1903.

VALÉRY (P.), *Œuvres*, vol. viii, Paris, 1937.

VIANEY (J.), *Le Pétrarquisme en France au XVIᵉ siècle*, Montpellier, 1909.

WARREN (A.), *Richard Crashaw, a Study in Baroque Sensibility*, Louisiana State University Press, 1939.

WELLEK (R.), 'The Concept of Baroque in Literary Scholarship', *Journal of Aesthetics and Art Criticism*, vol. v, 1946.

WILLEY (B.), *The Seventeenth Century Background*, London, 1946.

WILSON (F. P.), *Elizabethan and Jacobean*, Oxford, 1946.

WILSON (J. D.), *John Lyly*, Cambridge, 1905.

WÖLFFLIN (H.), *Principles of Art History*, London, 1932.

INDEX